THE
SHOCKING
HISTORY
OF
ADVERTISING!

Also by
E. S. TURNER

BOYS WILL BE BOYS
The story of Sweeney Todd, Deadwood Dick,
Sexton Blake, Billy Bunter, Dick Barton, etc.

ROADS TO RUIN
The shocking history of social reform

BY E. S. TURNER

THE SHOCKING HISTORY OF ADVERTISING!

MICHAEL JOSEPH
London

First published by
MICHAEL JOSEPH LTD
26 Bloomsbury Street,
London, W.C.1
1952

Set and printed in Great Britain by Unwin Brothers Ltd. at
the Gresham Press, Woking, in Times type, ten point, leaded,
on paper made by John Dickinson and bound by James Burn

CONTENTS

★

AUTHOR'S NOTE
page 7

INTRODUCTION
page 9

ILLUSTRATIONS

★

THE SHOCKING HISTORY OF ADVERTISING

AUTHOR'S NOTE

THIS is a study of commercial advertising in newspapers and magazines, on hoardings, on the landscape, on the sky and in the ether.

The book does not touch on advertising in the ancient world (gladiatorial shows were advertised on the walls of Rome), or in the Middle Ages. This is partly for reasons of space, partly because all that can usefully be written about advertising in those days has already been written at length. Nor does the book touch on the history of shop and inn signs, on bellmen or on old playbills, all of which have been adequately dealt with elsewhere.

State propaganda is rightly a separate subject; it is mentioned in this volume only in so far as it influenced commercial advertising. Such extensions of advertising as public relations, fairs and exhibitions are not treated here, nor are specialized fields like window-dressing and direct mail advertising. The book does take in its stride many unorthodox forms of advertising, as for instance on the coin of the realm or on the sails of yachts, but it does not set out specifically to deal with 'publicity'—of the kind which takes the form of hanging an elephant (as once described by Mr. H. L. Mencken) or swimming the English Channel for commerce.

The field is limited to Britain and America. To avoid repetition, the chapters on America are designed to be complementary to those on Britain, or vice versa as necessary.

Henry Sampson's much-quoted *History of Advertising* was published in 1874, before modern advertising began. Frank Presbrey's *History and Development of Advertising*, published in 1929, was devoted more to American than to British advertising, especially in its latter stages. Both these books contain a good deal more about the early origins of advertising than the present one. Sampson found much material in the long articles on advertising which appeared in the *Edinburgh Review* in 1843 and the *Quarterly Review* in 1855, to which the present writer is also indebted.

INTRODUCTION

Through the bright catacombs of the London Underground, in the spring of 1951, went a poster censor, with a bundle of strips of paper and a paste brush. For once, he was not concerned to obliterate parts of the female anatomy. Instead, he paused here and there to stick his strips of paper over offending words. The public, whose curiosity was understandably whetted, picked away at the stickers after he had gone. They found that the slogan 'Keeps you healthy, slim and attractive' had been converted to read 'Keeps you healthy, vital and attractive.' On another poster the word 'asthma' had been expunged from a list of afflictions for which solace was offered, and the phrase 'acts like a charm' had also been blotted out.

To the inquisitive public, who had hoped to find something more piquant, these excisions were puzzling. Who, they may have wondered, was the man with the brush? On whose authority did he operate? Was he a Government hireling? Probably few suspected that he might be the agent of the advertising interests themselves, making voluntary suppressions for the good name of the profession. The average man was unaware that the latest advertising Code of Ethics ruled out claims to promote slimness (which had been such a feature of advertising in the 'thirties) and even disallowed hints of magical properties, which was presumably the reason for obliterating the phrase 'acts like a charm.' This average man may have thought: Why delete a trivial flourish like 'acts like a charm' when so many much more romantic claims, in other quarters, go uncensored?

One or two advertising men who saw these acts of well-meant disfigurement in the Underground shook their heads. To them it seemed that advertising had sunk into such a slough of good taste, of inhibition, that it would be impossible to extract it. How much easier it had been in the good old days . . . the good old days of only twelve or so years ago.

The public at large little suspects the extent to which advertising has been made 'respectable' in the last dozen years. There is much wrong with it still, and always will be, so long as it remains a mirror of mankind; but the briefest glance at the newspaper files of the nineteen-thirties will show what a tightening-up there has been. The less fastidious twenty- and twenty-four-page news-papers to which the public were accustomed between the wars were sustained, on occasions, by advertisements which today would be illegal, and by others which wore so shifty a face that the advertising profession and the newspapers have agreed to renounce them. Fierceness of competition, presumably, was the only reason why these advertisements were accepted at the time. Which prompts the question: if newspapers were able to return to their former dimensions, and similar trade conditions pre-vailed, could the guardians of advertising and the Press lords prevent the same sort of thing happening all over again?

Today no reasonable persons—not even those who advocate an advertisement tax—will dispute that advertising is a necessary force, both in its informative and persuasive roles. No one doubts that it has done much to raise the physical standard of living, though there are some who, like the *New Yorker*, shy at 'the terrifying conception of the good life through accumulation of objects.' It is undeniable that advertising has introduced useful inventions to a wide, as distinct from a select, public, and that quickly. It has changed the habits of nations, usually (but not always) for the better. Its advocates assert with pride that adver-tising has abolished heavy underwear, made people clean their teeth and persuaded them to be far more careful about personal hygiene. These results have been achieved, not only by informative, but by persuasive and indeed by intimidating advertisements. It is worth remembering that the prime object of the advertisers was not to produce these gratifying results; it was to sell more silk, more toothpaste, more disinfectant.

To say that advertising is necessary is a long way from saying that all advertising is necessary. It is complete humbug to suggest that everybody ought to take a daily laxative or that every house-wife with frayed nerves is in need of tonic wine. The public's only defence against high-powered suggestion is its own common sense. Unfortunately that bulwark, though strong, cannot always be depended on to withstand the pounding and insinuating sea. 'Nobody believes the nonsense in any one advertisement,' wrote Mr. Herbert Agar in *A Time for Greatness*. 'Everyone is affected by the mist of deception which we continually breathe. The trouble is that we prefer to breathe that mist.'

Francis Bacon would have agreed. In his essay on truth, he wrote:

A mixture of a lie doth ever add pleasure. Doth any man doubt, that if there were taken out of men's minds vain opinions, flattering hopes, false valuations, imaginations . . . and the like, but it would leave the minds of a number of men poor shrunken things, full of melancholy and indisposition, and unpleasing to themselves?

Millions of words have been written on the ethics of advertising. It is a grim thought that several writers, including Bertrand Russell and Aldous Huxley, should have deemed it necessary to advocate teaching children distrust of advertising (a suggestion first made, as far as the present writer can discover, at the S.C.A.P.A. conference of 1896). Mr. Huxley in his *Ends and Means* (1937) said that children ought to be shown that there was no logical connection between the pretty girl in her expensive dressing-gown and the merits of the toothpaste she was intended to advertise. 'This lesson might be brought home by practical demonstrations,' said Mr. Huxley. 'Chocolates could be wrapped in a paper adorned with realistic pictures of scorpions, and castor oil and quinine distributed from containers in the form of Sealyham terriers or Shirley Temple.' Then, having mastered the 'art of dissociation' in the field of commercial advertising, the young generation would be on their guard against political and religious propaganda.

A schoolmaster, Mr. Denys Thompson, who powerfully criticized advertising methods in *The Voice of Civilization*, said in that book that he had already practised his pupils in the analysis of advertisements and oratory.

Mr. F. P. Bishop, author of that thoughtful book *The Ethics of Advertising*, argued that suggestions like those of Huxley and Russell amounted to 'cynical manipulation of the infant mind.' If that is so, what is the appropriate description of the tactics revealed in this extract from an American magazine, *The Sound Track*, in 1951:

Speaking of surveys, we tried an experiment the other evening. . . . To a curly-headed four-year-old being tucked under the covers we posed this question: 'Susie, which product brushes teeth whiter?' 'Colgate's, of course, Gramp.' We couldn't resist another. 'Which product washes clothes cleaner?' Without a moment's hesitation: 'Tide.' We tried once more. 'Which coffee gives the best value?' When she replied, 'A and P, and now good-night, Gramp,' we hurried out of the child's room with other questions beating at our brain.

Where else on earth is brand consciousness firmly fixed in the minds of four-year-old tots? How many pre-school age Americans are pre-sold on how many different products? How can we get reliable data? What is it worth to a manufacturer who can close in on this juvenile audience and continue to sell it under controlled conditions, year after year, right up to its attainment of adulthood and full-fledged buyer status? It *can* be done. Interested?

From this it can only be concluded that the advertising man— or this kind of advertising man—is the new Jesuit: 'Give me your children before they are five and they are mine for ever.' To him all values are different. Fog is not something which delays trains; it is something which prevents people seeing posters. Words have different meanings: loyalty means always buying the same hair oil. To him a bride is not a young woman on the edge of a great adventure; she is a conditioned consumer who, by buying the right cosmetics and right brassière has captured her man, and who, when she returns from her honeymoon will go into the grocer's and automatically recite those branded names which have been the most loudly dinned into her ears for the last twenty-one years. To him all problems can be solved in terms of advertising. The remedy for absenteeism in the mines is to make miners *want* more luxuries. He has made women adopt men's habits (smoking, wearing trousers) and now he wants to make men adopt women's habits (using perfume). If he opens a Bible it is only because he has read that such an exercise is valuable as a reminder of 'the value of iteration,' and because the late Sir William Crawford said that every copy-writer ought to do so.

It will be objected that the foregoing is a crude travesty of an advertising man, or at all events of the kind of advertising man to be found in Britain (compare Mr. Cyrus Ducker's more flattering picture on page 240). But all advertising men of ambition tend to think on these lines, to some degree.

Perhaps because he was captured young, the adult consumer is oddly tolerant of the button-holings, the shoutings in his ear, the pitfalls ingeniously dug in his path. Long ago he conceded, without giving the matter overmuch thought, that advertised goods were best. He may even have conceded that advertising, by widening markets, enables the cost of raw materials to be cut, fosters quicker turnover and allows smaller profits. In his heart he may suspect that a well-advertised brand of soap is no purer or 'sudsier' than another; if he continues to buy it, it is because he believes, quite genuinely, that the product of a firm with a reputation to keep up is likely to be more reliable than that of an anonymous maker. He would not buy a nameless motor-car put together in a back-street garage.

Yet sometimes he finds his faith in advertising put to a sharp test. If he goes into a chemist's and asks for aspirin the assistant will put before him a well-advertised proprietary brand at something like one-and-fourpence. If he hesitates the assistant may produce from under the counter a bottle of unbranded aspirin at one-fifth of the price. Now comes the struggle. If the customer has not been properly conditioned he will begin to wonder whether the additional cost of the branded aspirin can be wholly explained away by extra purity, extra potency, quicker solubility or whatever is claimed for it; whether, if he buys the dearer aspirin he will not be paying for copy-writers' salaries and (not least) for packaging. Only the firm that makes the branded aspirin knows what, in fact, he is paying for. And that is the crux of the problem. Unless every balance-sheet of every firm is broken down in detail, no one knows whether the customer is paying for advertising. Millions of words, also, have been written on this subject, and the only safe conclusion is that sometimes the advertiser pays for advertising and sometimes he does not.

That tolerance of advertising shown by the consumer takes on a cynical tinge when he considers what is today perhaps the least happy feature of advertising: the publishing of testimonials by the famous, the wealthy and the notorious. Does it help the dignity of advertising, does it help the dignity of the human race, to have titled women explaining how they rid themselves of blackheads, and actresses boasting of their 'all-over loveliness'?

Whether these testimonials are disinterested, whether they are venal, is beside the point; the point is that not two persons in a hundred believe them to be voluntary and disinterested. The public is resigned to the fact that anyone entering certain spheres of public life will feel impelled, sooner or later, to lend his or her name to some everyday product. George Bernard Shaw told in *Everybody's Political What's What* how a lady of his acquaintance had been paid £800 for a letter 'ascribing the beauty of her complexion, which was entirely and thickly artificial, to a well-advertised face cream.' He himself had been offered a big sum to attribute his mental powers to an equally well-advertised correspondence course.

Inevitably it will be retorted that an author has no cause to complain about the use of testimonials, since it is with the aid of them that his works are usually commended. The difference seems to be that reviewers, whatever their faults, are under no suspicion of venality. What is more, they write their own copy.

Is it not time that advertising, if it wants to be considered honest, should try to look honest—in this important respect? Would the loss of these 'vain opinions . . . false valuations . . . imaginations . . .' really leave the minds of many people 'poor shrunken things, full of melancholy and indisposition, and unpleasing to themselves'?

17th Century

THE MERCURIES

SOONER or later, the explorer seeking to track down the first advertisement in an English publication finds the trail petering out in a world of mermaids and two-headed children: the world of the Elizabethan broadsides and news-books which, at irregular intervals, purveyed 'miraculous newes' to the credulous.

Some of these publications were little more than elaborated versions of the handbills which were distributed at Bartholomew's Fair, calling attention to such attractions as 'a woman with three breasts, an admirable work of nature,' or 'a male child born with a bear growing on his back alive.' The Elizabethans had a relish for abominations, which they liked to believe were the result of whoredom and worse.

Since these accounts contained the addresses of the objects they described, and such phrases as 'to be seen without a moment's delay' or 'not unlikely to live long' they were in essence just as much advertisements as the handbills at the Fair.

Some of the earlier news-books had set out to give a sober and reliable service of news, both from home and overseas; but dispatches were slow, authority was obstructive and men of culture were often contemptuous. It was not surprising that the writers lost heart and filled out their sheets with improbabilities. However, the outbreak of the Thirty Years War in 1618 quickened the literate public's appetite for news. The first regular English periodical appeared in 1622; it was the *Weekly Newes* of Nicholas Bourne and Thomas Archer. Closely following came Nathaniel Butter's *Newes from Most Parts of Christendom*. It was a later publication by Archer—the *Mercurius Britannicus*—which carried on February 1, 1625 one of the earliest known advertisements in a periodical:

An excellent discourse concerning the match between our most Gracious and Mightie Prince Charles, Prince of Wales, and the Lady Henrietta Maria, daughter of Henry the Fourth, late King of France . . . with a lively picture of the Prince and Lady cut in Bronze.

The Star Chamber harassed the publishers of these early sheets. When it was abolished in 1641, English journalism faced the future with more confidence. With the outbreak of the Civil War in 1642 'mercuries' under all manner of extravagant titles began to appear, on both sides. In these, book advertisements were frequent. The *Mercurius Politicus* carried announcements of Izaak Walton's *Compleat Angler* and works by John Milton.

By mid-century most of the mercuries were printing advertisements, not only of books and freaks but of lost horses and of the earliest patent medicines. In 1652 Samuel Sheppard, one-time assistant to Ben Jonson, noted that the writers of news-books had adopted 'another quaint device in their trading,' explaining:

There is never a mountebank who, either by professing of chymistry or any other art drains money from the people of the nation but these arch-cheats have a share in the booty—because the fellow cannot lye sufficiently himself he gets one of these to do't for him.

Sheppard was sceptical, too, about those 'lost' horse advertisements. So was a writer in the *Man in the Moon*, who imputed deceit to Henry Walker, publisher of 'that Westminster catterwaule called *Perfect Occurrences*.' 'The sheet,' he said, 'was bumbasted out with a sixpenny story of a man that lost a wall-eyed mare at Islington,' when the truth was that Walker himself stole the animal 'to carry his fardle of nonsense, heresy and blasphemy to Uxbridge to infect his parish in the national sin of Atheisme.' Whatever the truth about the wall-eyed mare of Islington, it has to be recorded that the 'lost and found' advertisements soon began to cover a good deal of criminality.

The range of advertisements continued to widen in that decade which preceded the Plague. One historic announcement was this in the *Mercurius Politicus* of September 30, 1658:

THAT Excellent, and by all Physicians, approved *China* drink, called by the Chineans *Tcha*, by other nations *Tay* alias *Tee*, is sold at the Sultaness Head Cophee-House, in Sweeting's Rents, by the *Royal* Exchange, London.

That Prodigy in Nature,

By His Majesty's Authority,

At the Sign of *Charing-Cross*, at *Charing-Cross*.

THere is to be seen a strange and monstrous Child, with one Body, and one Belly, and yet otherwise it hath all the Proporsions of two Children, that is two Heads, two Noses, two Mouths, four Eyes, four Ears, four Arms, and four Leggs, four Hands, and four Feet, the monster is of the femal kind, it was born at Fillips Town on the Twenty Ninth of April, 1699 The Father of this monster is present where it is to be seen.

[British Museum

Among the earliest printed advertisements in England were handbills calling attention to monsters.

B

Tea was to be the subject of rather less restrained advertising ere long. Coffee, first drunk in the Jamaica Coffee House in 1652, had already been hailed by Pasqua Rosée, its importer, as an excellent remedy and cure for consumption, dropsy, gout, scurvy, the King's Evil and hypochondriac winds. 'It so incloseth the orifice of the stomach, and fortifies the heat within, that it is very good to help digestion . . . it much quickens the spirits and makes the heart lightsome.'

A year later came one of the earliest advertisements in a new class. It is from *Occurrences from Foreign Parts:*

At the *Rose* Tavern in Covent Garden, there is to be sold these Silks and Stuffs following at very reasonable rates: Silver Stuffs, Plushes, Sattains, Colour'd Tabbies, Colour'd Silk Mohairs, Silk Prunelloes, Podeswaies, Plower'd Tabbies, Taffaties, Silk Druggets, Tammies, Woosted Druggets, Serges and all sorts of Bombassenes.

Other advertisements of this type offered Confaloes, Dorees, Elatches, Gelongs, Lungees, Mulmuls, Pelongs, Romals, Tanjeebs, Shahagerries, Farendines, Hair Shags, and Shaloons.

Another early entrant in a form of advertising which was to sweep the board in centuries to come was this, from the *Mercurius Politicus* of December 20, 1660:

Most Excellent and Approved DENTIFRICE to scour and cleanse the Teeth, making them white as Ivory, preserves from the Tooth-ach; so that, being constantly used, the Parties using it are never troubled with the Tooth-ach; It fastens the Teeth, sweetens the Breath, and preserves the Gums and Mouth from Cankers and Imposthumes. Made by Robert Turner, Gentleman; and the right are onely to be had at Thomas Rookes, Stationer, at the Holy Lamb at the east end of St. Paul's Church, near the School, in sealed papers at 12d the paper.

If a gentleman had lost his teeth, there were dentists who advertised their willingness to insert in his gums teeth pulled from the jaws of impoverished youths.

The Merrie Monarch was not long on the throne before he himself sought the aid of the advertising columns. In the *Mercurius Publicus* Charles began to advertise for his missing dogs. The most renowned of these advertisements, in July of 1660, ran:

We must call upon you again for a Black Dog, between a Greyhound and a Spaniel, no white about him, onely a streak, on his Brest, and Tayl a little bobbed. It is His Majesties own Dog, and doubtless was stoln, for the Dog was not born nor bred in *England*, and would never forsake his Master. Whosoever findes him may acquaint any at Whitehal, for the Dog was better known at Court than those who stole him. Will they never leave robbing His Majesty? Must he not keep a Dog? This Dogs place (though better than some imagine) is the only place which nobody offers to beg.

It must not be supposed that Charles II used the advertisement columns solely for the recovery of dogs. A king had his responsibilities to his people. In the *Public Intelligencer* of 1664 appeared the following:

Whitehall, May 14, 1664. His Sacred Majesty, having declared it his Royal will and purpose to continue the healing of his people for the Evil during the month of May and then to give over till Michaelmas next, I am commanded to give notice thereof that the people may not come up to Town in the Interim and lose their labour.

By now the Press was again under restraint. Charles rewarded the loyal Roger l'Estrange, who had narrowly escaped execution by the Commonwealth, with the congenial task of supervision and suppression of newspapers. L'Estrange's personal conviction was that a newspaper 'makes the multitude too familiar with the actions and counsels of their superiors.' As justification for publishing two newspapers of his own—the *Intelligencer* and *The News*, both of which carried advertisements—he cited the need for prudent guidance of the public. He conducted night raids on printing shops, looking for treasonable works in the Press; nor was he disappointed.

The year of the Plague—1665—affords the first notable example of a mass assault on the public by advertisers, using not only the public prints but the public streets.

Daniel Defoe has told the story admirably in his *Journal of the Plague Year*. When the threat of the pestilence became real, he says, the public ran to 'conjurors and witches,' eagerly 'storeing themselves with such Multitudes of Pills, Potions and Preservatives' that they 'prepared their bodies for the Plague instead of preserving them against it.'

It is incredible and scarce to be imagined how the Posts of Houses and Corners of Streets were plastered over with Doctors' Bills, and Papers of Ignorant Fellows; quacking and tampering with Physick, and inviting the People to come to them for Remedies; which was generally set off with such flourishes as these, (viz.) INFALLIBLE preventive Pills against the Plague. NEVER-FAILING Preservatives against the Infection. SOVEREIGN Cordials against the Corruption of the Air. EXACT Regulations for the Conduct of the Body, in case of an Infection. Antipestilential Pills. INCOMPARABLE Drink against the Plague, never found out before. An UNIVERSAL Remedy for the Plague. The ONLY-TRUE Plague-Water. The ROYAL ANTIDOTE against all Kinds of Infection; and such a number more that I cannot reckon up; and if I could would fill a Book of themselves.

The claims, it is worth remarking, were no more sweeping than some of those advanced in our own century on behalf of 'cures' for cancer and tuberculosis.

Here are some more advertisements quoted by Defoe:

An Italian Gentlewoman, just arrived from NAPLES, having a choice Secret to prevent Infection, which she found out by her great Experience, and did wonderful Cures with it in the late Plague there; wherein there died 20,000 in one day.

An eminent HIGH-DUTCH Physician, newly come over from HOLLAND, where he resided during all the Time of the great Plague, last year in AMSTERDAM; and cured Multitudes of People that actually had the Plague upon them.

An antient Gentlewoman having practised with great Success, in the late plague in this city, ANNO 1636, gives her advice only to the Female Sex. . . .

Defoe noted that one advertiser offered 'advice to the poor for nothing.' This advice, it turned out, was to buy the advertiser's physic. The Lord Mayor of London instructed the College of Physicians to publish a list of cheap remedies, in order to save the public from throwing their money away; but nothing could prevent them now from buying not only physic but charms, philtres, exorcisms, incantations, and amulets.

Many of the quacks who stayed on to snatch the last profits were themselves felled by the Plague. Others dosed themselves liberally with their own specifics, and died just the same. It is possible that many of the vendors honestly believed in the virtues of their potions, or at least were convinced that their remedies were no less efficacious than those compounded by the doctors. The state of medical knowledge at the time was illustrated by a belief that if a sufferer from the Plague breathed upon glass, an observer with a microscope would see 'strange, monstrous and frightful shapes, such as Dragons, Snakes, Serpents and Devils, horrible to behold.' But, said Defoe, 'this I very much question the truth of.'

For two years after the Plague, says Defoe, no quacks were to be seen in the city. Some of the public thought they had been all swept away by the infection, as 'a particular mark of God's Vengeance upon them, for leading the poor People into the Pit of Destruction, merely for the Lucre of a little Money. . . .' Defoe preferred to believe that many of them had fled into the country, unloading the remainder of their wares on scared villagers, who were hourly awaiting the visitation from the cities.

During the Plague the journals of L'Estrange had advertised nostrums, official instructions and closing-down notices by inn-keepers and others. When the Great Fire succeeded the Plague, merchants whose businesses were burned out were invited to advertise their new addresses in the public sheets (a facility denied, for security reasons, to burned-out traders in the 'blitz' of the second world war).

London could take it, then as now. The business world struggled back to its feet. New and better coffee-houses sprang up, frequented by merchants, masters of vessels, lawyers, authors, gamblers, clergymen, promoters of the new joint stock companies. England was on her rapid climb to commercial greatness. The fear of another Great Fire was partly allayed by a new facility now advertised: fire insurance.

Lloyd's Coffee-House was a resort frequently mentioned in the advertisements—if only as a place at which news of runaway blackamoors and absconding clerks could be reported.

For the purpose of this book, the outstanding name in the latter part of the seventeenth century is that of John Houghton, a one-time apothecary and general dealer who saw a far greater future for advertising than anyone had done to date. He was not the first to conceive a paper published primarily for advertisements, but he was the first to propagate the idea with vigour and imagination. In 1682 he launched a modest sheet entitled *A Collection for the Improvement of Husbandry and Trade*. It had indifferent success, but Houghton kept on. The world must be informed of the possibilities of advertising. For instance, there were great and unrealized opportunities in the fields of 'situations vacant' and 'situations wanted':

If I can meet with a sober man that has a counter-tenor voice I can help him to a place worth £30 the year or more.

I want a complete young man that will wear a livery, to wait on a very valuable gentleman; but he must know how to play on a violin or flute.

I want a pritty boy to wait on a gentleman who will take care of him and put him out an apprentice.

I know of several curious women that would wait on ladies to be housekeepers.[1]

Houghton was concerned in the exchange of commodities and services, too:

If any want all kinds of necessaries for corps or funerals, I can help to one who does assure me that he will use them kindly; and whoever can keep their corps till I get to London and have a coffin set down may have them afterwards kept any reasonable time.

At one Mr. Packer's in Crooked Lane, next the Dolphin are very good lodgings to be let, where there is freedom from noise, and a pretty garden.

Houghton stimulated a peculiar traffic which persists down to the present day—in second-hand sermons. He advertised books, read and recommended them gratuitously. At one point he had to chide booksellers for putting new titles on old books. He published quack advertisements, but told his readers that they were under no obligation to read them.

'Anything to oblige' might have been Houghton's motto. He even went so far as to enter the matrimonial field:

I know of several men and women whose friends would gladly have them match'd, which I'll endeavour to do, as from time to time I shall hear of such whose circumstances are likely to agree; and I'll assure such as will come to me it shall be done with all the honour and secrecy imaginable. Their own parents shall not manage it more to their satisfaction and the more comes to me the better I shall be able to serve 'em.

Houghton seems to have been one of those men whose passion it is to 'do business,' no matter of what type. He has been called the 'father of advertising' and his naïve-sounding offers and

---

[1] 'Curious' was used in the sense of 'careful' or 'bestowing care.'

protestations have been quoted widely at advertising clubs and conventions in the last hundred years.

He had sounder ideas about the stimulation of business than the publisher of the *Country Gentleman's Courant,* who wrote in 1685:

Seeing promotion of trade is a matter which ought to be encouraged, the price of advertisements is advanced to twopence a line.

18th Century

'NEAR TO PERFECTION'

DURING the early years of the eighteenth century, the years of Steele and Addison, publications of all kinds sprang into life, flourished for a day and subsided into oblivion. In 1702 appeared the first daily newspaper in Britain—the single-sheet *Daily Courant*.[1] Two years later Defoe started his *Review*, and poured his prodigious energies into it for the next nine years. Next came 'social' journalism, with a deliberate appeal to women, as exemplified by the *Tatler* (1709) and the *Spectator* (1711). These papers were usually in financial straits. When, in 1712, on Crown instigation, the Government set out to curb the activities of the Press, it did so by imposing a punitive stamp duty and an advertisement tax. Each paid announcement, whether it occupied a line or a column, was charged at the rate of one shilling; if this was not paid within thirty days the tax was trebled, one-third being paid to the informer. With many others, the *Spectator* went to the wall, while the more disreputable sheets continued to flourish.

For a century to come, the advertisements in all these publications were directed only at a limited circle: the frequenters of coffee-houses, where the newspapers were read. There was little or no advertising of household goods. The advertiser was content to offer the wealthy their coffee, their tea, their turtles, their books and wines and wigs, their purges and 'cosmaticks'; to notify them of new plays and concerts; to offer them lottery tickets; to engage them servants and slaves. He was also prepared (as will be seen) to offer even more intimate help.

[1] The first daily newspaper in America appeared in 1704: the *Boston News Letter*. It carried advertisements.

It was a day when Scotsmen anxious to seek their fortunes in London had to endure thirteen days of jolting and pay £4 10s. for the pleasure. (In the *Tatler* Henry Mills, Gentleman, drew attention to his steel springs which lessened the rigours of coach riding.) On the Continent of Europe Marlborough's armies were shuffling to glory; and in the news-sheets of the day poets advertised their congratulatory odes. Queen Anne kept up the practice of touching the faithful to rid them of the King's Evil; one of those on whom she was to lay hands was a youngster called Samuel Johnson. Country girls journeyed to town to sell their tresses to the wigmakers. Prodding the lunatics in Bedlam was regarded as a good afternoon's fun. Half the country was ready to argue that a woman could give birth to rabbits. An inventor, ahead of his time, installed near St. James's Coffee-House the 'Globe Light,' which (according to an advertisement in the *Tatler*) 'is observed to enlighten the street and all parts near it with a true steady light no way offensive to the eyes.' Unfortunately this new form of lighting had to be abandoned because it served to make the shadows darker, and rogues gathered there.

For a progress report on the art of advertising at the end of the first decade, it is necessary to turn to Addison's essay in the *Tatler* of September 14, 1710.

'It is my custom in a dearth of news to entertain myself with those Collections of Advertisements that appear at the end of all our Publick Prints,' wrote Addison. He saw advertisements as 'instruments of Ambition'—'A man that is by no means big enough for the *Gazette* may easily creep into the Advertisements; by which means we often see an Apothecary in the same paper of news with a Plenipotentiary, or a running Footman with an Ambassador.'

Addison noted how advertisements during late years had been used for the furthering of controversy: 'The Inventors of "Strops for Razors" have written against one another this way for several Years, and that with great Bitterness.' He went on:

The third and last use of these writings (advertisements) is to inform the world where they may be furnished with almost every thing that is necessary for life. If a man has Pains in his Head, Cholic in his Bowels, or Spots on his Cloathes he may here meet with proper Cures and Remedies. If a man would recover a Wife or a Horse that is stolen or stray'd, if he wants new Sermons, Electuaries, Asses' Milk or anything else, either for his Body or his Mind, this is the Place to look for them in. . . .

Addison told how a puff for Spirit of Lavender had been sent to him, with five shillings, for insertion among his advertisements; it was written in such a Ciceronian manner that he felt he ought to include it in the body of his paper. It ran:

The highest compounded Spirit of Lavender, the most glorious, if the expression may be used, enlivening scent and flavour that can possibly be, which so enraptures the spirits, delights the gusts, and gives such airs to the countenance as are not to be imagined but by those that have tried it. The meanest sort of the thing is admired by most gentlemen and ladies; but this far more, as by far it exceeds it, to the gaining among all a more than common esteem. It is sold in neat flint bottles, fit for the pocket, only at the Golden Key in Wharton's Court, near Holborn Bars, for three shillings and sixpence, with Directions.

'At the same time that I recommend the several Flowers in which this Spirit of Lavender is wrapped up, if the expression may be used,' went on Addison, 'I cannot excuse my fellow-labourers for admitting into their papers several uncleanly advertisements, not at all proper to appear in the works of polite writers.'

Among them I must reckon the 'Carminative Wind-Expelling Pills.' If the Doctor had called them 'Carminative Pills' he had been as cleanly as anyone could have wished; but the second word entirely destroys the decency of the first. There are other absurdities of this nature so very gross, that I dare not mention them; and shall therefore dismiss this subject with an admonition to Michael Parrot, that he do not presume any more to mention a certain worm he knows of, which, by the way, has grown seven foot in my memory; for, if I am not much mistaken, it is the same that was but nine feet long about six months ago.[1]

Addison commented on some of the more elementary devices employed by advertisers to attract attention:

Asterisks and Hands were formerly of great Use for this Purpose. Of late Years the N.B. has been much in Fashion; as also were Cuts and Figures, the invention of which we must ascribe to the Author of

---

[1] The worm was 16 feet long in an advertisement in the *Post Boy* of April 27, 1710.

Spring Trusses. I must not here omit the blind *Italian* character, which being scarce legible always fixes and detains the eye and gives the curious reader something like the satisfaction of prying in a secret.

He noted, too, the fomenting of controversy between rival merchants, who for the next 150 years were to accuse each other of 'base impositions,' 'fallacious subterfuges' and so on. Also he noted how the advertiser was expected 'to mention the universal Esteem or general Reputation of Things that were never heard of.'

The 'cuts and figures' mentioned by Addison were of varying standards, according to the skill of the block-maker. Announcements of ship sailings were often introduced by small pictures of barques or brigantines in full sail. The column listing runaway apprentices was sometimes headed by a picture of a fugitive with his head turned back over his shoulder. Advertisements for horse thieves and men suspected of the more serious offences would be decorated by a neat little picture of a gallows, laden or otherwise. In due course embellishments came to be stipulated by almost every advertiser, so that the effect of them was lost and valuable space was wasted (shipping pages were strewn with more ships than ever sailed in the Armada). The newspapers then imposed a ban on illustrations which lasted until almost the end of the nineteenth century.

Evidently Addison found no occasion to complain of rogues resorting to advertisement. During the years immediately following, an ingenious offender in this line was scaling the ladder of infamy: Jonathan Wild. In the *Daily Post*, which enjoyed the distinction of serializing *Robinson Crusoe*, appeared this innocent-looking announcement on July 31, 1724:

LOST, the 28th inst. at the Installment at Windsor, a Gold Watch. . . . Whoever will bring the aforesaid Watch to Mr. Jonathan Wild in the Old Baily shall have eight Guineas Reward; or if anyone will discover the Person who took the gold Watch, he shall have ten guineas Reward for such discovery to be paid by the aforesaid Mr. Wild.

There was another advertisement in the same issue, in respect of a lady's watch. At this time Wild, the self-styled thief-taker, was at the height of his nefarious career. Under him served a corporation of thieves and highwaymen, who stole from wealthy victims nominated by himself; the pillaged goods were then sold back to the victims after such eye-washing formalities as public advertisements. In January of 1724 Wild petitioned to be granted the freedom of London in return for his thief-catching services; for he handed over to justice many free-lance thieves (notably Jack Sheppard) and any members of his organization who defected. But already, by the time the above advertisement appeared, Wild was under strong suspicion. Six months later he was clapped in Newgate, where he still carried on business as best he could. Soon, however, he fell foul of a newly passed law making it a capital offence to take a reward for restoring stolen goods unless the thief was apprehended by the person rewarded. Wild was hanged at Tyburn on May 24, 1725. One result of his activities was that advertisers offering rewards were no longer allowed to say 'No questions ask'd'; a rule which had to be reinforced a century later.

The year 1728 saw friction between the coffee-house keepers and the publishers of newspapers. Grievances of the former were set out in a truculent pamphlet entitled *The Case of the Coffee-Men of London and Westminster: or an Account of the Impositions and Abuses put upon them and the whole Town by the present Set of News Writers*. Not least of the complaints was that the coffee men were 'made tools and properties of in the business of advertising.'

They [the coffee-house keepers] stipulate for news, not advertisements. Yet the papers are ordinarily half full of them. The *Daily Post*, for example, is often equipped with thirty, which yields £3 15s. that day to the proprietors for the least. And sometimes that paper has more. Well may they divide TWELVE HUNDRED POUNDS A YEAR AND UPWARDS! They are paid on both hands—paid by advertisers for taking in Advertisements and paid by the coffee men for delivering them out; which (to make use of a homely comparison) is to have a good dinner every day and be paid for eating it. Here's luck, my lads! Never was there so fortunate a business.

If the coffee-houses were closed, said the writer of this pamphlet, the advertisers would be forced back on their 'old habitations,' namely gates, corners of streets, tavern doors and (to bowdlerize) conveniences. 'And what would they be worth in such situations?'

The coffee-house keepers threatened to start their own publications, but the storm gradually subsided.

The next noteworthy report on the state of advertising comes from Dr. Samuel Johnson, who wrote in the *Idler* in 1759:

Advertisements are now so numerous that they are very negligently perused, and it is therefore become necessary to gain attention by magnificence of promises, and by eloquence sometimes sublime and sometimes pathetic. Promise, large promise is the soul of an Advertisement. . . .

As instances, Dr. Johnson cited 'a washball that has a quality truly wonderful—it gave an exquisite edge to the razor,' and a blanket 'warmer than four or five blankets and lighter than one.' However, a vendor of a 'beautifying fluid' had been candid enough to admit that it would not restore 'the bloom of fifteen to a lady of fifty.'

The technique of 'scaring the mother' had already been discovered. The Doctor noted how the manufacturer of an anodyne necklace 'warned every mother that she would never forgive herself if her infant should perish without a necklace.'

Dr. Johnson was unhappy about the way in which 'a famous Mohawk Indian warrior, who took Dieskaw, the French general, prisoner' was being advertised as on exhibition 'with his face and body painted, with his scalping knife, tom-axe, and all other implements of war.' This noble warrior, Dr. Johnson thought, suffered by being juxtaposed in the advertising columns with an offer of a fresh parcel of Dublin butter.

The doctor then made the observation which has not failed to amuse later generations: 'The trade of advertising is now so near to perfection that it is not easy to propose any improvement.' But he thought it time to administer a caution:

. . . as every art ought to be exercised in due subordination to the public good, I cannot but propose it as a moral question to these masters of the public ear, Whether they do not sometimes play too wantonly with our passions? as when the registrar of lottery tickets invites us to his shop by an account of the prizes which he sold last year? and whether the advertising controversists do not indulge asperity of language without any adequate provocation? as in the dispute about strops for razors, now happily subsided, and in the altercation which at present subsists concerning Eau de Luce. In an advertisement it is allowed to every man to speak well of himself, but I know not why he should assume the privilege of censoring his neighbour. He may proclaim his own virtue or skill, but ought not to exclude others from the same pretensions. Every man that advertises his own excellence should write with some consciousness of a character which dares to call the attention of the public. He should remember that his name is to stand in the same paper with those of the King of Prussia and the Emperor of Germany, and endeavour to make himself worthy of such association. Some regard is likewise to be paid to posterity. There are men of diligence and curiosity who treasure up the papers of the day merely because others neglect them, and in time they will be scarce. When these collections shall be read in another century, how will numberless contradictions be reconciled? and how shall fame be possibly distributed among the tailors and bodice-makers of the present age?

Dr. Johnson's appeal to the advertiser to refrain from 'censoring his neighbour' is possibly the first move (an unavailing one) against 'knocking copy.'

In the latter part of the eighteenth century daily journalism entered a more responsible period. It was still an age of licence and frivolity in high places. It was the age that lost the American colonies, but it was also the age that founded an empire in India. Already the Industrial Revolution was on its way; the Black Country was beginning to stretch its shadow; mill towns were springing up on the northern moors; canals were streaking the green fields.

Henry Woodfall's *Public Advertiser* (which published the Letters of Junius) was an organ of distinction in mid-century. His brother William's *Morning Chronicle*, launched in the 'seventies, began to print long reports of debates in Parliament (thanks only to its editor's astonishing feats of memory).

In 1772 the *Morning Post* appeared. In its early years it was a disreputable sheet, one of its first editors being a reverend rake who allowed both contributors and advertisers extraordinary latitude. It was a long time before respectability overtook the future organ of the squirearchy, a respectability fortified by lucrative columns of horse-and-carriage advertisements.

Then, in 1785, John Walter issued his *Daily Universal Register*, which three years later changed its name to *The Times*. From the beginning it promised to carry nothing which could tend to 'wound the ear of delicacy or corrupt the heart.' Advertisements, it was promised, would be inserted without fail the day after receipt, no matter how inconvenient this might be. John Walter's view was that 'A News-Paper in this particular ought to resemble an Inn, where the proprietor is obliged to give the use of his house to all travellers who are ready to pay for it and against whose persons there is no legal or moral objection.'

The Times had been in existence only a few months under its new name when the Bastille fell. From this point onwards the British Press found itself under stricter government surveillance, and the advertisement tax and stamp duty were still further increased, in a despairing attempt to drive journals with radical tendencies out of business. The advertisement tax, which had been raised to 2s. in 1757, now jumped in 1789 to 2s. 6d. It was a blow to new and struggling journals; but if a newspaper found advertisements were scarce it was better to lift some from its contemporaries than to go without (a practice not unknown in a later day). 'In an emergency,' says *The History of The Times 1785–1841*, 'the official announcements of the Victualling Office could be inserted without authority and the Minister afterwards brought by political pressure to pay for their insertion.'

The radical sheets refused to die; they were powerfully spiced with news of vice and crime. *The Times* itself was regarded with deep suspicion by the Government, and in the first year John Walter found himself imprisoned for libels on the royal dukes.

In those days of dangerous ideas an editor could not keep too careful a watch on his advertisement columns. John Mennons, editor of the *Glasgow Advertiser* (forerunner of the *Glasgow Herald*), explained to his readers one day in 1793 that he would have to suspend publication in order to answer an indictment in Edinburgh. He had innocently published, at the instance of a Gorbals gunsmith, an inflammatory announcement telling how 'the Sons of Liberty in Partick, having attentively perused the whole works of the immortal author of "The Rights of Man," Thomas Paine, declare it as their opinion that if the nations would adopt the practical use of these works tyrants and their satellites would vanish like the morning mist before the rising sun, that social comfort, plenty, good order, peace and joy would diffuse their benign influence over the human race. . . .'

Mennons escaped punishment, and resumed publication after nothing more than a bad fright. He was luckier than some who followed.

* * *

Many of the advertisements of the eighteenth century add such piquant footnotes to social history that the temptation to over-quote is strong. Some of the more general types of announcement may be noted here, leaving over the more scandalous ones, and those of the quacks, for separate attention.

There are curious glimpses of the entertainments of the day. Steele has told how, on going to the Bear Garden at Hockley-in-the-Hole, he had a paper thrust in his hand which read:

I, James Miller, sergeant, lately come from the frontiers of Portugal, master of the noble science of defence, hearing in most places where I have been of the great fame of Timothy Buck, of London, master of science, do invite him to meet me and exercise at the several weapons following:

Backsword	Single falchion
Sword and dagger	Case of falchions
Sword and buckler	Quarter-staff

For those who liked their fun unrefined, there was another kind of match, like this one advertised to take place near Whitechapel Mount:

I, *Mary Brindle*, of *New England*, well-known through the Provinces in *North America*, particularly that of Massachusetts, for my extra-ordinary Skill, Judgment and peculiar Dexterity in the noble Science of handling the Members, having by a series of Good Fortune dis-comfited all those who have hitherto encountered with me, as well on the public as private Stage, throughout the American Colonies; and being desirous of aggrandizing my Character in this Part of the World, do hereby invite the famous Miss *Elizabeth Sturdy* to meet and fight me . . . for the Sum ten pounds old Tenor, and hope to convince the mistaken World that though born in the new-discovered Country we are no wise inferior in Point of Courage to any Woman upon the Face of the Globe.   *Mary Brindle*

I, *Elizabeth Sturdy*, from the Kingdom of *Ireland*, do readily accept to the above Challenge; and notwithstanding my present Indisposition, occasioned by the Scars lately received at *Guy's* and *St. Thomas's*, *will not fail* of meeting this celebrated Heroine, and doubt not that I shall soon convince her, as I have several others before, of her Folly and Vanity in attempting to contend with one who possesses so great a Share of innate Courage so peculiar to her famous Hibernian Ancestors.
                                    Elizabeth Sturdy

For this encounter, which was to be preceded by numerous 'bye-battles' between cinder-wenches and oakum-pickers, it was announced that 'commodious Seats are provided for the Ladies to separate them from the Mob; and if the Weather proves cold, Mr. Smarvey intends to accommodate the Ladies with Pans of Charcoal-Dust gratis.'

An advertisement of a similar combat at Hockley-in-the-Hole stipulated that each woman should hold half a crown in each hand 'and the first woman that drops the money to lose the battle.'

If women were pitted against each other in public, how much mercy could animals expect? Alan St. H. Brock, in his *History of Fireworks*, has recorded how the ingenuity of his forbears used to be misapplied, to judge from this advertisement of an entertainment at the Bear Gardens, Hockley-in-the-Hole:

Likewise a green Bull to be baited, which was never baited before, and a Bull to be turned loose, with Fireworks all over him; also a mad Ass to be baited. With a variety of Bull baiting and Bear baiting and a Dog to be drawn up with Fireworks. To begin exactly at three of the Clock.

A later announcement (1730) promised 'a Mad Bull dressed up with Fireworks is to be turned loose in the same place; likewise a Dog dressed up with Fireworks; also a Bear to be turned loose. N.B. a Cat to be tied to the Bull's Tail.'

Not always were fireworks put to such dubious uses. The advertisements of the London pleasure gardens throughout this century tell of many ingenious and spectacular pyrotechnic novelties. Those who visited Cuper's Gardens on September 4, 1749, were promised 'a curious and magnificent firework which has given great satisfaction to the nobility, wherein Neptune will be drawn on the canal by sea horses and set fire to an Archimedean worm and return to the Grotto.' Equally imaginative was a spectacle at Bermondsey on September 25, 1792—'By particular desire the Battle of the Fiery Dragons and the line comet to come from the Rock of Gibraltar and cause the Dragons to engage.'

Brilliant feats of arms overseas were followed by brilliant pyrotechnic displays at home, the sieges of Quebec and Gibraltar being favourites. Occasionally the advertisements contained apologies for breakdowns on account of damp powder. Ranelagh, towards the end of the century, staged a volcanic eruption which was a favourite for many years. There was a scene representing Mount Etna and the Cave of Vulcan, with the Cyclops forging armour for Mars 'as described in the Aeneid of Virgil,' all to the accompaniment of music 'compiled from Gluck, Haydn, Giardini, and Handel.'

'Black boy' advertisements were a constant feature in the newspapers of this century. Those who are under the impression that slavery never existed in these isles will here find a rude awakening. To show that the keeping of black boys was not just a Metropolitan fad, here is an announcement from the *Edinburgh Advertiser* of January 20, 1769:

To be Sold

A BLACK BOY, about 16 years of age, healthy, strong and well made, has had the Measles and Smallpox, can shave and dress a little and has been for these several years accustomed to serve a single gentleman both abroad and at home.

For further particulars, inquire at Mr. Gordon, Bookseller, Parliament Close, Edinburgh, who has full powers to conclude a bargain.

Some of these boys came from Spain and Portugal, others may have been brought to Britain by the masters of slavers. Not infrequently, a boy fled his master, and then his virtues were sung less praisefully. He was described as pock-marked, instead of 'has had the smallpox.' He became bandy legged and wall-eyed, instead of handsome. Almost all runaways, whether black boys, apprentices, serving maids, or absconding clerks, seem to have been ugly, misshapen creatures. In an appeal for information about thieves who had stolen fishing tackle, an advertisement of 1775 said: 'The above banditti may be discovered by the following marks: they all walk *on one side*, are *short-sighted* and most of them are marked with the King's Evil.'

After describing a missing youth, another advertisement said 'Whoever meets him at a Billiard Table, or at a Bawdy House. . . .' Occasionally, however, a missing youth was given the benefit of the doubt, as in an announcement in the *Daily Advertiser* in 1772: 'It is feared he has been surprised and engaged by some of those Persons employed to pick up Men for the India Company and is confined and deprived of Pen, Ink, and Paper.'

An artificial society needed instruction in artificialities. The perfumer Charles Lillie offered to teach readers of the *Spectator* 'the exercise of the Snuff Box according to the most fashionable airs and motions.' There were different ways of offering snuff to a stranger, a friend or a mistress, and there were appropriate gestures to each, all of which should be known to a gentleman. In *Parker's London News* of 1722 an advertiser offered to teach ladies and gentlemen how to walk the streets in bad weather without *dirtying* themselves.

A learned monograph might well be written, with the aid of advertisements from this century and the next, on the bear's grease trade. Here there is room to quote only the following from the *Daily Universal Register*:

H. LITTLE, Perfumer, No. 1 Portugal Street, Lincoln's Inn Fields, acquaints the Public, that he has killed a remarkable fine RUSSIAN BEAR, the fat of which is matured by time to a proper state. He begs leave to solicit their attention to this Animal, which, for its fatness and size, is a real curiosity. He is now selling the fat, cut from the Animal, in boxes at 2s 6d and 5s each, or rendered down in pots, from One Shilling to One Guinea Each.

A generation like our own, accustomed to smearing its hair with the 'scientifically prepared' contents (animal, vegetable or mineral—who knows?) of some highly advertised jar, recoils fastidiously when assured that its great-grandfathers used raw, unprocessed bear's fat to nourish their scalps. The enterprising Mr. Little was only one of a big band of bear's grease men. Unlike a certain rival in the trade, he did not caution his buyers to keep the grease off the backs of their hands, lest they grow hairy paws. Nevertheless, his announcement was probably sufficient to ensure a procession of customers to No. 1, Portugal Street. But Mr. Little did not say enough to satisfy the speculations of the modern reader. Where did he obtain his bears? Where and how did he keep them? How did he fatten and exercise them? How did he mollify those neighbours who were downwind of the bears?

If bears were a nuisance, so were bugs—in spite of the heroic efforts of men like Andrew Cooke, of Holborn Hill, who boasted in the *Public Advertiser* of 1775 how, over 20 years, he had 'cured 16,000 beds with great applause.' He professed to be the oldest bug-destroyer in England, and was angry with a rival who styled himself 'Bug-Destroyer to His Majesty.' If anyone had a right to this title, said Cooke, it was himself, for he had worked at sundry apartments in the King's Palace.

Almost every social foible was reflected sooner or later in the

advertising columns. At the end of the century a country gentleman in Lancashire was advertising for a recluse to sit permanently underground in his hermitage, for £50 a year. The
successful candidate had to be willing to let his hair and nails
grow as long as possible.

Public and Personal

The advertisements of the latter part of the eighteenth century
project a startling light on urban morals. In the daily newspapers there is an unending succession of paragraphs in which
some 'beauteous fair one' who smiled in the direction of a gentleman at such-and-such a place and time is implored to keep a
rendezvous with him. Clearly it was not shyness which prevented
these amorous gentlemen from making the lady's acquaintance
in the first place, but the fact that she was under escort. Occasionally the advertiser received an encouraging reply; sometimes a
stinging rebuff, possibly from the lady's escort. On its lowest level,
this type of advertising was not far removed from the type of
solicitation to be found on lavatory walls.

An enterprising publisher issued, in 1750, a symposium of contemporary advertisements under the title *Love at First Sight*, or
The Gay in a Flutter. One announcement reads:

Being at Covent Garden Play-house the fifth instant, saw a gentleman
there that belonged to the Army, and afterwards went to a House in
the Strand; if the Gentleman is of the same Mind, as he was then,
and will leave a line at the said House for *M. B.*, where I can see him,
I will certainly meet him.

Note.—If the Gentleman has forgot, the last Words were, *To Trust
to Chance*.

One of M. B.'s sisters in the profession also sought to re-
establish contact with a military friend:

Whereas on *Tuesday* night last between the Hours Nine and Ten
a certain well and strong Backed Officer did go into a Lady's Bed-
Chamber in a house in Dean Street and take from the Head of the
Bed while she was in it a gold Watch with a Steel polished Woman's
Chain with several seals, etc. hanging to it; this is therefore to give
notice that unless he delivers the Watch etc. to the Owner within four
days from the Publication hereof, or comes in Person to perform what

was that Night expected, his Name will be published at Length and his Person described. . . .'

Threats to publish the names of offenders were quite common. 'An old Fornicator whose sins have rendered his Limbs incapable to support him' was informed that he would be exposed if he did not stop annoying persons at a certain address; a warning which must have worried quite a number of aged gallants. Another threat of exposure was addressed to a lady who 'persuaded a gentleman to meet her on the other side of the water a month ago,' and who had given him 'a most severe C——p'; but if the lady was prepared to render, in writing, a good explanation for her incivil action, the advertiser was prepared to hold his tongue.

Sometimes the motive of the advertiser is obscure. Was it merely a disinterested moralist who inserted the following announcement, or a woman jealous of her more adventurous neighbours?

This is to advise certain ladies to pay no more Visits to a certain House near Covent Garden; for it is a Place where Reputation may be lost but I have never heard of any got there.

Matrimonial offers are ten a penny. It was usual for a gentleman to stipulate that the lady must be in possession of a private income, and *vice versa*; and at the same time the partner had to be capable of returning 'a most sincere and ardent love.' Sometimes a gentleman politely deprecated his personal appearance, which probably meant he was little removed from Caliban; but usually he would make the most of any modest asset, as 'a gentleman of Hampshire, wearing his own Hair. . . .' There were plenty of brash announcements of this type (from *Love at First Sight*):

If any Lady not yet past her Grand Climacterick, of a Comfortable Fortune in her own Disposal, is desirous of spending the Remainder of her Life with a tolerably handsome young Fellow of *great* Parts, about five feet six inches, she may hear of such a one to her mind by inquiring at the *Theatre* Coffee-House for Mr. F., a Sophister of —— College, Cambridge.

In May 1750 the *Daily Advertiser* carried the following:

WANTED: Tall and graceful in her Person, more of the fine Woman than the pretty one . . . good Teeth, soft Lips, sweet Breath, with Eyes no matter what Colour so they are but expressive . . . her bosom full, plump, firm and white . . . a good understanding without being a wit, but cheerful and lively in Conversation, polite and delicate of Speech, her Temper humane and tender and to look as if she could feel Delight where she wishes to give it. If such a one there be! there is a Gentleman of £2,000 a year, 52 years next July, but of a vigorous Strength and amorous Constitution that will marry her, be her Fortune ever so small, and settle on her a clear Jointure of £600 a year . . . she must consent to live entirely in the Country . . . she must not be more than 14 years, nor less than seven years younger, than the Gentleman.

There were many dubious requests by impoverished single ladies for loans of money. One lady wishing to borrow £100 announced that 'the Security, though personal, may probably be very agreeable to a single Gentleman of Spirit.' She is more likely to have obtained her loan than the lady who inserted the following in the *Daily Advertiser* of October 27, 1752:

GENTLEMEN. It's well-known that many of you spare neither Pain nor Cost, when in pursuit of a Woman you have a Mind to ruin; or when attached to one you have already undone; But I don't remember to have heard of any considerable Benevolence conferred by any of you on a virtuous Woman: I therefore take this Method to let you know, that if there should be any among you, who have a desire to assist (with a considerable Present) an agreeable Woman, for no other Reason, than because she wants it; such a Person or Persons (if such there be) may, by giving their address in this Paper, be informed of an Occasion to exercise their disinterested Generosity.

As the century progressed the 'personal' advertisements became more and more bare-faced. Here is an item from *The Public Advertiser* of January 3, 1775:

This Day is Published
Price 2s 6d with the original Introduction HARRIS'S LIST OF COVENT GARDEN LADIES; or, Man of Pleasure's Kalendar for the Year 1775. Containing an exact Description of the most celebrated Ladies of Pleasure who frequent Covent Garden and other parts of the Metropolis.
Printed for H. Ranger, Temple Exchange Passage, Fleet Street. Where may be had Harris's List for 1771, 1772, 1773 and 1774.

Who was Harris? And how did he compile his popular year-book? Was it a one-man task? Who (if anyone) reviewed it? Even though it did not sell out every year, the guide must have been profitable enough to repeat. There was even a companion guide to the ladies of Piccadilly.

Either this was an age of unusual looseness, or it was one of unusual candour. Henry Sampson quoted numerous personal advertisements of the 1770's which must have shocked mid-Victorian readers; but the morals of many of his contemporaries were no better than those of their eighteenth century forbears. The difference was that Victorian men-about-town did not *advertise* for gentlemen of honour to take over their unwanted mistresses. They made private arrangements, or none at all. Nor is there any instance of an elderly Victorian legislator, anxious to save his estates from being broken up, advertising for a bride in an advanced state of pregnancy. Yet who will say that such accommodations were never forthcoming in the nineteenth century?

In the *Morning Post* in 1775 could even be discovered a young gentleman anxious to devote his services to 'a lady of real fashion and fortune, who may wish to have some particular deficiencies thoroughly supplied, without subjecting herself to any disagreeable restraints.' Shaking his head, Sampson suggested that young gentlemen like this, who 'knew what was marketable,' may have done much 'to prevent the titles and fortunes of noblemen and gentlemen who married late in life from passing to remote branches.' On the other hand, the advertisement may simply have been that of an eighteenth century gigolo-blackmailer.

There were numerous advertisements by benevolent ladies anxious to help homeless girls, or to remedy any inconveniences suffered by young women of spirit and fashion. Here is one of many in the *Morning Post* of 1772:

LADIES may be accommodated to lie-in, where care, tenderness, humanity, honour and secrecy may be depended on. Inquire of Mr. Jenkins, grocer, Rathbone Place.

In what other age could ladies have hired humanity, honour and secrecy at their grocer's?

Running through all these personal columns was the oft-repeated advertisement of the 'respectable young woman with a good breast of milk.' There is something rather endearing about these announcements. It is pleasant to think that the young woman really was respectable; that she had not forfeited, and never would, her 'undeniable character.' Sometimes there was a sad, circumstantial tale explaining how the breast of milk came to be available. In one instance a couple who had lost their infant said that they were anxious to assuage their grief by helping some mother in distress.

There *was* generosity and humanity in this age—though the advertising columns have to be searched hard for it.

The Great Empirics

The eighteenth century was an age of magnificent quacks, or 'empirics,' if a kinder word must be used. Some, but not all, were blatant humbugs. A few were men of powerful personality and a high level of culture, personal friends of the literary men whose works they subsidized by their advertisements, and whose lives (in regrettable instances) they cut short by their pills and elixirs. In the empirics' favour it can be said that they often believed passionately in their nostrums, that they did not descend to inventing new illnesses, and that on the whole they did not market their goods by 'scare' tactics, being content to sing their virtues in extravagant language. Although they made the crudest claims for their purges, and went into revolting details about the length, hairiness and voracity of the worms they conjured from the human gut, they did not proclaim that nine out of ten suffered from gravel. Their promises to cure stuttering by the application of ointment were no more absurd than some latter-day offers to stimulate the growth of hair by 'magic combs.' When they told a lie they told a resounding one to attract attention, leaving it to a later age to sell rubbish by false suggestion, by half-truth and by words carefully chosen to mean nothing when challenged in a court of law. The modern medicine vendor is entitled to retort that even if his specifics do no good they do no harm; whereas the eighteenth-century quacks killed right and left.

In medical knowledge, such as it was, there was often little to choose between the empiric and the physician. Had not Voltaire described a physician as 'one who pours drugs of which he knows little into a body of which he knows less'? In one direction, the prosperous empiric gave better value for money: his arrival, by coach, in an unsuspecting village, with a retinue of acrobats, clowns, dwarfs and trumpeters was a spectacle in itself well worth the price of a bottle of elixir.

One of the more successful empirics at the beginning of the century was Sir William Read, described by Addison as 'that learned knight, my very worthy friend.' Read had started life as a tailor and travelling charlatan, and rose to become oculist in ordinary to Queen Anne. His knighthood was awarded for 'curing' numbers of seamen and soldiers of blindness, gratis. Besides doctoring cataracts, Read also offered to cure wry necks and hare lips. He advertised widely, giving lists of patients treated 'at their request and for the public good'—'the lady Yollop, aged 70, Couch'd of a Cataract and restor'd to sight; Mr. Carter, an Attorney, aged 75, restor'd to perfect sight,' and so on; and he added names of constables, churchwardens and curates as witnesses. Swift wrote of Read's hospitality—'he makes admirable punch and treats you in golden vessels.' After Read's death his widow carried on the practice with vigour, claiming fifteen years' experience of her own in couching cataracts. Her husband had left her, among other receipts, that of 'his styptic water so famous for stopping all fluxes or effusions of blood.' She promised to continue the practice of treating soldiers and sailors gratis.

No knighthood came the way of Joshua, or 'Spot,' Ward, whose notoriety exceeded that of Read. This grave-diggers' ally, who entered Parliament by false pretences and had to flee the country for a while, achieved an enormous sale for his pills. Compounded variously of antimony or arsenic, they had all the subtlety of a depth-charge, and would sometimes bring on convulsions or temporary blindness. Ward had friends in high places. Despite the ravages of his pills, and the failure of his action for defamation against the *Grub Street Journal* in 1734, he was specifically exempted, in 1748, from a Bill aimed at preventing unlicensed persons from compounding medicines. Ward hired 'patients' at half a crown a week and instructed them in the simulation of symptoms; a superior class of patient, at five shillings, travelled by coach. Dr. Johnson thought Ward a dull dog; Pope mocked him as a benefactor of 'batter'd beaux'; but Henry Fielding (whom Ward had tapped for dropsy) sat at his deathbed. Ward took his life's work seriously enough to request that he be buried in Westminster Abbey.

A contemporary of Ward was Dr. Robert James, who also thrived on the sales of a much-advertised preparation of antimony.

Oliver Goldsmith thought so highly of this powder that he took
it, in large doses and against all advice, in his last illness. The
powder undoubtedly accelerated his death, and afterwards the
proprietor was at pains to put out a pamphlet in his own defence.
In 1788 the medical advisers of George III tried out James's
treatment in an effort to rid the monarch of his mania. Another
leading, and misleading, empiric was Van Butchell, whose
advertisements were eccentric to the point of incoherence. When
his first wife died he embalmed her body and kept it on view in his
home for his friends to view by appointment; but his second wife,
feeling that eccentricity was being carried over-far, persuaded him
to send the remains to the Hunter Museum.

Some of the more audacious quack advertisements of this
century appeared in Steele's *Spectator*. 'Imposters and murderers'
was the phrase used by Steele to describe quacks who distributed
bills at street corners, yet he admitted into his columns advertisements like this:

Loss of Memory, or Forgetfulness, certainly cured by a grateful
Electuary peculiarly adapted for that end; it strikes at the primary
source, which few apprehend, of Forgetfulness, makes the Head clear
and easy, the Spirits free, active and undisturbed, corroborates and
revives all the noble Faculties of the Soul, such as Thought, Judgment,
Apprehension, Reason and Memory, which last in particular it so
strengthens as to render that Faculty exceeding quick and good beyond
Imagination; thereby enabling those whose Memory was before almost
totally lost to remember the minutest circumstances of their Affairs
etc. to a wonder. Price 2s. 6d. a pot. Sold only at Mr. Payne's at the
Angel and Crown in St. Paul's Churchyard, with directions.

Here is another from the *Spectator*:

Famous Drops for Hypocondriack Melancholy: Which effectually
cure on the Spot, by rectifying the Stomach and Blood, cleansing them
from all Impurities, and giving a new Turn to their Ferment, attenuating
all viscous and tenacious Humours (which make the Head Heavy,
clog the Spirits, confuse the Mind, and cause the deepest Melancholly,
with direful Views and black Reflections), comforting the Brain and
Nerves, composing the hurried Thoughts, and introducing bright lively
Ideas and pleasant Briskness, instead of dismal Apprehension and dark
Incumbrance of the Soul, setting the Intellectuals at Liberty to act
with Courage, Serenity and steady Cheerfulness, and causing a visible,
diffusive Joy to reign in the Room of uneasy Doubts, Fears, etc., for

which it may be truly esteem'd infallible. Price 3s 6d a Bottle, with Instructions. Sold only at Mr. Bell's, book-seller at the Cross Keys and Bible in Cornhill, near the Royal Exchange.

In other words, 'Wake up your Liver Bile.'

Readers of the *Spectator* were offered cures for all kinds of bodily ravages (though no advertiser emulated John Archer, Charles II's Court Physician, in promising immunity beforehand from the possible consequences of debauchery). Susanna Kirleus, daughter of an eminent doctor, offered to cure 'the secret Disease,' without hindering the patient's business occasions. 'An experienced Operator,' living near Temple Bar, was ready to cup sufferers 'with an Engine, without Fire, scarcely to be felt.' Another offered a 'Chymical liquor' which, in a moment, would make 'the most Nauseous Breath smell delicately Fine and Charming,' as well as fastening any loose teeth and making the gums grow again 'when almost eaten away.' There was a Chymical Balsam for 'green Wounds and running Sores.' And there was 'an incomparable pleasant tincture that restores the Sense of Smelling though lost for many Years.'

When the *Spectator* died the fleas left the body and were made welcome elsewhere. In almost every paper were earnest offers to alleviate Defluxions of Rheum, Hyppo, hectic disorders, scorbutic humours, griping of the guts and even writer's cramp. A Dr. Lowther offered a nerve powder to counter 'frightful dreams, confused ideas, failure of memory and horrors.' Freeman's Grand Restorer of Human Nature was directed against 'horrid Thoughts, Startings in the Sleep and Decay of Nature.' There was the 'true Royal Chymical Washball' mentioned by Dr. Johnson which, besides ridding the skin of all Deformities, Tetters, Ringworm, Morphew, Sunburn, Scurf, Pimples and pits or redness of the Small pox,' was warranted to 'give an exquisite edge to the razor, and so comfort the brain and nerves as to prevent catching cold.'

Advertisers freely sneered at each other's products, often opening their announcements with such phrases as 'Whereas an ignorant pretender . . .' or asserting that their notices were 'not the hasty composition of an illiterate schemer or self-created Doctor.' Dr. Radcliffe, creator of a savoury elixir which cured the effects of hard drinking along with the King's Evil, warned readers of the *Edinburgh Advertiser* in 1767 against 'sweet slops' and 'nauseous pills' which make 'thousands puke at the sight of the phial or pill box. . . .' Perhaps it was this queasiness of the public stomach that inspired Molyneux's Smelling Medicine (*Edinburgh Advertiser*, 1770), for curing 'scurvy, pimpled faces, bald heads and all cutaneous eruptions by smelling only'; no bleeding, no physic, no anointing the body, and—a noteworthy advantage—no need to 'change either bed clothes or wearing apparel.' Not that cleanliness was entirely at a discount. An advertisement in the same newspaper announced the opening of 'A Neat Bath' for Gentlemen and Ladies near Edinburgh, and added, 'Every person is served with fresh water.'

Apart from pills and elixirs, some of the most extravagant claims were made on behalf of tobaccos and snuffs, medicated or otherwise. As far back as 1604 James I had noted some of the contradictory claims made by quacks on behalf of tobacco:

'. . . it cures the Gowt in the feet, and (which is miraculous) in the very instant when the smoke thereof, as light, flies up into the head, the vertue thereof, as heavie, runs downe to the little toe. . . . It helpes all sorts of Agues. It makes a man sober that was drunke. It refreshes a weary man and yet makes a man hungry. Being taken when they goe to bed, it makes one sleeps soundly, and yet being taken when a man is sleepie and drowsie, it will, as they say, awake his brain and quicken his industrie. . . .'

'Cephalick'[1] tobaccos were widely advertised in the eighteenth century; one of them, announced in the *General Advertiser* of 1749, professed to cure insanity.

'It hath set a great many to rights that was never expected, but there is but few, or none, that careth to have it published they were a little out of their Senses, although it be really an Ailment. . . .'

Some of the tallest claims on behalf of a tobacco—'The Famous Cephalick and Opthalmick Tobacco'—were advanced in early numbers of *The Times*. It was a miraculous weed:

Which by Smoaking a Pipe of it, is good for the *Head, Eyes, Stomach, Lungs, Rheumatism* and GOUT, Thickness of Hearing, Head-Ach, Tooth-Ach or Vapours.

And to Restore Ancient Sight and preserve Young Eyes.

So that by using this *Tobacco* Persons may never come to wear *Spectacles*; And if they have already used them may leave them off, by its so *Strengthening*, and *Clearing* the SIGHT.

Likewise to bring away *Phlegm, Rheum* and *Foul Humours* from the

---

[1] 'Cephalic': relating to the head.

Breast, Stomach and Lungs, and such terrible Wheezings that Persons can hardly fetch their Breath.

This Fine Tobacco is Prepared *Only* Up One Flight of Stairs, at the Sign of the *Anodyne Necklace*, against *Devereux Court*; at Mr. Bradshaw's, at the Golden Key behind the Royal Exchange and at Messrs. Peter and Abraham Brown's, in Bristol. Price 4s a pound, or Any LESS Quantity proportionately down to Three Pence.

Another engaging field was that of aphrodisiacs, notably

'. . . viper wines, to make old age presume
To feele new Lust and youthful Flames again.'

Baldwin's London Weekly Journal of 1772 contained numerous repetitions of the following:

The true Cordial Quintessence of Vipers.

The most noble and grand Preparation in the whole Materia Medica, for the real substantial Cure of Impotency in Men and Barrenness in Women, and is vastly preferable to Viper Wine or any other preparation of Viper whatsoever as being replete with the full and whole Virtues of them.

A few Days of it only give such a general Warmth, and so exceedingly delight the Vital and Animal Spirits, Senses and Nerves, as soon to show what it will do upon a little Continuance of it; for it not only promotes and prompts Desire, but also furnishes proper Matter for the Support and Establishment of a true and lasting Power and Inclination. Price 10s 6d. a bottle.

In the *Morning Post* of 1776 was offered a 'Bath Restorative' of which the vendor wrote: 'In the late decays of life it will supply the vital lamp with some recruits; it is admirable for those who have been almost worn out by women and wine . . . where persons are not early happy in their conjugal embraces it will render their intercourse prolific and be of service to our rising generation.' The restorative was also guaranteed to remedy deficiencies caused by sins best left unspecified.

Those who peddled snake-juice *et alia* in the service of Aphrodite were outshone from 1779 onwards by the ineffable Dr. Graham with his Celestial Bed, designed 'for the propagation of Beings, rational and far stronger and more beautiful in mental as well as in bodily Endowments than the present puny, feeble and nonsensical race of Christians.' The 'Temples of Health' run by this handsome Edinburgh quack have often been described; it was in the Adelphi establishment that the future Lady Hamilton made her thinly-draped debut as 'Vestina, the Rosy Goddess of Health.' Graham, during a two years' stay in America, had watched Benjamin Franklin's experiments and had seen possibilities in electrical mumbo-jumbo. On his return to London he installed ornate and preposterous electrical machines in his Temples, the interiors of which were as lush as his prose style— 'Oriental odours and aetherial essences will perfume the air while the hymeneal sopha blazes forth in the plentitude of the soft lambent celestial fire.' The great bed, made for £12,000 by a coiner who was hanged at Tyburn, was an extravaganza of crimson silks and glass pillars, perfumed with essences from 'the Grand Turk's seraglio.' It could be rented at £100 a night by childless couples, the fee including the Doctor's 'magnetico-electric' treatment. 'In a neighbouring closet,' he explained, 'is placed a cylinder by which I communicate the celestial fire to the bed-chamber, the fluid which animates and vivifies all, and those cherishing vapours and Oriental perfumes, which I convey hither by means of tubes of glass.'

Somewhere else there were 1,500 pounds of compound magnets which were 'continually pouring forth in an ever-flowing circle.' As for the mattresses, they were filled with 'the strongest and most springy hair, produced at vast expense from the tails of English stallions.'

The Doctor took leave to doubt whether there existed anyone 'frigid enough to resist the influence of the pleasure of those transports which this enchanting place inspires. It furnishes the grossest imaginations with the means of refining its enjoyments, of multiplying its pleasures and of carrying them to their highest degree.' But he warned potential customers that 'such refinements of the pleasures of the senses abridge the period of life and relax the springs both of body and mind.'

The Celestial Bed made its appeal to a few jaded voluptuaries, but soon the fee dropped to £50 a night and even less. There is no evidence to show that any richly-endowed Christians were sired in it. In 1782 creditors began to close in, and Graham returned by devious ways to his native heath. Soon he began to preach the virtues of earth-bathing; and in 1791 he and a young lady, each wearing one modesty garment, were publicly buried up to their necks. Their hair was elegantly trained and powdered, so that the two heads reminded an observer of a pair of fully-grown cauliflowers. Three years later Graham died; possibly insane, and even worse, poor. He had sparked the trail for the electrical quack, who was to flourish so freely in the next two centuries.

The century, and this chapter, may fitly be rounded off with an epitaph which was inscribed in a churchyard at Godalming, Surrey:

Sacred
To the Memory of
Nathaniel Godbold Esq
Inventor and Proprietor
of that Excellent Medicine
The Vegetable Balsam
For the Cure of Consumption and Asthmas
He Departed this Life
The 17th day of Decr 1799
Aged 69 Years
Hic Cineres, Ubique Fama

1800–1850

THE 'BLAST OF PUFFERY'

THE most rousing advertisement with which to start the nineteenth century is a non-commercial one: Sergeant Hammond's recruiting poster. When this famous call to arms was reproduced in a London exhibition in 1949 it inspired a fourth leader in *The Times*, which praised the writer for the 'rich perfection' of his simultaneous appeal to the nobler sentiments and the human love of comfort.

A HORSE! A HORSE!
MY KINGDOM FOR A HORSE!
Now, my lads, for the
14th LIGHT DRAGOONS
or the
DUCHESS OF YORK'S OWN

All you who are kicking your heels behind a solitary desk with too little wages, and a pinch-gut Master, all you with too much wife, or are perplexed with obstinate and unfeeling parents
may apply to
SERGEANT HAMMOND, ROSE & CROWN, WHITECHAPEL

You are quartered in the fertile County of Kent, where you have provision remarkably cheap. Luxurious living to the brave and ambitious mind, is but a secondary object, else thousands would repair to the Standard of the gallant 14th, could they obtain the honour of being received.

Those of address and education are sure of preferment, your comforts in this Service surpass all clerks or mechanics, an hospitable table and capacious bowl of punch that will float or sink the little Corsican Chief.

N.B. Four Farriers are wanted, and a Master
for the Band.
'GOD SAVE THE KING'

As an example of the 'psychological attack' more than a century before that tainted technique began to be developed, Sergeant Hammond's poster is indeed notable. It leaves a better taste in the mouth than some of the recruiting posters ('Is Anyone Proud of *You*?') issued during World War One.

Other regiments, also, directed their appeals to 'young fellows whose hearts beat high to tread the paths of glory.' There were vacancies, not only for private soldiers, but for commanding officers, in the enlisting of whom a less heroic note was sounded. Here is a bargain offer from the *Morning Post* of April 21, 1803:

ARMY. A LIEUT-COLONELCY in an Old Regiment at home to be DISPOSED OF. There are advantages attending this Commission, which render it peculiarly profitable. Letters, post-paid, addressed to Y. Z., Cannon Coffee-house, Charing Cross will be immediately attended to.

In those fateful days nepotism and place-hunting were carried to startling lengths. Here is an appeal from *The Times* of April 16, 1801:

FIVE HUNDRED GUINEAS will be given to any lady or gentleman who can procure the Advertiser a Permanent Situation of proportionate value in the Exchequer or any other office under Government where not more than three hours daily attendance is required. Strict secrecy may be relied on if requisite. Address to Mr. Mason at 4 Salisbury Street, Strand. None but principals will be treated with.

Two years later the market appeared to have stiffened. An advertiser in the *Morning Post* of May 26, 1803, dangled a bigger sum and even offered to do an honest day's work:

A PREMIUM of One Thousand Pounds will be presented to any Person who can procure to the Advertiser a SITUATION in any of the PUBLIC OFFICES under Government. The Advertiser's object is to be employed six, eight or ten hours of the day. Letters addressed to G. H. G., Orange Coffee-House, Haymarket will reach the Advertiser.

Sometimes an applicant specified the exact post he required— in one instance, that of Commissary of the Forces—and invited the existing incumbent to resign (for a consideration) in his favour.

The eighteenth century was still dying, lustily and lustfully. The 'naked fashion' was in vogue; a fashionable woman's dress weighed as little as seven ounces. Belles of society had false faces, false hair, false breasts and false bellies (for the fashion of the anterior bustle, giving an illusion of pregnancy, died hard). Mantraps and the pillory had still to be abolished. But reform was unmistakably in the air. Sir Samuel Romilly was seeking to whittle down the monstrous list of felonies for which a noose was the penalty—there were two hundred of them at the start of the century. In 1801 the *Aberdeen Journal* carried this announcement:

WANTED, AN EXECUTIONER

For the City of Aberdeen. Such persons as may wish to be appointed to the office are desired immediately to apply to George Turriff, Dean of Guild's Officer, who will give information respecting the salary and emoluments, which are considerable, besides a free house.

The Scots prided themselves that their law was less barbarous than the English, yet evidently there was sufficient work to justify the supposedly frugal city of Aberdeen keeping a full-time executioner, and providing him with a free house.

It was a grim age, and not even the grave could always be relied upon for shelter. One advertiser boasted, however, that his patent coffins were 'on such a principle as to prevent their being opened.'

During the Hundred Days, the advertising columns of the newspapers gave little hint of tremendous events on the Continent. The respectable young woman with a good breast of milk, the pedlar of lottery tickets, the young orphan lady seeking the protection of a single gentleman, the pox-doctor, the Society for Suppression of Mendicity, the vendor of cauls (for those in peril on the sea), the promoter of panoramas, the auctioneer, the ventriloquist, the rakes of Ranelagh—all these were conducting business as normal. A Mr. Gray, of the Royal College of Surgeons, announced an 'unprecedented' development in dentistry: artificial teeth could now be provided without springs, wires or other anchoring devices—'the teeth may be taken out with the greatest facility, cleansed and replaced by the wearers themselves.' The cry of 'no springs, no wires' was soon to be taken up by dozens of competitors. There was internecine strife among the truss-makers; the firm of Salmon, Ody and Company tried to work up public indignation against one of their number who had canvassed Army and Navy contracts by offering self-adjusting trusses, whereas the ones he was in a position to offer were not self-adjusting and did not even have universal joints. There was a whiff of a pre-Revolutionary world in the announcement of a powder which would give any woman 'the incomparable bloom of Ninon de L'Enclos.' On the day that the *Morning Post* carried the heading 'Glorious Intelligence—Defeat of Bonaparte by Duke of Wellington' it is unlikely that many readers had time to read the persuasive announcement on the front page of Slater's Patent Steam Kitchen and Range—'Its various operations of steaming, boiling, roasting, baking, stewing and broiling, and supplying constantly from one to fourteen gallons of boiling water ... are all performed by the use of one small fire.' The advertiser went on to make a claim familiar to modern ears—that his range used only half the fuel of any other.

During these years the Press was straining for its liberty. William Cobbett, back from exile in America, had launched his journal *The Porcupine* in 1800. This short-lived sheet was notable for the fact that it contained one of the first attacks on disreputable advertising:

Not a single *quack* advertisement will on any account be admitted into the *Porcupine*. Our newspapers have been too long disgraced by this species of falsehood, filth and obscenity. I am told that, by adhering to this resolution, I shall lose five hundred a year, and excite the resentment of the numerous body of empirics; but their money I hope I shall never be so graceless as to covet, and as to resentment, I have nothing to fear from that, so long as I abstain from their death-dealing nostrums.

Cobbett ascribed the *Porcupine's* ill-success, not to lack of advertising, but to his inability to stoop to the prevailing fashion of smirching reputations in the expectation of being paid to keep silence. It is worth noting that Leigh Hunt's brother John, on starting the *Examiner* (1808), declined even trade advertisements lest they impair the dignity of the paper.

The 'taxes on knowledge' were so severe at this period that only the best and the worst publications prospered. In 1803, as a war measure, the advertisement tax was raised to the crippling figure of 3s. 6d. Yet even under this handicap *The Times* and the *Morning Post* continued to make headway. Government advertising—an important source of revenue—was withheld from those papers which had the temerity to criticize the way the country's affairs were conducted. In 1803 Cobbett was deprived of Post Office advertisements; next year *The Times*, after a strong and well-warranted attack on the First Lord of the Admiralty, also lost its Government announcements. Ingeniously, John Walter the Second surmounted the many obstacles the Government put in his path, and the mounting circulation of *The Times* was reflected in the increased number of advertisements (about 100 a day in 1800, 150 a day in 1810). Lesser publications suffered, flouted or evaded the 'taxes on knowledge' as best they could. Lord Ellenborough, in 1819, complained of the 'continued stream of falsehood and malignity' from the 'pauper Press.' When it was suggested that the lower classes had a right to political information, he said he 'saw no possible good to be derived from having statesmen at the loom and politicians at the spinning jenny.'

Cobbett's England gave way to Dickens' England. The rotten boroughs were banished; a police force sprang into being; the railway boom began; illiteracy began to recede. Yet, because of the 'taxes on knowledge,' there were fewer newspapers in the 1840's than there had been in the 1740's; even though the advertisement tax was lowered—in 1833—to 1s. 6d. Often enough the new literacy was nourished on the 'last confessions' of criminals, the early 'penny dreadfuls' and the tasty *réchauffages* of police news served up by Edward Lloyd, founder of *Lloyd's Weekly Newspaper* (1842).

A powerful whiff of radicalism rose from this obstreperous organ, which vigorously defended the under-dog. At first it was only lightly supported by advertisers, who favoured those papers circulating among 'carriage trade.' Both Lloyd's paper and *Bell's Life in London* carried announcements which would scarcely have been welcomed by the *Morning Post*; for example, the following from *Bell's Life* on June 7, 1835:

Read the Pocket BLACK BOOK, containing Authentic Details of the Revenue, Expenditure and Taxation of the United Kingdom. The Income and Patronage of the Church, amounting annually to nearly Ten Millions! The Enormous Income and Patronage of the Bishops! A complete list of 1500 Ladies and Gentlemen, pensioners, place-men, sinecurists etc. who receive annually upwards of one million of the public money!

There was still much to outrage a good radical. In 1844 an

advertisement in the *Cheltenham Free Press* by the Earl of Ducie's agent offered 'the ENTIRE VILLAGE of Nymphfield, wherein are SIXTY-SIX HOUSES and the DUCIE ARMS, WITH POLITICAL INFLUENCE extending over 1200 HONEST YEOMEN.'

Commented *Punch*: 'Has the Earl no *droits de seigneur*? . . . Can he not lump in with the yeomen their wives and daughters?'

A new type of advertisement which began to appear in *Lloyd's Weekly Newspaper* was the undertaker's announcement.

The Metropolitan Cemetery and Funeral Company offered a First-Class Funeral at £14 14s., with carriages built in the new Gothic style, Use of Cloaks, Hatbands, Hoods and Scarfs for eight Mourners, and—a considerable inducement—Superintendent on Horseback. Two Mutes on Horseback, with Appendages, cost £2 2s. extra.

The Superintendent on Horseback was still included in the fee for a Second-Class Funeral, but in a Third-Class Funeral he was present only on foot. The Fourth, Fifth and Sixth Class Funerals he left to his assistants. Incidentally, the Sixth Class Funeral, at £2 2s., appeared to offer very sound value.

* * *

Gradually the nature of the advertisement columns was changing. The reproach that the advertiser was the rich man's pander could no longer fairly be made. Manufacturers of hair dressing and tooth powder were beginning to woo the mass market. Even household goods—blacking, polish, soap—were being lauded in print. They were also being lauded, with increasing blatancy, in the streets, where the 'fly posters' were beginning to scramble for every vacant patch of brickwork, and the sandwichmen trudged in lugubrious procession.

This increasing trend towards 'puffery' aroused much disdain in those who wrote for the reviews. The *London Magazine* offered some 'hints' to advertisers of the day in its issue of February 1825:

The style should be firm and forcible, calculated to command respect and attention, and not going tenderly and gingerly to work merely to solicit observation. Judgment must be passed, not prayed for. The public must be cautioned against every thing on earth but the identical article advertised. The world must be challenged for a certain amount (a hundred guineas is an approved sum). The trade must be defied.

The inventor must be 'ever anxious' or 'always emulous' to check imposition.

The *London Magazine* went on to tell how a 'certain prose writer of the present day' had been commissioned to write lottery puffs, but had had his efforts returned as being too modest. 'He thought that he could write,' commented the magazine, 'and the florid Mr. Atkinson with a pen dipped in his own curling fluid wrote a flourishing paragraph that put him quite beside himself.' There is good reason to suppose that the writer whose copy was spurned was Charles Lamb.

In the literary world the advertising methods of Henry Colburn (who published among others Disraeli, Mrs. Shelley, Hood, and Fenimore Cooper) were the scandal of the day. Colburn was the proprietor of several papers which he used to push his own publications. He also had a share in the *Literary Gazette* which on one occasion (as the *Athenaeum* pointed out) carried twenty-one columns of extravagant commendations of his own works, and one-eighth of a column on a publication by John Murray. *Frazer's* and the *Athenaeum* belaboured Colburn regularly. They were incensed that he should seek to advertise literature on the same lines as blacking and tooth powder. In April 1830 *Frazer's* noted how Colburn kept clerks and writers solely to look after his papers and advertisements and said: 'And does not the little man boast of being able to stuff his uncomfortable trash down the reluctant maws of the public in spite of magazines and newspapers and critics?' His puffs appeared in all newspapers, said *Frazer's*, except *The Times* and the *Morning Herald*.

On July 17, 1830, the *Athenaeum* returned to the attack:

There can be little doubt that the stupidest cluster of trashy papers, the most insignificant articles, may by dint of eternal paragraph be forced into sale. It could not otherwise happen that Day and Martin, Rowland, Colburn and Bentley, Eady, Warren and those after their kind could lavish so much money in the praises of their oils, their books, their pills and their polish if there did not exist a class of human being who are greedy of belief. It is the duty of an independent journal to protect as far as possible the credulous, confiding and unwary from the wily arts of the insidious advertiser.

Flagrant though his methods might be, there was no doubt that many authors sighed to be published by Colburn. His annual expenditure on advertising reached as high a figure as £9,000.

At this period publishers and booksellers accounted for much advertising space. The first full-page advertisement in *The Times*, in 1829, was of a book: Edmund Lodge's *Portraits and Memories of the Most Illustrious Personages of British History*, published by the firm of Harding and Lepard, of Pall Mall East. In passing, it may be noted that Wordsworth is probably the only author to have complained that his publisher over-advertised his works. As he received only £9 8s. 2d. for the first edition of one of his books, and a bill from Longman's for advertising amounting to £27 2s. 3d,[1] his protest is perhaps understandable.

In 1843 the *Edinburgh Review* devoted a long article to the history of advertising. 'There is no disguising it,' said the writer, 'the grand principle of modern existence is notoriety. Hardly a second-rate Dandy can start for the moors or a retired Slopseller leave London for Margate without announcing the "fashionable movement" in the morning papers.'

The writer mourned the passing of that cautious attitude once expressed in the 'well-known aphorism':

> Be not the first to lay the old aside,
> Be not the first by whom the new are tried . . .

a piece of advice which, if practised to-day, would bring civilization down in ruin.

The *Edinburgh Review*'s approach to advertising was one of wry, but on the whole good-humoured, resignation. By contrast, Thomas Carlyle was sourly unamused by what he called the 'all-deafening blast of puffery.' In his *Past and Present* (1843) he wrote:

We take it for granted, the most rigorous of us, that all men who have made anything are expected and entitled to make the loudest possible proclamation of it, and call upon a discerning public to reward them for it. . . . Nature requires no man to make proclamation of his doings and hat-makings; Nature forbids all men to make such. There is not a man or hat-maker born into the world but feels, or has felt, that he is degrading himself if he speak of his excellences and prowesses, and supremacy in his craft; his inmost heart says, to him, 'Leave thy friends to speak of these; if possible thy enemies to speak

[1] Quoted in *The Athenaeum*: Leslie A. Marchand.

of these; but at all events, thy friends!' He feels that he is already a poor braggart; fast hastening to be a falsity and speaker of the Untruth.

Some of the advertisements which drew such heavy disapproval must now be reviewed. The names 'Warren' and 'Rowland' were cited by the *Athenaeum* in its list of wily puffers. Robert Warren is generally supposed to have marketed the first nationally advertised household article: Warren's Shoe Blacking, which was launched on a sea of poetry. Little is known about Robert Warren. The advertising appears to have been taken over after some years by Mrs. Warren, presumably his widow. Said the *Edinburgh Review*: 'The praises of blacking were sung in strains which would have done no discredit to Childe Harold himself, even in his own opinion—for when accused of receiving £600 a year for his services to Mrs. Warren—of being, in short, the actual personage alluded to in her famous boast, "We keeps a poet"—he showed no anxiety to repudiate the charge.'

The reader may, or may not, be able to detect the hand of Byron in this specimen verse, which appeared in *Bell's Life* in January 1835:

> 'Friend,' said Aminadab to Obadiah,
>   'Why such amazement do thy features show?'
> 'To see, Aminadab, thy Boots on fire,
>   And thou stand harmless in the burning glow!'
> 'Ah! Friend, dost thou so of discernment lack—
>   Art thou so far to common knowledge barren,
> Not to perceive 'tis but the radiant black
>   That's manufactur'd by Friend Robert Warren?'

Mrs. Warren could also have boasted 'We keeps an artist'— and a distinguished one at that. Her much-admired picture of a cat spitting at its reflection in a Hessian boot was drawn by George Cruikshank, who was not the man to turn up his nose at Mrs. Warren's profession. On occasions, Mrs. Warren could be very much on her dignity, as the following extract from one of her announcements will show.

Imposture Unmasked

The progress of MERIT, although frequently assailed, is not impeded by Envy and Detraction. The aggression of ambuscade terminates in defeat; and conscious rectitude ultimately triumphs in the attainment of the grand object—public approbation. The test of experience is the guarantee of favour and has established Warren's Blacking in general estimation; of which there exists not a stronger proof than the tacit acknowledgment of a host of servile imitators who surreptitiously obtrude on the unwary a spurious preparation of the genuine article. . . .

'Rowland'—Alexander Rowland—was the originator of a commodity (still on the market) which became so popular that society was forced to defend itself—and it did so with the antimacassar. Rowland's Macassar Oil first appeared about 1793. Twenty-one years later it was widely enough known for the Emperor of all the Russias to ask that ten guineas' worth should be sent him without delay, through Foreign Office channels. In due course the firm was able to boast the patronage of 'Her Majesty, His Royal Highness Prince Albert, the Royal Family and nobility and the several sovereigns and courts of Europe.'

If Byron was in the pay of Mrs. Warren, it seems unfair that he should have chosen to bestow lasting fame on Rowland in his *Don Juan:*

> In virtues nothing earthly could surpass her,
> Save thine 'incomparable oil,' Macassar!

Rowland's announcements were remarkable, in the opinion of the *Edinburgh Review*, for their 'confident tone of conscious superiority.' The 'elegant, fragrant and pellucid' oil was 'of vegetable ingredients,' possibly a slap at the bear's grease trade, which still flourished in Dickens' day.[1] Its fame inspired Grimaldi to one of his stage illusions—turning a deal box into a hair trunk.

Rowland had other commodities to offer: Odonto, a dentifrice; Cerelaum, for headaches; Kalydor, 'an Oriental botanical preparation,' for redness and pimples. One advertisement told of 'a whimsical occurrence' which had befallen a customer who had used Rowland's Essence of Tyre. A writ had been made out against

---

[1] In *Master Humphrey's Clock* Dickens introduces an ill-starred barber who over-spends on bears. When taken ill, he loses all interest in life until the bears are 'stirred up a bit' and made to growl. In the year of the Great Exhibition *The Times* had an advertisement of a bear's grease 'depot' off Belgrave Square, containing an invitation to 'any gentleman desirous of shooting the bear' to communicate with the proprietor.

him for some dereliction. As he walked past the bailiffs in the
street he heard one say to the other, 'That's the man.' The other
said, 'Why, you fool, that gemman has black hair, and you
know Mr. —— has grey.' Said the advertisement: 'This is one
among the thousand instances of the beneficial effects of Rowland's
Essence of Tyre in changing the colours of the hair.'

For those beset by bailiffs, there was also Spencer's Chinese
Liquid Hair Dye, which 'changes in a few minutes without trouble
red or grey hair, whiskers, eyebrows, moustaches, etc. to dark
brown or black by simply using a comb wetted with this liquid
. . . a pleasing and permanent change.'

The admiration of many was aroused by a Mrs. Harden, with a
place of business off Oxford Street, who announced herself ready
to display to all comers her own hair dyed in stripes to demonstrate the full range of colours available. Anyone who was unable
to stimulate the growth of his hair by the foregoing preparations
could have recourse to Cantharides Oil ('Spanish Fly is the acting
ingredient'). And if that failed there was always the assiduously
advertised 'Gentlemen's Real Head of Hair, or Invisible Venti-
lating Peruke.'

Another original advertiser at this period was Richard Tanner,
who was trying to revolutionize the art of writing. Apparently the
public clung to the quill, distrustful of Tanner's claim that his
steel pens were 'the noblest invention of which mankind can
boast.' So Tanner tried what would now be called the emotional
appeal. He assured his readers that the stripping of geese, as
practised in Lincolnshire and Cambridgeshire, was a reproach to
civilization. He dwelled on 'the streams of empurpled dye, and the
half-expiring contortions of these birds,' and asked: 'Cannot the
science of writing be improved and increased without inflicting
such violence?'

Tanner, like so many of his contemporaries, had a fatal affec-
tion for polysyllables. In one advertisement he told of his 'Tobago
Permanent Anti-Corrosive Limpid Ink, and Immarcessible Atra-
mental Fluid—That facilitates writing, by flowing from the
pen in a certain gradual stream to the paper, obviating the
unpleasant obstruents which are so justly complained of in other
inks.'

No one can read the advertisements of this period without
marvelling at the cumbrous Latin compounds, the grotesqueries

of 'Greek' with which the advertiser sought to impress his public. Teeth were stopped with 'mineral marmoratum' or 'mineral succedaneum'; raincoats were 'siphonias'; hair cream was an 'aromatic regenerator'; hair dye was an 'atrapilatory.' There were 'pulmonic wafers' for the chest; there were Aethereal Oleine, Elmes's Arcanum, Winn's Anticardium, Olden's Eukeirogenion, and Rypophagon Soap. Some critics feared (as many have feared since) that the English language would never recover from the abuses of the advertiser.

The 'hungry 'forties' offered wide, if not perhaps lucrative, employment for those poets who were prepared to twang the lyre on behalf of commerce; Mrs. Warren's example was widely imitated, not only in Britain but overseas. The *Illustrated London News* drew attention to itself in a saga 128 lines long. Goodman, a saucemaker of Berkshire, kept a poet who could praise his product in many languages. A stanza from the English advertisement went as follows:

> The goose that on our Ock's green shore
> Thrives to the size of Albatross,
> Is twice the goose it was before,
> When washed with Neighbour Goodman's sauce.
> And ye, fat eels and trout, may feed
> Where Kennet's silver waters toss,
> Proud are your Berkshire hearts to bleed
> When drest with Goodman's prime Vale Sauce.

In America, unhappy couples derived what cheer they could from stanzas like this:

> Lucina Cordial!—Barren wives
> It turns to mothers fair,
> And the fond name of father gives
> To husbands in despair.

Then, as now, advertising had its MacGonagalls; and the worse the style, the longer the poem. In a Sydney newspaper land speculators were urged to make up their minds to buy plots in a certain favoured area, or . . .

> At last there'll be no 'lotments to be had,
> And many a one will say, 'My slowness was too bad.'

In Britain, another patron of poets was the firm of Moses and Company, sellers of cheap clothes. What the firm paid per stanza is not known, but it is on record that its women shirt-makers received two-and-sixpence for every dozen shirts.

An advertising fashion exploited *ad nauseam* in the 'forties was that of printing in bold type an arresting phrase like:

A Beautiful Young Girl Strangled

to be followed, in small type, by something like 'a cry of admiration when she saw our new blouses.'

Or perhaps:

The Duke of Wellington Shot

followed by 'a glance of admiration at our hats.'

Punch's celebrated 'Advice to Those About to Marry—Don't' stemmed from one of these advertisements. In the original the word 'Don't' had been followed by a phrase on the lines of 'fail to visit our store.'

The inventiveness of the age was constantly finding its reflection in the advertising columns. In *The Times* were not only appeals 'To Capitalists' but appeals *from* capitalists, like the following dated May 1, 1845:

To Inventors and Patentees: From £1000 to £2000 will be given for any chymical or mechanical invention not expensive to manufacture and for producing economically some article of general consumption.—Apply, to Mr. Dircks, King William Street, City.

Some article of general consumption . . . something which a growing population could be persuaded to swallow, to smear on its hair or to ride on, or in. . . . It was a confident, forward-looking age, and no better evidence is to be found than in the railway advertisements of the 'forties. In these columns of small-type advertisements can be read the story of a brave new world in the making—a new world which was no less brave because many fortunes were lost in the building of it. It is easy to see, even at this remove, how the minds of the Victorians must have been fired by the contents of these arid-looking columns.

By the early 'forties, gangs of Irish navvies were laying the glittering metals throughout the length of Britain. But that was only a fraction of the picture. The same issue of *The Times* that contained the announcement of the Coventry and Leicester Junction Railway would carry solicitations on behalf of the Great Mediterranean and Adriatic Junction Railway ('connecting the cities of Genoa, Turin, Milan and Venice'); the Enniskillen and Sligo Railway; the Namur and Luxembourg Railway ('shortest route to Baden'); the Northern Trunk Railway of France; the Jamaica South Midland Branch Railway; the Austrian and Sardinian Railway Company; the Central of Spain Railway; the Great India Peninsula Railway; the Alto Douro Railway ('will connect the harbour of Oporto with the entire wine district'); the South London Suburban Railway; and a score of others.

Distended to many times their normal size by these advertisements, the popular newspapers of 1845 reaped an immense revenue. Special newspapers were started with no other idea than that of tapping the flow of gold. *The Times*, which carried as many as forty-four columns of railway advertisements in one issue, attacked the craze for speculation and turned away a great many advertisements which appeared over-reckless; these easily found harbour elsewhere. Very few editorial voices were raised in warning. Right until the end, some newspapers egged on their readers to invest, but were quick enough to abuse the public for its folly when the crash came.

It was a poor prospectus which offered less than a 15 per cent return. The more ambitious companies hinted at profits which would be so great that the directors were hesitant to name them. To justify the building of railways in improbable places, some extraordinary reasons were advanced, as, for example, on behalf of the Somersetshire and North Devon Junction Railway. Said the promoters:

'The advantages which this Railway presents, in a national point of view, are of great importance and cannot fail to ensure the consent of Parliament to the line in question. It is evidently a Coast line, and is connected with the remarkable historical fact, that in the reign of Alfred the Great the vicinity of this line of coast was the seat of an actual invasion by the Danes, under HUBBA, their leader; but to the honour of the brave men of Devon, that hostile armament was wholly destroyed, their Chief HUBBA slain with all his followers and their supposed invincible standard, Reafan, taken. Supposing, therefore, that a modern or future HUBBA should attempt a renewal of invasion

on this line of coast, what other fate could he expect in the face of
a whole nation eager and hastening to receive him? Such are the
advantages of defence which Railways afford to distant and apparently
unprotected coasts.

Most of the advertisements follow a standard pattern and are
over-long for quoting. But tucked among them are such curiosity-
rousing announcements as that of Pilbrow's Atmospheric Railway
and Canal Propulsion Company (director: The Earl of Essex).
Said the advertisement in *The Times* (1845):

The prominent advantages of this system of atmospheric traction
are that the continuous valve is dispensed with, roads are crossed upon
a level without interruption of main, one atmospheric railway can be
intersected by another, thus saving bridges, approaches and leakage,
and it is confidently expected that a stationary engine every ten miles
will be sufficient.
Increased safety is insured, also obstruction and destruction by
weather and other sources are placed beyond probability by the mains
being buried.

The bursting of the bubble ruined many besides George
Hudson, the 'railway king'; but the railways went on. In 1848—
a fact to discomfit moderns—a special train, chartered by W. H.
Smith and Son, was run from Euston to Glasgow, *via* York and
Newcastle, in ten hours and twenty minutes, a distance of 472
miles.

It is worth remembering that the railway boom occurred
during the golden age of coaching. Faced at last by serious
competition, the coach operators had begun to do all in their
power to make their services attractive. The stage coach died
hard, and died respected.

The Hygeist—and Holloway

In 1849 an advertiser calling himself Y.Z. offered to readers of
The Times the recipe for a 'superior' patent medicine. He ended
his eulogy: 'It is a *gentlemanly employment*, requiring but little
attention and from which a fortune may speedily be made.' The
last claim was perhaps nearer the truth than the first one. It has
been said that in the second half of the nineteenth century anyone
with £10,000 to spend on pushing a patent medicine could not

fail to make a large fortune. Whether or not the medicine had any virtue was of small consequence.

Out of the legion of medicine men in Victorian times (no one called them empirics any more) it will suffice to single out three leading pill-makers. The most provocative of the three, in an advertising sense, was probably James Morison, self-styled 'the Hygeist,' creator of the Universal Pill. So assiduously and ingeniously did he advertise this concoction (chiefly gamboge) that Thomas Carlyle felt impelled to draw morals from it in two of his essays in *Past and Present*. Men and women, complained Carlyle, 'fancy that their religion, too, shall be a kind of Morison's Pill which they have only to swallow once and all will be well. . . . I advise thee to renounce Morison; once for all, quit hope of the Universal Pill.'

Morison was another of those enterprising Scots—this time from Bognie, Aberdeenshire—who exploited the credulous southerners to great purpose. According to his autobiography, of which excerpts were freely given in his advertisements, he himself endured 'thirty-five years inexpressible suffering' (spent mostly between Hanau, Riga, and Bordeaux) before discovering, about 1822, his simple secret—the swallowing of a few vegetable pills at bedtime, followed by a glass of lemonade in the morning. Morison's headquarters were in Hamilton Place, New Road, London, and were dignified by the name of 'The British College of Health.' His advertisements often included a picture of the building, which was imposing, detached and surmounted by a couchant lion.

Morison claimed to have been the first to attack the medical practice of bleeding. He missed no chance to mock the doctors, and when well-known personages died he did not hesitate to criticize their medical treatment and imply that his Universal Pill would have saved them. If confronted with instances in which the pills had failed to fulfil expectations, he would simply assert that the sufferer had not taken enough of them. No one could say that he had not the courage of his convictions, for when he died in 1840 he was (so the story goes) in the act of reaching for another box of his own medicine.

Morison's vigorous tradition of advertising was maintained by his heirs and assigns. A specimen in the best popular style is the following, from *Lloyd's Weekly Newspaper* of December 11, 1842:

DIFFERENCE BETWEEN A DOCTOR'S BILL AND A
HYGEIAN'S BILL

A Doctor's Bill

Mr. John Bull,
To Bleed 'em and Kill 'em

	£.	s.	d.
To Pills, Draughts, Bleeding, Leeching, Blistering, Cupping etc. for yourself and family during the last six months	£10	10	
To 182 visits at 5s per visit	£45	10	
	£56	0	

A Hygeist's Bill

Mr. John Bull (now in his senses)
To Purge 'em and Cure 'em

	£	s.	d.
To 12 boxes at 1s 1½d (No 1 and 2) of Morison's Vegetable Universal Medicines for yourself and family during the last six months . . .	£0	13	6
To 12 boxes of vegetable cleansing powders .		13	6
According to the Hygeian System *no* visits are necessary since you have only to take the pills whenever you feel pain or are unwell . .		0	0	0
	£1	7	0
Difference between the doctor and the hygeist .	£54	13	0

Note—All the Patients are radically cured and
some of the Pills still left in the house.

The scope of Morison's operations may be gauged from the
fact that he paid the Government £60,000 in stamp duties between
1830 and 1840, and also from the reports he used to print in his
advertisements from such far-flung agents (since he scorned
chemists) as 'John Mackinnon, Esq., of Her Majesty's 104th
Regiment, now on half-pay, Hygeian agent for the islands in the
Gulph of St. Lawrence.'

The Hygeist's successors seem to have had a go-ahead agent in
the region of Exeter, for in 1851 seventy-year-old Samuel Crabb, of
Pinhoe, a man of infirm mind, was reported in the local Press to

have been 'thoroughly restored to reason' by taking the Universal Pill. There was another instance in the same neighbourhood 'where a young man was effectively cured in a single night of insanity by swallowing the whole contents of a thirteen penny-halfpenny box of No. 2 Pills which had been inadvertently left in the bedroom.' And it was almost certainly a Morison pill which, at Winchcomb, 'fetched a man out of the Union Workhouse and sent him to provide for himself with his own hands.'

'Parr's Life Pills' were less sensationally, but no less widely, advertised. They were said to be concocted from a secret recipe handed down by Old Parr, a venerable Salopian whose span of life is entered in the *Dictionary of National Biography* as '1483?–1635.' Reputedly, Parr threshed corn when he was 130 years of age, and then was taken to London to be exhibited at the Queen's Head in the Strand. After his death William Harvey carried out an autopsy and asserted that the air of London had killed him.

The recipe of Old Parr was acquired by Herbert Ingram, co-founder of the *Illustrated London News*, who employed a school-master to write the Pill's history. The advertisements were often introduced by statements like the following (from *Lloyd's Weekly Newspaper* in 1843):

The spring and fall of the leaf has been always remarked as the periods when disease, if it be lurking in the system, is sure to show itself. The coldness of winter renders torpid the acrimonious fluids of the body and in this state of inactivity their evil to the system is not perceived; but at the spring these are roused, and if not checked mix up and circulate in the blood, and thus the whole system is con-taminated. . . .

At other times Parr's Life Pills were said to increase the beauty of women, lending 'brightness to the eyes, cheerful animation to the features and agreeable vigour to the whole frame.' Dickens, no doubt, had Parr's Life Pills in mind when he published a skit on the 'Methuselah Pill' in *Household Words* on October 5, 1850.

The third of the pill-making trio, 'Professor' Thomas Holloway, was a man with strong claim to be classed as the first world-wide advertiser. Probably no single name was more widely blazoned over the earth in Victorian times than that of Holloway. It assaulted the eye on every wall in London; it was to be found in the ill-printed newspapers of China, India, and Peru; once it

E

screamed from no less a hoarding than the Great Pyramid. But it
failed to find its way into the pages of Dickens, who refused an
offer of £1,000 for a 'puff.'[1]

Holloway was a soldier's son from Devonport, a fastidious
town which later declined to accept largesse from him. His early
rise is shrouded in apocrypha. One version has it that, as a
merchant in London, he helped to obtain a hospital testimonial
for one Albinolo, a leech-seller from Turin, who was seeking to
popularize an ointment with the resounding name of 'Albinolo's
or the St. Come and St. Damien Ointment.' Soon, to the leech-
seller's chagrin, Holloway put an ointment of his own on the
market, also fortified by a testimonial from a hospital, and followed it with a brand of pills. The leech-seller went to a debtor's
prison, and in due course so did Holloway. He owed large sums to
newspaper proprietors, most of whom he eventually persuaded to
accept a composition. Later he paid them all in full, with a
10 per cent bonus for those who had trusted him. The pill had
been slow to take on; in one week Holloway spent £100 and
disposed of two boxes. For years the self-styled professor worked
an eighteen-hour day seeking to expand the sale of his pills and
ointment. He would visit the docks almost daily, introducing his
commodities to captains of vessels and their passengers, in the
hope that goodwill for Holloway would thus be built up along
the trade routes.

In 1842—four years after starting his business—Holloway was
spending £5,000 a year on advertising. He had richly decorated
offices in the Strand (on the site of the present Law Courts). By
1850 his advertising expenditure had risen to almost £20,000,
which was twice the budget of either Rowland or Moses. In this
year he was faced with a family embarrassment, and found it
necessary to obtain an injunction against his brother, who was
also selling 'Holloway's Pills and Ointment' from an address in
the Strand.

For his more cultured readers Holloway liked to quote the
'celebrated lines of Dante'—'And Time shall see thee cured of
every ill.' How gratifying, said Holloway, that this prophecy was
now 'literally fulfilled' in nineteenth-century England! *Punch*
twitted Holloway on numerous occasions; in 1843 it recorded

---

[1] 'Authoritatively' reported in Sell's *Dictionary of the World's Press*, 1886.

how 'Mr. Holloway with the modesty which is the invariable attendant on real merit declares that his "Universal Ointment" will mend the legs of men and tables equally well and will be found an excellent article for frying fish in.' In 1855 (when Holloway's advertising budget had exceeded £30,000) the *Quarterly Review* wrote: 'It does seem incredible that one house should expend upon the mere advertising of . . . pills and ointment a sum equal to the entire revenue of many a German principality. Can it possibly pay? asks the astonished reader. Let the increasing avenue of assistants to be seen "from morn to dewy eve" wrapping up pills in the "Professor's" establishment within the shadow of Temple Bar supply the answer.' A later historian was to marvel that Holloway should employ 'two intelligent females whose sole duty it is to see that all the advertisements, whether at home or abroad, for the publication of which he has paid, are duly inserted.'

Holloway's career may as well be followed through, though it means running ahead of the period under review. He opened an agency in America in the 'fifties, and soon established an acknowledged supremacy. In 1870 the American advertising agent George P. Rowell wrote: 'Millions who have never heard of Napoleon, his victories and defeats, the sad story of his invasion of the frozen North [*sic*] and his woeful return, have heard of Holloway, the most general advertiser of to-day.'

Holloway's Press advertisements lacked the piquancy of Morison's. It was the scale, not the impudence, of his announcements which impressed the world. Like his rivals, however, he could produce some notable tributes when required. In 1850 the Earl of Aldborough professed to have been cured by Holloway's Pills after all the doctors on the Continent, and even the waters of Carlsbad and Marienbad, had failed. A lady living in Sydney, 'after having for twenty years been unable to make the slightest exertion,' found it possible, since taking the pills, to run up mountains.

By the 'seventies Holloway, who now had offices in New Oxford Street, was spending between £40,000 and £50,000 a year on advertising, and taking a similar sum in profit. He had quietly dropped the title of 'Professor.' Friends now began to suggest ways in which he could atone for his wealth. Lord Shaftesbury recommended him to build a shelter for the mentally afflicted of the lower middle classes, and Holloway duly set up a sanatorium for this purpose at Virginia Water. In memory of his wife, he also created and endowed the Holloway College at Egham (now the Royal Holloway College, London University) which was opened by Queen Victoria. On the two buildings he spent more than a million pounds.

In his later years, Holloway watched without undue alarm the rise of a rival pill, one which, in the succeeding century, was to support an immense financial empire. Thomas Beecham had laid the modest foundations of his business in St. Helen's in the 'fifties, but it was not until the end of the next decade that his thrustful brother, Joseph, joined forces and adopted the slogan 'Worth a guinea a box.'

When Holloway died at Sunninghill in 1883, *The Times* referred to his 'enormous property, valued perhaps with exaggeration at more than five million sterling.' The London Stock Exchange, it added, was already in a flutter at the news. In a long leading article, the newspaper said this of the soldier's son from Devonport: 'He was one of that remarkable class who seemed destined to become rich, who roll wealth together in a way which ordinary men either fail to follow or understand.' Making money had been his 'steady, unvarying purpose.' Of the pills which brought his fame, *The Times* leader-writer contented himself with saying: 'If they possessed one-tenth part of the wonderful virtues which have been assigned to them, their discovery may safely be set down as marking an era of no small importance in the progress of the curative art.'

This is perhaps the place to note that, throughout the Victorian age, the crowned heads of Europe, and many of the lesser lights of the *Almanach de Gotha*, were by now freely giving testimonials to patent medicines, though freely is perhaps not the right word. In 1848 (the year of revolutions) *Punch* said: 'We perceive that the Emperor of Russia has been swallowing a lot of Revalenta Arabica for the sake of testifying to the merits of the article, when so many of the Continental kings are so badly off that it would be a charity to let them have the job of puffing the Revalenta if there is anything to be got by it.'

The Czars, the Grand Dukes and the Grand Duchesses nevertheless continued to praise a variety of commodities. Not far behind them were the members of the royal house of Greece; but the easiest testimonials to obtain were those of the German princelings.

Numerous articles were advertised as in use by Queen Victoria's household, often no doubt without authority. One of these was the Balm of Syriacum, 'a sovereign remedy for both bodily and mental decay.'

The *Edinburgh Review* discovered that Mr. Cockle's Antibilious Pills were recommended by, among others, ten dukes, five marquises, seventeen earls, eight viscounts, sixteen lords, one archbishop, fifteen bishops, the adjutant-general and the advocate-general. 'This list,' commented the *Review*, 'may give rise to curious speculations about the comparative biliousness of the higher classes.'

Personal Again

It is tempting to linger among the 'classified' advertisements of Dickens's day. Here were mirrored the earnestness, the unction, the condescension of the middle classes.

Punch paid much attention to the 'situations vacant,' pillorying presumptuous employers, championing ill-paid clerks and governesses. Once, after quoting a £2-a-month offer for a governess of lady-like manners 'capable of imparting a sound English education with French, music, singing, dancing and drawing, unassisted by masters,' *Punch* commented: 'We have recently read the statistics of insanity and have found governesses to be in a frightful disproportion to other educated classes. Can this be wondered at?'

If the 'English Miss' could expect little, the French Miss could expect less. In 1846 *Punch* quoted the following from *The Times*:

WANTED with no salary or a MERE TRIFLE for the sake of a comfortable and respectable home where she would be treated with the greatest kindness and her morals attended to, a YOUNG FRENCH PERSON, of the Established Church of England, who can speak no English or scarcely any. She would be required to perform no menial office except dressing and attending to the wardrobe of three little girls; the rest of her time would be occupied in needlework. She must be able to read her own language well and have enough knowledge of writing and arithmetic to teach children of six or seven years old. The object chiefly being for the children to have practice in talking French, the less English known the better. If a young lady she would often be admitted into the parlour and would have her meals in the schoolroom.

Reference as to respectability required. To the daughter of a reduced gentleman this would be a desirable home. Direct to C. B., Post Office, Exmouth.

The number of young French persons, speaking no English, who belonged to the Church of England must have been limited, the reader may feel; and of those, the number content to become a household drudge, privileged to make occasional appearances in a drawing-room was even smaller, perhaps. Many were the advertisers who dismissed the idea of wages as something no decent girl would ask for. In advertisements for governesses, seamstresses and so on would occur, monotonously, such phrases as: 'It is expected that a comfortable home and the opportunity of improvement will be considered a sufficient recompense for the first twelve months.' Governesses in their own appeals for work often stressed that 'salary is not of the first importance.' In many instances no doubt the chief desire of a would-be governess was to obtain shelter under a respectable roof. It was a hard world for an educated young woman, forced to earn her living. Not only were governesses driven to insanity; newspaper reports of the day had tragic stories to tell under such headings as 'Determined Suicide of a Young Woman.' And lurking on the Continent was the iniquitous Mr. Fynn, who was always advertising in the London papers for a governess, preferably under twenty-one, to accompany himself and his two boys on a tour of the East. A substantial deposit—as much as £70—was requested as security; and a succession of wretched girls travelled to Hamburg or Heidelberg to make a gift of the money to Mr. Fynn.

In offers of employment 'below stairs' a note of asperity often crept in. A perfumer in the Strand, seeking a cook-housemaid, stipulated: 'The sobriety . . . which consists in drinking deep without staggering will not do; nor will the honesty suffice which would make up for the possible absence of pilfering by waste. Neither will the cleanliness answer which is content with bustling only before the employer's eyes—a sure symptom of a slattern.'

At times the details of the employment offered were set forth in curious detail. Any maidservant who applied for a post in a certain seminary for young gentlemen could hardly complain that she did not know what was in store for her. The advertisement ran (in part):

On Saturdays she will have to comb their [the boys'] heads with the small tooth comb and after the servant has washed their feet she will cut their toe nails; but on no account must she chastise the children— the ladies of the Establishment reserve to themselves the privilege, having a peculiar method of their own.

It sounds an ominous establishment, but clearly not one without delicate distinctions; one in which a hard-working conscientious girl could rise from the washing of feet to the cutting of nails, and thence, by who knows what edifying stages, to the blissful position of being able to mete out 'peculiar' punishment.

It was one thing for a woman to be expected to work for nothing. But she might even be expected to pay for the privilege, to judge from this cry in the *Essex Standard*, in 1850:

HOUSEKEEPER WANTED. The Advertiser (without any family) wishes to meet a respectable Female, of limited income, who would be willing to act as housekeeper and pay him £10 a year towards the expenses of a comfortable home.

The following advertisement from *The Times* of 1853 would appear to have been penned by one of the less engaging characters of Dickens:

As LEDGER CLERK, Manager and Correspondent—A gentleman, of close-sticking business habits who does nothing by halves, whose references as to character etc. are first-rate and whose devotion to his employers' interests ever has been unbounded, is just now open to a Re-ENGAGEMENT. The advertiser is of ripe vigorous middle age and so undeviatingly systematic as by restless force of example to be qualified to establish in all round him habits of perseverance, self-denial and fagging industry such as could not fail to tell wonderfully as those habits became more and more fully developed, on any set of people so organised. Clever men of business who, one and all, admire cleverness in others and especially when it makes to them its own peculiar bow of the most profound obeisance, are most respectfully required to address their replies to ALPHA DELTA etc.

Though pillorying unreasonable employers, *Punch* frequently mocked those would-be employers who allowed themselves to be bullied into paying butlers high wages for working in unfashionable areas, and for expressing the timid hope that applicants for posts would have 'no objection to the country,' 'no objection to wait at table occasionally,' 'no objection to look after a cow,' and even 'no objection to a tradesman's family'—surely the ultimate in self-abasement.[1] 'Wanted, in a respectable family, where all the washing is put out, a steady GOOD COOK . . .' began one advertisement. Every other announcement said 'no followers,' or 'no encumbrances.' Couples seeking employment proudly used the latter phrase to describe their own unblessed state. There was another stipulation encountered from time to time: 'No Irish need apply.'

Employers frequently stipulated the religion required of an applicant. 'A Christian Lady' sought as helpmeet 'a lady of evangelical principles,' expressing the hope that 'no lady with Tractarian views will apply.' An employer seeking an apprentice said, 'A Dissenter would be preferred.' Sometimes it was the person asking employment who stipulated 'religious principles indispensable' in his employer. An advertiser who wished to augment his small annuity by taking on copying work 'in a respectable attorney's office' ended his appeal: 'As the advertiser is a man of extremely High Church principles, no high Calvinist, Socinian or Unitarian need notice this.'

Even appeals for money were cloaked in religious sentiments. One which appeared in *The Times* in 1843 inspired deep nausea in the *Edinburgh Review*:

TO THE LORD'S PEOPLE.—A dear Christian tradesman, who about four months ago drew from the Savings Bank L. 60 his all therein, to give to a fellow-Christian who urgently required that sum, 'thus lending and hoping for nothing again.' But from a bountiful 'God, whose name is Love,' is now in WANT OF FORTY POUNDS to pay all demands upon him, ere he accepts a call to the ministry of the Everlasting Gospel, which he believes his Heavenly Father is about to make known unto him. A lady, his friend in Christ the Lord as revealed, in the power of God the Holy Ghost, thus ventures in simple faith to try the door of Providence in his behalf; and would leave the issue in the hands of Him who has heart, hand, breath and purse of men at sovereign command. The smallest help will be gratefully acknowledged by the Advertiser. Address to B. B., care of Mr. Evans, butcher, Store Street, Tottenham Court Road.

There was a falling-off in the vogue for matrimonial advertisements, traceable perhaps to the extravagant publicity which had

---

[1] In Australia at this time 'help wanted' advertisements often contained 'no objection to ticket-of-leave man.'

attended the trial of William Corder, the Red Barn murderer (executed on August 11, 1828). It emerged that Corder, after stealthily disposing of Maria Marten, had inserted the following advertisement in the *Morning Herald*, of November 13, 1827:

MATRIMONY—A Private Gentleman, aged 24, entirely independent, whose disposition is not to be exceeded, has lately lost the chief of his family by the hand of Providence, which has occasioned discord among the remainder, under circumstances most disagreeable to relate. To any female of respectability, who would study for domestic comfort, and willing to confide her future happiness in one every way qualified to render the marriage state desirable, as the advertiser is in affluence. The lady must have the power of some property, which may remain in her own possession. Many very happy marriages have taken place through means similar to this now resorted to, and it is hoped that no one will answer this through impertinent curiosity; but should this meet the eye of any agreeable lady, who feels desirous of meeting with a sociable, tender, kind and sympathising companion, they will find this advertisement worthy of notice. Honour and secrecy may be relied on. As some little security against idle applications, it is requested that letters may be addressed (post-paid) to A.Z. care of Mr. Foster, stationer, No. 68 Leadenhall Street, which will meet with the most respectful attention.

According to J. Curtis's account of the Red Barn case, the stationer Foster delivered forty-five letters to William Corder, one of them from Mary Moore, whom Corder married. Corder also advertised in the *Sunday Times* of November 23, but did not bother to go through the fifty-three letters sent in. Curtis quotes from several of the letters. Some sound genuine enough, and more than one applicant admits to being not very handsome.

Curtis may safely be left to point the moral:

'We heartily hope that the sad experience of the unfortunate Mrs Corder will deter our female readers from embarking in a speculation where the chances are five hundred to one against them. An upright, prudent and moral man would hardly, we conceive, make his desires in matrimony known through the medium of a newspaper. There may be here and there a platonic lover, a quixotic sentimentalist or a *timid being*, who might resort to such a measure; but what female would like to link her destiny through life with either of those characters, however unobjectionable he might be from a moral point of view?

Our experience is, and it is founded upon considerable experience arising from a long acquaintance with the public press, that those advertisements generally emanate from speculative, sensual and sordid men, whose aim is to obtain a *mistress*, or a *fortune*, rather than a wife. How many there have been who will ever curse the day when they were induced to form an alliance with such adventurers!

*   *   *

The 'agony' column of *The Times* in the middle of the nineteenth century is worth special study. It contained a great deal of what Sherlock Holmes, at a later date, was to describe as 'Bleat, Watson, unmitigated bleat.' That is, cries of 'Come home, all is forgiven,' 'Would Philip like to hear of his Mother's Death?' and professions of undying passion. Some were in the most melodramatic language composed regardless of cost; for instance, this of May 29, 1850:

To A xxxxxx If humanity has not entirely fled from your breast, return, oh! return ere it is too late, to your heart-broken, distracted wife you have forsaken—ere the expression of those soft eyes that won you be lost in the bewildered stare of insanity—ere they may gaze on you and know you not; write, tell her, oh! tell her where you are, that she may follow you—her own, her all—and die. See her once more.

Sometimes the agony was disguised in code. The breaking down of such messages seems to have provided the more leisured readers of *The Times* with mental recreation akin to that to be obtained nowadays by solving the newspaper's cross-word puzzle. A large number of these cryptic advertisements were assembled in book form a generation later by a Miss Alice Clay, who seems to have been a code-breaker of more than ordinary talent.

Some of the codes were dismayingly naïve. It is doubtful whether the master of 35, Upper Seymour Street, Portman Square, would have been baffled for very long if, suspecting a domestic intrigue, he had turned to the agony column of *The Times* on the morning of June 27, 1861:

ABZ si yltsenrae detseuqer ot etacinummoc tuohtiw yaled. ma ni yrev taerg elbuort. Dna eriuqer etaidemmi ecivda. 53 Reppu Ruomyes-teerts, Namtrop eraqus.

It was an equally unoriginal advertiser who inserted the following on July 12th:

Smude. Eht tsop eciffo ta Hgiel si dehctaw, Lotsirb lliw od. Ekat erac.—July 11.

A trifle more ambitious was the coding of this one on October 11, 1869:

SKZPCJJY. BCYP Dyllw, kccr wmsp bgqrpyarcb dpgclb zclcyrf rfc ugjjmu zw rfc jyic.

Solving of this merely involves moving each letter forward two positions in the alphabet; the message is then seen to be an assignation with Dear Fanny. Other codes were of considerable complexity, as even the *Quarterly Review* admitted. Occasionally a solver was caddish enough to play the marplot, inserting his own message to the confusion and alarm of the parties concerned. Sometimes a marplot intervened even when the messages were in clear. For instance, Miss Clay quotes:

Eighth May. You are not despised—quite contrary. (May 13, 1852)
Eighth May. I feel delighted and shall get mad with joy. Pray do answer. (May 14, 1852)
Eighth May. Heed not yesterday's advice. (May 15)
Eighth May. The advertisement under this head on the 15th is not inserted by the same party as that of the 14th. (May 17)

Certain personal columns were used for negotiations with 'finders' of 'lost' property. The Larceny Act of 1861 banned anew the use of the phrase 'no questions asked.' Common informers have since collected money when publications have erred in this respect.

The agony column of *The Times* was as well conducted as such a column can be, which is more than can be said for that of the *New York Herald*. On occasions *The Times* would go to pains to help readers in genuine difficulties, as when, in 1845, it broke its firm rule not to allow illustrations and reproduced a specimen of the handwriting from a threatening letter addressed to one of its readers.

Probably the 'finest hour' of *The Times* agony column was at the time of the siege of Paris, in 1870. French residents and refugees in England greatly distended the column in their anxious efforts to communicate with relatives and friends in the French capital. The front page was photographed, at the behest of *The Times*, on thin transparent paper one and half inches long and one inch wide. Nothing, except the title words 'The Times,' was legible save under a microscope. The photographs were sent to Bordeaux, thence flown by pigeon to besieged Paris. There they were enlarged by magic lantern and projected on to a screen. Clerks transcribed the messages and sent them off to the addresses indicated by the advertisers. It was all part of *The Times* service.[1]

'External Paper Hangers'

Many ambitious merchants of Dickens's England were far from convinced that the Press was the best advertising medium. There were hundreds of thousands of people who did not read newspapers, and who were yet, in a sense, literate. Their attention was best secured by enlisting the aid of the 'external paper hanger,' as the billposter of the day liked to be described. Moreover, bills pasted on walls were not subject to the advertisement tax.

In the 'thirties and 'forties London was papered over, nightly and often twice-nightly, until it vanished from view. Everywhere prowled fustian-jacketed guerrillas with their big pockets bulging with posters, their paste boxes suspended from their shoulders, their long rods at the ready. A householder leaving his home in the morning might find a poster stuck on his own front door, an undertaker's announcement chalked on the flags outside and every vacant wall pasted and overpasted with shrieking announcements barbarously printed. The Metropolitan Police Act of 1839 made it an offence to post up bills without the consent of the owner of the property, but it seemed impossible to enforce the law. Even the Fleet Prison was treated as a hoarding. Charles Knight says that some of the bill-posters had 'consuetudinary bye-laws of their own'; that is, they made it a point of honour not to paste over another man's poster until it was dry. The real problem for the 'external paper hanger' was to operate early enough in the day to escape interference, yet late enough to be able to cover a rival's posters. Contractors banded together some of these guerrillas, with the result that pitched battles occurred from time to time between rival gangs. Since the fly-poster's stock-in-trade consisted not only of paste but of blacking to deface the enemy's

---

[1] In February 1950 Mr. G. R. Pope, assistant manager of *The Times*, told members of London Publicity Club that frequent attempts were made to abuse the advertisement columns of that newspaper. The classified advertisements manager had a close link with Scotland Yard, and there was a 'black list' of 5,000 names.

A *Fly-poster* of 1815.

handiwork, these encounters were as spirited as anything in a Keystone comedy.

Engaging details about the days of unregulated bill sticking are to be found in an article by Charles Dickens in *Household Words* of March 22, 1851. If the 'King of the Bill Stickers,' who is interviewed in this article, is to be believed, bill-posting in its heyday was by no means an ill-paid profession. When lotteries were still legal (that is, up to 1826), the 'trampers' employed by the State Lottery Commissioners were paid 10s. a day and expenses. Sometimes they might be on the road for six or eight months at a time. As the day of the draw neared, London bill stickers in the service of the Commission would earn as much as £8 or £9 a week. They often dined ceremonially together. With the banning of lotteries, however, all the good fellowship vanished, and cut-throat rivalry took its place. The new élite were the auctioneers' men, 'mostly respectable and intelligent,' who were paid 7s. for a day's work, a shilling for a night's lodging and a shilling for paste.

A few bill-posters were illiterate. Their sheets were handed to them right side up, and in a fixed order, and the men took such good care not to confuse them that it was rare to find a bill posted upside down. But the 'King of the Bill Stickers' was contemptuous of the intelligence of some of his rivals. He himself took pride in having been the first to post bills under the arches of the Thames bridges. His imitators had posted their bills at low tide, and in consequence these had been washed away.

The 'King of the Bill Stickers' told his interrogator how, after the passing of the Metropolitan Police Act, one poster contractor had employed a gang of ruffians to beat up those free-lance bill stickers who refused to respect his territory. After spending £500 in a fruitless attempt to rout the guerrillas, the contractor capitulated, but not before he had shaken hands with the enemy and congratulated them on their tenacity.

By mid-century, it appeared, the bill sticker had fallen on lean times. In order to prosper, a man had to erect and maintain his own hoarding, unless he was prepared to spend his time haggling with piermasters and builders' foremen for permission to post bills on premises under their control. If a building was found to be tenantless or derelict, fly-posters still descended on it in droves. Dickens cited 'an old warehouse which rotting paste and rotting paper had brought down to the condition of an old cheese . . . it was so thickly encrusted with fragments of bills that no ship's keel after a long voyage could be half so foul.' The doors and even the water spout had been billed over. Finally the whole place had become so rank and encrusted that even the fly-posters had abandoned it.

Not only towns were plastered with posters. Edward Lloyd carried his message far and wide into the country-side. According to Thomas Catling, who worked for him, 'the more remote the place for sticking a bill the more tempting it was to Mr. Lloyd.' In the head office the cry was always for 'more slips for palings and gates,' and 'six-sheet bills for the rocks in Wales.' Lloyd gave free copies of his newspapers to toll-keepers to induce them to post his bills at the roadside.

The trade of 'external paper hanger' was not one that could be learned in a day. Nor, it seems, was the art of handing out leaflets, as practised by those hypnotic, and often distinguished-looking, gentry who stood at every other street corner. 'Any man,' said Charles Knight, 'can stick up a bill upon a wall, but to insinuate one gracefully and irresistibly into the hands of a lady or gentleman is only for one who, to natural genius, adds long experience.' Reluctance on the part of ladies and gentlemen to accept these leaflets was heightened by the well-founded suspicion that many of them were concerned with 'cures' for disreputable diseases. Eventually the street leaflet scandal became such that Parliament passed the Indecent Advertisements Act (Chapter Four).

Another form of outdoor advertising enjoyed a vogue at this time. Down-and-outs by the score were rounded up and sent out in droves carrying placards back and front (it was Dickens who invented the phrase 'sandwich-men'). Sometimes they were made to patrol carrying banners on long poles, like down-at-heel heralds. The sandwich-men were the infantry of advertising; but the more resourceful advertiser threw cavalry and mobile columns into the battle. A man on horseback could carry a more imposing placard than a man on foot, and a vehicle could be adapted to carry all manner of ingenious devices.

Knight has mentioned one vehicle—'an undescribable column mounted like the tower of Juggernaut upon the body of a car—a hybrid between an Egyptian obelisk and the ball-surmounted column of an English country gentleman's estate. It bore an inscription of "washable wigs". . . .' Another had a revolving device full of Gothic niches in which tailoring styles were displayed.

Dickens's interview with the 'King of the Bill Stickers' was conducted on board one of a procession of advertising carts touring the streets of London. There is no detailed description of the vehicles, but each one drew violent attention to the contents of a sensational Sunday newspaper (presumably Lloyd's). 'Robbery, fire, murder, and the ruin of the United Kingdom—each discharged in a line by itself, like a separate broadside of red-hot shot—were among the least of the warnings to an unthinking people.' Yet, says Dickens, 'the Ministers of Fate who drove the awful cars leaned forward with their arms upon their knees in a state of extreme lassitude, for want of any subject of interest.' During the frequent traffic hold-ups, angry carters struck blows with their whips on the sides of the advertising carts.

Carlyle found time to complain of one vehicular monstrosity in *Past and Present*. He wrote:

> The Hatter in the Strand of London, instead of making better felt-hats than another, mounts a huge lath-and-plaster Hat, seven-feet high, upon wheels; sends a man to drive it through the streets; hoping to be saved *thereby*. He has not attempted to *make* better hats, as he was appointed by the Universe to do, and as with this ingenuity of his he could very probably have done; but his whole industry is turned to *persuade* us that he has made such! He too, knows, that the Quack has become God.

There were advertisements on London passenger vehicles before Queen Victoria came to the throne. Madame Tussaud paid £90 a month to the Atlas Omnibus Company for the privilege of putting her bills on the outside of their vehicles. When the proposal was made that advertising should be allowed *inside* the vehicles (1848), *Punch* was scandalized:

> How will you feel sitting for an hour opposite to a pleasant list of the wonderful cures of some professor's ointment? . . . The testimonials of these gifted gentlemen are as little noted for their delicacy as for their truth, and do not form the kind of reading we should exactly prescribe to the fairer portion of the public who patronise omnibuses. . . . Do in mercy allow us to ride for a day's pleasure to the Bank to receive our dividends without compelling us to sit vis-a-vis to Moses and Son, or having Rowland's Kalydor perpetually thrown in our faces.

Let us be a nation of shopkeepers as much as we please but there is no necessity that we should become a nation of advertisers.

It may not be out of place here to mention that the city of Glasgow held out against allowing advertisements on its trams and buses for more than a hundred years after London succumbed.

Punch kept a critical eye on all extravagances of publicity; noting how advertising boats were making a nuisance of themselves in the middle of the Thames during regattas; recording with sharp disapproval how Barnum's visit with Tom Thumb had resulted in a rash of posters over the Egyptian Hall shouting the attractions of the *lusus naturae* within ('deformity seems to grow by what it feeds upon'). On another occasion *Punch* sarcastically observed that people would be advertising on umbrellas next; and the suggestion was gratefully put into practice.

Any award for audacity in advertising at this period must inevitably go to Edward Lloyd. He began to stamp the copper coin of the realm with the words 'Lloyd's Weekly Newspaper,' paying half the wages of his men with this money in order that it should be well distributed. Belatedly the Government took action and frustrated this enterprise; quite a sizeable sum had to be voted to replace the mutilated coinage. The writer has searched *Hansard* in vain for any expression of indignation at a practice which now carries the penalty of a year's imprisonment. Oddly enough, this was not the end of advertising on coins. Thomas J. Barratt, of Pears' Soap, hit upon a scheme of much ingenuity; it belongs to a later chapter.

F

1850–1890

THE TAX IS LIFTED

BY the middle of the nineteenth century the agitation against the advertisement tax and the stamp duties could no longer be brushed aside. As operated, the tax was unjust. The catalogue of the Great Exhibition contained fifty-three pages of advertisements, all tax-free; the announcements in the railway carriages paid no tribute; nor did the posters of Thomas Holloway. Yet a clerk in search of a job had to pay a tax of 1s. 6d. if he advertised in a newspaper.

Tax officials showed great zeal in discovering what they called 'separate interests.' That is, if a steamboat announcement contained a reference to a hotel and an omnibus service, the tax collectors demanded an additional 1s. 6d. for each. Even news items about the arrival of early fruit or vegetables were decreed to be advertisements. The *Publishers' Circular* avoided payment of advertisement tax only by omitting the publisher's name from the announcement of a new book. More ludicrous was the practice of taxing a favourable review as an advertisement; an author whose book was savaged by an impecunious periodical could be pardoned for harbouring base suspicions.

One simple argument in favour of abolishing the advertisement tax was that a single small advertisment could easily elicit as many as 200 letters, all of which bore postage stamps and thus contributed to the revenue; if the advertiser answered some proportion of those letters, that meant a further expenditure on postage stamps. Thus, if small advertisements were allowed to multiply, the Exchequer would soon recoup the modest £178,000 received from the tax. The Chancellor of the Exchequer remained unconvinced. As a gesture he suggested cutting the tax to sixpence, but the abolitionists carried the day. That was in 1853.

It was a momentous period for the Press. Two years later the stamp duty on newspapers was abolished, and in 1861 the last remaining 'tax upon knowledge'—a duty on paper—was lifted. 'Of all decades in our history, a wise man would choose the 1850's to be young in,' a historian has said. Certainly of all decades it was the one in which to start a newspaper (the *Daily Telegraph*, for instance, made its appearance in 1855). There were some 640 newspapers in Britain in 1855; by the end of the century there were more than 3,000. It is perhaps ungenerous to speculate how many of these would have appeared if it had not been for the open-handed advertising of quacks. Truth, knowledge, culture, piety, and wit—these, whether the world likes it or not, were propagated by pills, salves, pick-me-ups, elixirs, and aphrodisiacs.

The golden age of the 'fifties and 'sixties was not yet the golden age of advertising. In spite of the manifest success of Thomas Holloway, all but a few manufacturers had yet to be convinced that advertising was necessary. They were quite certain that it was ungentlemanly. Some may even have agreed with Carlyle that it was against nature. The ideal, the traditional way to do business was to surround oneself with a circle of customers and to cultivate personal relations with them; excellence of goods, and word-of-mouth recommendation would do the rest. If wider markets were necessary, the way to tap them was to send respectable travellers out on the road, and pay them commission. The last thing to do was to chalk the firm's name on the sides of quarries or to insert furtive little paragraphs in the newspapers, in the contaminating company of truss-mongers, snuff-sellers, pox-doctors, body-snatching undertakers and cut-price abortionists.

That was the only attitude a gentleman could adopt towards advertising, which he preferred to call 'puffing.' Yet what if an honest capitalist, in this inventive age, planned to build and market a complex machine like a steam cultivator or a traction engine, or a mechanical piano? Hundreds of separate processes were involved in the making of these things. If only half a dozen articles were to be turned out in a year, the selling price would be prohibitively high. Unless a ready market could be assured, how was such an enterprise to be sustained? Similarly, if a man invented a new processed food—and scores of these were now being created—how could he offset the cost of plant if there was no certainty of buyers? How could people buy a product when they had never heard of it? Distasteful though the idea might be, there seemed to be no other way of ensuring a market than by advertisement, or perhaps—was this a way out?—by *announcement*. Thomas Russell, a former advertising manager of *The Times*, has argued that it was because advertising, at this period, was still held in such widespread contempt that manufacturers contented themselves with little more than a bald statement of the firm's name and product; the technique of proclamation rather than persuasion. Since all advertisers' announcements were assumed to be mendacious, it was better to make no claims at all, but to let the public investigate for themselves, and having assured themselves of the excellence of the product, to tell their friends.[1]

Hence, contends Russell, the unsubtle and monotonously repetitive advertising of the latter part of the century—'Pears' Soap,' 'Reckitt's Blue,' 'Hot Bovril,' 'Mellin's Food,' and so on, reminder phrases which were regarded as complete and sufficient advertisements in themselves. There may be much truth in this theory, but it is hardly the whole story. For as yet there was no difficulty in selling novel and need-filling goods once their existence was made known. There was no necessity to bludgeon or cajole people into buying. The population was fast expanding, and it was a population which was anxious enough to be wooed by the advertiser. An ambitious, lightly taxed middle-class demanded the outward trappings of prosperity and progress. It is worth noting that this class lived for the most part within its income. The passion for keeping up with the Joneses was a latter-day disease; and though the seeds of hire-purchase had been sown— a Singer sewing machine could be hire-purchased in 1856 for 35s. down and 35s. monthly—it was not until the twentieth century that the 'never, never' system reached its monstrous flowering.

The older generation's fierce distrust of advertising and the advertiser was rooted deep in newspaper editors. Abolition of the 'taxes on knowledge' had enabled the selling price of newspapers to be lowered, but the costs of running a newspaper, with all the news services and features which the public had grown to expect, were becoming ever heavier. Editors were curiously reluctant to admit that it was the advertiser who enabled them still to publish at a penny. They looked on the man as a pariah to be frustrated

[1] *Commercial Advertising:* Thomas Russell.

and disciplined as much as possible. He must be made to pay in
advance, and he must bring his copy, cap in hand, to be edited.
Why, some of the more importunate quacks were even demanding
display advertisements, as if the newspapers were a public
hoarding! They were asking to use big black type, and pictures of
voluptuous women with billowing manes of hair. They wanted to
abolish column rules in the interests of more vulgar presentation.
Apart from disfiguring the newspaper (ran the editorial argument)
such concessions would only play into the hands of the biggest
advertisers, at the expense of the little men. By common consent
the newspapers put a ban on the use of any type larger than minion.
So, from the 'sixties onwards, began that tiresome era when the
advertising columns were filled with endless repetitions of a firm's
name:

> JOHN JONES AND SON
> JOHN JONES AND SON
> JOHN JONES AND SON

for as many as 1,000 lines. Small though the type was, the cumulative effect was often impressive. It could be made more eye-
catching by resorting to tricks like these:

> SHINO   SHINO
> SHINO   SHINO
>   SHINO
>   SHINO
> SHINO   SHINO
> SHINO   SHINO
>   SHINO
>   SHINO
> SHINO   SHINO
> SHINO   SHINO

The idea, possibly, was to goad the newspaper proprietors into
relaxing their rules against display by making the columns look
as foolish as possible. All over the world the same childish game
was being played, in the *Sydney Morning Herald* as well as in the
New York Herald. (American advertisers revealed a special gift in
this direction—Chapter Five.) *The Times* enforced a rule against
the endless repetition of the same phrase; each line had to be
followed by explanatory matter. Thus:

ROSSETTER'S HAIR RESTORER
is not a dye

ROSSETTER'S HAIR RESTORER
contains no oil

ROSSETTER'S HAIR RESTORER
prevents hair falling

ROSSETTER'S HAIR RESTORER
promotes the growth of hair

And so on, for as long as the advertiser cared to spin it out.

Then, in an evil moment, the trick was discovered of building up large capital letters by grouping together single, small letters, in appropriate shapes, thus:

```
TTTTTTTT     HH     HH     EEEEEE
TTTTTTTT     HH     HH     EE
   TT      HHHHHHH         EEEE
   TT      HHHHHHH         EEEE
   TT        HH     HH     EE
   TT        HH     HH     EEEEEE
```

If the letters were built up sufficiently, capitals three or four inches deep could be constructed. The name CUTICURA could be, and was, spelt out, one letter to a column across the top of an eight-column paper, subsidiary headings being constructed on a lesser scale. Many papers refused to allow column rules to be removed, with the result that words were arbitrarily split. Other gruesome feats of typographical topiary were perpetrated. A hatter would stipulate that the type in his advertisement be set out in the shape of a top-hat; an oculist would mangle his message into the shape of a pair of spectacles. These advertisements, which must have caused unspeakable profanity among compositors, now appear to be eyesores of the most futile kind; it is impossible to turn over the files of those days without shuddering. But the editors thought that anything was better than to let advertisers loose among the big black type.

It was perhaps not surprising that some of the more frustrated manufacturers began to concentrate on outdoor advertising. There was no ban on the size of letters which could be painted on the side of a cliff.

It is time to review some of the new commodities which were invented in this fast-expanding age—commodities which carried the names of their backers into every household and into every mouth, yet rarely into the reference books. From now on a man could make a million pounds yet never rate an obituary in *The Times* or *Daily Telegraph*.

It was the age of new foods. In 1850 it was discovered that the virtues of beef could be stored in a small bottle, but it was fifteen years before the Liebig Extract of Meat Company (LEMCO, parent company of Oxo) was founded and began to advertise aggressively. During those years, Baron Liebig had been content to keep 200 or 300 cattle, and to supply extract of beef for purely medicinal purposes. By 1867 the LEMCO Company had been awarded a gold medal in Paris for originating 'a new industry productive of an article eminently cheap and useful.' Not until 1884 did Johnson's Fluid Beef come on the market under the name of Bovril, and the frisky bull ('I hear they want more Bovril') became familiar to millions.

Almost simultaneously with the condensing of the cow came the condensing of its milk. This lucrative feat was achieved, not without numerous setbacks, by Gail Borden in Connecticut; and by Henri Nestlé in Switzerland. In 1868 a restless young chemist from Heligoland, Gustav Mellin, invented an infant food in powder form. Soon Nestlé and Mellin were unable to move far without being confronted by their own names. In 1869 a French chemist, Mège Mouriés, was commissioned by Napoleon III to find a butter substitute; out of his test tubes he conjured margarine, on the popularizing of which many fortunes were to be spent.

If a common commodity like milk could be processed and patented, why not bread? Richard Smith, in the 'eighties, produced a loaf with the singularly unappetizing title of 'Smith's Patent Germ Bread.' Rechristened Hovis (from *Hominis Vis*) it was swiftly propelled to fame. Others took the view that bread had enjoyed too long an innings, and began to devise breakfast foods of much ingenuity. These foods had the advantage that weight for weight they could be sold at many times the price of bread.

So it went on. An American firm marketed a new kind of cocoa and forced the Quakers to abandon some of the old-world reticence with which they shrouded their products. Cocoa had always been a problem to advertise: was it soothing, stimulating, nourishing, or just a pleasant drink? The Cadburys and Frys had

The Lady with the Lamp
c. 1900.

never seemed quite sure; but they proclaimed that their brands were 'absolutely pure,' 'soluble,' 'highly concentrated,' and 'fully developed,' and in due course they became millionaires—one of the first examples of firms being hounded along the road to riches by their advertising rivals.

Then there were the mechanical inventions which changed the business and social habits of the age. In 1874, after scores of patents had been taken out—the American firm of Remington put the first effective typewriter on the market. It typed only in capitals; but four years later a shift key was triumphantly announced. At the Great Exhibition of 1851 a model of a sewing machine had aroused no especial interest (ten years previously the Paris mob had wrecked the establishment where Barthelemy Thimmonier was using sewing machines on Army contracts); but as the century wore on, and patent litigation began to abate, Singer sewing machines began to conquer the world. One sewing machine firm abandoned the trade, however, in favour of making bicycles—the Coventry Sewing Machine Company (later the Swift Company). Hobby horses and velocipedes had long since been laughed off the streets; the cycles which the Coventry firm marketed were low-built machines and had originally been intended for France, but the outbreak of the Franco-Prussian War compelled the firm to seek a home market. Bicycle races helped to 'improve the breed' and winners were much publicized. Ball bearings came in the late 'seventies, and in 1889 arrived John Boyd Dunlop's pneumatic tyre, paving the way for the great cycling boom of the 'nineties.

George Eastman, in America, announced the first portable roll-film camera in the late 'eighties, and a new popular hobby was born. 'You press the button—we do the rest' was the slogan on which Kodak sales subsequently soared. The gramophone had a long way to go before its makers could boast 'purity of tone,' but ingenious player-pianos were being marketed.

Modernized baths, furnaces, stoves and water-closets also began pressing on to the market. In the latter years of the century there was a campaign to instal a Turkish bath in every middle-class home. Many of the pictures of these advertisements suggested scenes of penance. In one cabinet a naked male is about to sit gingerly on a skeleton stool under which burns what appears to be an equally naked lamp. From another emerges the head of a woman bearing an expression such as might be found on an elderly governess who has had the misfortune to be buried up to her neck by Touaregs. As time went on the bathers' expressions became less strained and most of them were depicted reading books.

All these were new commodities, new inventions, and the public had to be told about them. But there were also old commodities, about which the public had never been sufficiently informed. As long ago as 1789 Andrew Pears had devised his transparent soap, but until the middle of the nineteenth century it had been very modestly advertised. In 1865, when the firm's annual bill for advertising was £80, a young man of twenty-four, Thomas J. Barratt, became a partner in the firm, and ushered in a vigorous new regime. It was too vigorous for Francis Pears, grandson of the founder, who thought that such reckless expenditure on advertising could bring only ruin. He withdrew from the business in 1875, while (as it seemed to him) there was still a business left; luckily for himself, he left £4,000 in the firm.

One of the many 'fathers of modern advertising,' Barratt is on record as saying, 'Any fool can make soap. It takes a clever man to sell it.' When he finally took over control of Pears he raised his expenditure on advertising to between £100,000 and £130,000. In justification he never tired of pointing out that he was enabled to sell soap 30 per cent more cheaply than if he had not advertised it.

Barratt's policy was summed up with perfect simplicity in one of his own advertisements: 'How do you spell soap?'— 'Why P-E-A-R-S, of course.' 'Pears' and 'soap' had to be linked so deeply and ineluctably in the public mind that it would be impossible to think of one without the other. Ultimately the public would be so conditioned to the association that they would go into a shop and instead of asking for soap would ask for 'Pears' Soap,' or even for 'Pears.' That was, and is, the advertising man's dream. It accounts for the tens of thousands of tedious and apparently futile signs bearing the names of household products—notably the indestructible enamel signs which stud the approaches to railway stations. It is wrong to say that no one reads them; they are not there to be read, but to be absorbed, just as a capsule is not meant to be tasted, but to be swallowed.

Barratt's policy has been called one of hypnosis. Certainly his puzzle posters, in which crowds of perhaps fifty persons stood for as long as twenty minutes staring at optical illusions, suggested hypnotic trance. If the crowds did not quite fathom the illusion, at least they went away, it is said, with 'Pears' Soap' tattooed on their sub-conscious.

The visual attack did not satisfy Barratt, however. He decided he must have a catch-phrase which would make the whole country say 'Pears' Soap.' His staff were invited to nominate the commonest phrases in daily use. Inevitably, somebody suggested 'Good morning.' The result was the notorious 'Good morning! Have you used Pears' Soap?' which scourged two continents. There were many who never forgave Thomas Barratt for debasing this traditional, friendly greeting. The sensitive shrank from saying 'Good morning,' knowing that it would only spark off the exasperating counter-phrase in the mind of the person addressed.

The opposition from rival soap firms was far from negligible. Since the 1840's Hudson's had been boasting that their new soap powder spelled 'washing without tears'—a cry which was still being dinned in the ears of British housewives by a score of rival manufacturers a century later. In the mid-'eighties a grocer's son from Bolton, William Hesketh Lever (the first Lord Leverhulme), who had been casting around for an attractive name for his soap, decided that he could do worse than use the word 'Sunlight.' In 1888, after studying publicity methods in America, he cut the first sod of Port Sunlight. Lever's was to prove the most formidable competition of all. Many of his advertisements and catch phrases—like 'Why does a woman look old sooner than a man?'—were to enjoy as wide a currency as anything conjured up by Barratt. In 1890 he had an advertisement of an old woman washing clothes in a tub. It was headed 'A CHEERY OLD SOUL' and the copy ran: 'It is possible for a woman with increasing years to continue to do laundry work. Thousands who would have been laid aside under the old system of washing have proved what Sunlight Soap can do in reducing labour.' When the soap war became really sharp, some of the advertisements took on a certain sharpness, too. One firm ran a 'knocking' campaign directed specifically at Pears.

By the 'eighties, several new-style advertising agencies were themselves beginning to advertise. The original agents had owed allegiance to the newspapers rather than to the advertisers; they had been debt-collectors at best and fee-snatchers at worst. Now agents began to identify themselves with the advertiser. The number of newspapers was so great that only a specialist could keep track of them all, and form a view as to their usefulness. Some of the leading agents were even undertaking to prepare the advertiser's copy and illustrations for him.

From the handbooks issued by agents in the 'eighties an interesting idea of the advertising methods and philosophy of the day can be gained. Two of the livelier (not the first) directories were Samuel Deacon's *Newspaper Handbook* and Henry Sell's *Dictionary of the World's Press and Philosophy of Advertising*. Both Deacon and Sell solemnly warned their readers against the folly of the argument: 'The father did not advertise, why should the son?' Henry Sell deplored that many old-established businesses of undisputed probity were crumbling away from dry rot. Fifty years previously, the public had been obliged to patronize these firms. The world had been smaller then and there was little rivalry.

Straightforwardness and honesty are as necessary, and we believe as frequently met with, now as heretofore, but even these qualities in a business house, unassisted by publicity, will fail to keep it in the leading rank. The public like to be asked for their custom and they naturally go to the people who invite them.

Henry Sell understood perfectly the art of marketing an everyday commodity. 'By the exercise of a little ingenuity it is easy to make a speciality. . . . Give it a name, register it and Advertise it, so that the public *must* come to *you* for it.' Then came a few elementary lessons in what would now be called psychology. Many people, he said, would have seen this sign in the window of a house:

A

MANGLE

KEPT HERE

How much better to put up signs in the windows of near-by houses reading:

MANGLING WITH A
NEW PATENT MANGLE
IS CAREFULLY DONE
BY MRS. JONES
NO. 20 IN THE NEXT COURT

Another of Sell's stories has been often told, but is worth retelling. It is about the man whose umbrella was stolen from church. When he complained that, after spending double the price of the umbrella in advertisements for its recovery, it had not been returned, a business man asked him what he had said in his announcement. It had been worded:

Lost from the vestibule of the —— Church last Sunday evening a black silk umbrella. The gentleman who took it will be handsomely rewarded by leaving it at No. —— High Street.

The business man, who said he was 'a liberal advertiser,' asked permission to rewrite the announcement, and did so on these lines:

If the man who was seen to take the umbrella from the vestibule of the —— Church does not wish to get into trouble and have a stain cast upon his Christian character which he values so highly he will return it at once to No —— High Street. He is well-known.

Next day the man who had lost the umbrella found twelve of them propped up in his porch, and the front yard strewn with many more.

Samuel Deacon told an equally amoral story, supposedly true. He said that the late M. Millaud, founder of the prosperous *Petit Journal*, had assured a gathering of Paris editors that the most worthless article could be sold if advertised sufficiently. Emile de Girardin, of *La Presse*, had joined issue with him. 'What will you bet,' said Millaud, 'that I cannot sell in one week 100,000 francs worth of the most common cabbage-seed under the pretext that it produces mammoth cabbage heads? All I have to do is advertise it once in a whole-page insertion in the daily papers of this city.' Emile de Girardin said he would present a page of *La Presse* free if Millaud was successful; so did the other editors. At the end of a week Millaud had sold twice as much

When soap competition became severe in the 'nineties,
one manufacturer who used only vegetable fats set out
to discredit its rivals—with pictures like this.

cabbage seed as he had promised, and the orders were still
flooding in. It was decided to fulfil no more orders, on the
grounds that the joke (if joke it was) had gone far enough.

The authors of both handbooks quoted advertisements of the
day which had caught their fancy. Deacon thought highly of the
following:

MR. BRADLAUGH. The Struggle in the Lobby of the House of
Commons. B. S. WOOLF, the celebrated City and Anglo-American
tailor of 9 and 10 Poultry EC and 292 and 294 Edgware Road W.,
having witnessed the struggle in which Mr. Bradlaugh's coat was
unfortunately torn, will be glad to replace the same if Mr. Bradlaugh
will honour him with a call at either of his establishments.

Deacon was impressed, too, by the vigorous advertising of the
Royal Insurance Company, which had expanded its business
greatly in consequence. He urged some of the older-established
and ultra-conservative insurance firms to advertise more, in order
to restore their virility. When they did take space in the Press, he
said, their manner was so apologetic as to recall the impoverished
gentleman, reduced to crying fish in the streets, who exclaimed,
'I hope to goodness no one hears me.' Those who remember the

attempts made, in quite recent days, to persuade certain big insurance companies to advertise may be surprised to learn that some insurance firms did advertise in quite lively fashion in the 'eighties. The Royal was not the only one. During the 'seventies the Railway Passenger Assurance Company had column-length advertisements in the *Daily News*, inviting readers to insure against a variety of risks, few of them connected with railways.

Each handbook contained aphorisms on advertising from newspapers and magazines of the day. To American newspapers were attributed such sayings as: 'Advertising is a blister that draws trade'; 'Trying to do business without advertising is like winking in the dark. You know yourself that you are keeping up a powerful winking but no one else is aware of your exertions'; 'The chap who could get all the business he wanted without advertising has been compelled to advertise at last. The advertisement is headed "Sheriff's sale" '; 'Don't fear to have a small advertisement by the side of a big one. The big one can't eat it up.' Horace Greeley, of the *New York Tribune*, had said that to do without advertising was 'to close one's eyes to the light and insist upon living in perpetual darkness.' In Greeley's view advertisements were now read by between five and ten times as many people as twenty years before. No less a figure than Lord Macaulay was quoted as saying: 'Advertising is to business what steam is to machinery—the great propelling power.'

One truth which had already been discovered in the 'eighties was contained in an unascribed quotation: 'Ceasing to advertise in dull times is like tearing out a dam because the water is low.' Henry Sell told a cautionary tale of the (unnamed) manufacturer who for twenty years had been spending £10,000 a year on advertising. Convinced that his product must at last be familiar enough to the public, he cut his appropriation to £5,000. In the following year he had to spend £20,000 to recover his position.

Between them, Deacon and Sell did their utmost to convince an advertiser that he could get nowhere without enlisting the aid of an agent. 'Would you leave or enter a port without a pilot?' asked Sell. 'Would you commence to prosecute a law case without a legal adviser?' Like Mrs. Warren, of blacking fame, Henry Sell could boast 'We keeps a poet.' He offered copy in prose or verse, explaining, 'I am in constant communication with gentlemen of literary ability.' Deacon assured his clients that he was trying to break down the reluctance of many newspapers to declare their circulations—the beginnings of a campaign which was to go on for fifty years.

Although, as late as 1887, Henry Sell was still boasting of his firm's virtuosity in typographical pattern-making, many newspapers—among them the *Daily News*—were beginning to allow display advertisements, in light-face type across two columns, even with an occasional thumb-nail illustration. The first slogans were beginning to appear. Many were inapt and inept, and only a few were witty. 'Absolutely pure,' 'Grateful, comforting,' 'In the highest class' or 'Leads the world' were typical specimens. The cleverest slogans came from America, like Kodak's. The artful alliteration of 'Dr. Williams' Pink Pills for Pale People' may have done much to build up the £1,111,000 fortune which George Taylor Fulford acquired from this property.

By the 'eighties, ambitious pictorial advertisements were beginning to appear in illustrated magazines like *The Graphic*. Some of these were creditable efforts; the worst of them were appalling. Having commissioned and accepted a drawing, the advertiser (or his agent) would frequently begin to disfigure it. If it showed a family at table, he would run his slogan for sauce along the bottom of the tablecloth. If it showed a beauty leaning forward in her box at the theatre, he would inscribe his message vertically up the pillars of the box. Some advertisers, less inhibited, stamped their name or slogan on a lady's bare back or chest. Others again went in for symbolism. A nude girl rising from the Borax lakes waved her wand at a flight of unclean shapes, labelled 'Disease' and 'Decay.' She was an attractive nude, and to ward off possible criticism she was labelled 'Spirit of Purity.' Undraped females were more plentiful in the advertisements of this period than might have been expected. Cadbury's also had a 'Spirit of Purity' which would have encountered criticism today (and would no doubt have been disallowed on the hoardings even then). Nude children abounded, too; so did odiously winsome little girls, into whose mouths were put words like 'I'm helping dear Mother by taking Ridge's to my baby Brother.' In 1890 'pretty girl' advertising was firmly established. Even the cigarette firm of Player had a girl with a cigarette in one of their advertisements. She was holding it in her hand, upraised above her head, and the expression on her face was one of near-ecstasy. If challenged, she would probably have explained that she was holding it for her brother. At this period there was a noticeable tendency to associate girls with cigarettes, without going so far as to put the cigarettes between their lips. If people chose to assume that these girls were smoking, well and good.

Player's famous bearded sailor had a predecessor, also framed in a lifebuoy. He was a very young-looking sailor, and the new face, adopted in 1898, was undoubtedly an improvement. It came as a surprise to many, in the summer of 1951, to learn that this was the portrait of a real sailor, Thomas Huntley Wood, who died in that year. Wood's likeness first appeared in the *Army and Navy Illustrated* in 1898, whence it was borrowed for advertising purposes. A friend of Wood's wrote to the firm suggesting payment of a fee of £15; Wood reduced this to a sum of two guineas 'and a bit of baccy for myself and the boys on board.' The firm paid, in cash and kind. Some time later, tiring of people pulling out a packet of Player's and asking, 'Is that really you?' Wood shaved off his beard. An O. Henry or a Damon Runyon could have built an enchanting whimsy round the story of Thomas Wood— the man who sold his face for a song, only to be haunted by it ever afterwards. The sailor was not the only unknown individual to be pitchforked into fame by the whim of an unknown man at an advertiser's desk.

Not every Victorian advertiser, by a long way, was willing to yield the composition of his advertisements to an agent. The most eccentric, the most obstinately 'different' advertisements in late Victorian magazines (and for a long time afterwards) were those personally devised by the founder of Eno's Fruit Salts. Three-quarters of his space would be taken up by high-flown quotations on the theme of man's unconquerable mind, from the ancient and modern philosophers. The underlying thesis (as far as it was distinguishable) was the sin of allowing the human intellect to be harnessed to a sluggish gut; but often the quotations came so thickly and haphazardly that it was impossible to trace a continuity of thought behind them. Now and again the compiler would throw in an uplifting poem which had taken his fancy, and he kept an artist busy drawing scenes in which lost wanderers stumbled into forest glades and found words like 'Integrity' mysteriously carved on the rocks, or in which seated greybeards solemnly drew the attention of milkmaids to moral phrases graven on the ground before them. Sometimes the descent from

☞ The Bottle Imp of Disease Germs, contamination and malodorous vapours, the remnant of a wreckage on the shores of health, speedily succumbs to the powerful antidote, CALVERT'S CARBOLIC, the Popular Disinfectant.

Advertising art of the 'eighties.

G

the cloudless peaks of the intellect to the mucous walls of the intestinal canal was achieved almost in one sentence. For a generation the strong-minded founder of the firm fought off any suggestion that he should 'modernize' his announcements. To-day his commodity is advertised, like all the others, with the aid of pretty girls.

No review of this period can omit the highly individual publicity methods—adapted, some said, from Barnum himself— which were being popularized in the city of Glasgow by one of her most resourceful sons, Thomas Lipton. The stunts began with the driving of fat pigs through the streets under a banner 'Lipton's Orphans'; they continued with parades of cadaverous males inscribed 'Going to Lipton's' and parades of fat men labelled 'Coming from Lipton's.' Then came the importing of gigantic cheeses, drawn by traction engine or elephant to Lipton's shops, there to be stuffed with sovereigns and sold to milling crowds. Alec Waugh tells of these exploits in *The Lipton Story*; not omitting Lipton's offer of a monster cheese to Queen Victoria to mark her Jubilee in 1885. 'The cheese which I purpose present-ing to your Majesty . . . would weigh about 11,200 pounds or not less than five tons and be made from one day's milk of 8,500 cows,' he wrote. The Queen replied that she could not accept gifts from persons to whom she had not been introduced; however, in due course the Sovereign who refused this humble tribute conferred a knighthood on the man who had offered it.

As a national, and international advertiser, Lipton did not get into his stride until the late 'eighties, when he took Ceylon for his colony and began to plaster the world with 'Lipton's Teas.' About 1890 he boasted of paying £35,000 Customs tax on his teas; but ten years later it was Mazawattee who claimed to have written the world's largest duty cheque: £85,862 8s. 8d.

The Law Steps In

The year 1853 had seen the 'emancipation' of advertising. It had also seen the passing of measures designed to frustrate two of the more importunate classes of advertiser: one, the contractor who cluttered the streets with purely advertising vehicles; two, the betting shop proprietor. The first of these measures was more effective than the second; even though in years to come there were to be occasional court wrangles over vehicles shaped like

Crowning Glory

baths or bottles—were they primarily load-carrying vehicles, or
were they primarily advertisements?

The Betting Bill, which had sought to shut down betting shops
and make it illegal to advertise them, merely had the effect of
driving the owners out of England and into Scotland or the
Channel Isles. From these tolerant sanctuaries they were at liberty
to advertise as seductively as they wished in English sporting
papers, and to flood the whole kingdom with circulars.

When a new Betting Bill came up in 1874, the House of
Commons was regaled with some of the unscrupulous 'discretionary' advertisements from current sporting papers. A typical
one from a Guernsey address read: 'Three Splendid Speculations.
Great Success. For the trifling stake of 15s. you can realise £3,000;
for £1, £12,000; and for £8, £37,000.' A 'discretionary' bet was
so called because the punter handed over a stake to be invested
at the discretion of the advertiser, who afterwards rendered to his
client an account of the transactions. Most often, the punter who
had been assured that he could not fail to win a fortune received
a letter saying that, inexplicably, and for the first time since the
business was founded, the system had failed; but that, as it was
clearly impossible that such a cruel stroke of luck could happen
twice, a further investment should be sent without delay. Sometimes a promising client was allowed to make modest wins at the
outset.

The House was told that 'discretionary' advertisements were
refused by all reputable papers. Those publications which accepted
them, knowing that they were mostly fraudulent, adopted the
curious ethical course of charging three times the usual rate for

them. Occasionally the editors warned their readers not to be ensnared by the specious offers in their pages. What more could they do?

Not all Members of Parliament were convinced that it was necessary to prevent rogues from exploiting fools, but the Bill was passed and the loophole plugged.

Another stage in the clean-up of advertising came in 1889 with the passing of the Indecent Advertisements Act. The discussions in Parliament on this measure are couched in such veiled language that it is not easy, at first glance, to ascertain what the offending advertisements were about; but the Earl of Meath permitted himself to say that the Bill was directed against vendors of cures for 'a certain class of disease of a nameless character.' He added: 'It is quite impossible that I can bring before your Lordships' house all the evidence I have to show the need of such legislation.'

No one, said the Earl, could pass down certain streets of London without having thrust into his hands 'indecent and filthy publications which ought not to come before the eyes of any decent man or woman,' leaflets which were 'inducements to promiscuous sexual intercourse.' Within recent years, 'a person connected with one of the societies interested in this subject' had had 20,000 papers thrust into his hands, whether he wished them or not. In less populated districts it was usual for these leaflets to be stuck on gates and posts.

The Archbishop of Canterbury told how pernicious leaflets were given away in school recreation grounds. 'While some girls were taking their recreation in a meadow attached to their school,' he said, 'two men drove rapidly by in a gig and flung over the wall packages of literature of the most horrible description. Fortunately one of them happened to fall at the feet of one of the mistresses and the mischief intended was not done.'

It was characteristic of the age that these advertisements should be attacked on the grounds of indecency and not because the treatments they offered were useless. Possible contamination of the mind was regarded as a greater peril than corruption of the body.

One speaker on the Bill in the House of Lords thought it odd that newspapers were still to be allowed to advertise cures for venereal diseases. Others thought it no less odd that the Press should be allowed to publish advertisements of abortifacients.

That same year the country read the exploits of the rascally Chrimes brothers, whose profanation of the medium of advertisement outclassed even the efforts of Jonathan Wild. Richard, Edward and Leonard Chrimes were charged at the Central Criminal Court, London, with attempting to extort two guineas from a married woman, Kate Clifford. It appeared that, under various aliases, and by heavy advertising, they had worked up a brisk business in abortifacients, one of their lines being entitled 'Lady Montrose's Miracle Female Tabules.' The newspapers which accepted these advertisements charged five times the normal tariff—'a somewhat significant increase,' as the prosecution pointed out. In all, the Chrimes brothers spent more than £2,000 in advertising their products; then dissatisfied with the rate of flow of wealth, they conceived a plot of classic effrontery. On the morning of October 8, 1898, between 8,000 and 10,000 women up and down the country received a disturbing letter in the post. It ran:

> Trafalgar Buildings,
> Northumberland Avenue.

Madame, I am in possession of letters of yours by which I can positively prove that you did on or about —— commit, or attempt to commit, the fearful crime of abortion by preventing or attempting to prevent yourself giving birth to a child. Either of these constitutes a a criminal act punishable by penal servitude and legal proceedings have already been commenced against you, and your immediate arrest will be effected unless you send me on or before Tuesday morning next the sum of £2 2s, being costs already incurred by me, and your solemn promise on oath before God that never again by whatsoever means will you prevent or attempt to prevent yourself giving birth to a child. No notice whatever will be taken of your letter unless postal orders (cheques, stamps etc will not be accepted) for the above amount are enclosed and received by me on the aforesaid day. Failing to comply with these two requests, you will be immediately arrested without further warning. All legal proceedings will be stopped on receipt of the £2 2s and the incriminating documents . . . will be returned to you and you will hear nothing further of the matter.

> I am, Madame etc
> (signed) Charles J. Mitchell, Public Official

The letter addressed to Mrs. Kate Clifford was opened by her husband, who showed it to the police. Between October 14 and October 17 detectives intercepted 1,785 letters addressed to

'Mitchell,' 413 of which contained money. Excerpts from one letter were read by the judge:

. . . the child that you are alluding to is a big fine girl, as healthy as any child could be, and is eight months old. . . . But if I have done wrong I ask you to forgive me as I did not know I was doing wrong. I will promise that I will never do wrong any more, for Christ's sake. Amen.

This letter was one of those which contained two guineas.

The jury which found the three men guilty added a rider saying that:

. . . such a vile plot, even with all the ingenuity displayed in it, could only have been possible by the acceptance of such immoral advertisements by a section of the Press—religious and secular—well knowing their nature.

The hint was not taken, not even by the religious Press. The Chrimes brothers were awarded a total of thirty-one years' penal servitude and ten thousand wives breathed freely again.

Two years later another anti-social advertiser came under a legislative ban—the moneylender who made a speciality of sending circulars to boys at boarding school. The Earl of Aberdeen assured his fellow peers that no other body of individuals in the country suffered more from the importunities of moneylenders than did the members of that House, as sons or fathers.

I have a boy of twelve, and therefore not old enough yet to be in a public school, who has received a good many of these circulars at his private school, in which he is told that if he borrows any money his father need not know anything about it, but that if in due course it becomes necessary he should know it, he would no doubt be delighted to pay the money.

For a moneylender to be able to ensnare the scion of a noble house at an early age was excellent business. With luck the victim would be on the firm's books for a lifetime.

As was to be expected, the Betting and Loans (Infants) Bill suffered no obstruction in the Lords. Moneylenders' methods of advertising continued on unseemly and often outrageous lines, but Parliament was slow to take further action.

The year 1892 brought a legal case which deeply disconcerted the more conscienceless class of advertiser—the Case of the

Carbolic Smoke Ball. In this, Mr. Justice Hawkins laid down the vexatious rule that words, in certain circumstances, mean what they say.

In the *Pall Mall Gazette* of November 13, 1891, had appeared this advertisement:

£100 REWARD

WILL BE PAID BY THE

CARBOLIC SMOKE BALL CO.

To any person who contracts the increasing Epidemic,

INFLUENZA,

Colds, or any diseases caused by taking cold, AFTER HAVING USED the BALL 3 times daily for two weeks according to the printed directions supplied with each Ball.

£1,000

Is deposited with the ALLIANCE BANK, REGENT-STREET, showing our sincerity in the matter. During the last epidemic of Influenza many thousand CARBOLIC SMOKE BALLS were sold as Preventives against this Disease, and in no ascertained case was the disease contracted by those using the CARBOLIC SMOKE BALL.

One **CARBOLIC SMOKE BALL** will last a family several months, making it the cheapest remedy in the world at the price—10s., post free. The BALL can be RE-FILLED at a cost of 5s. Address :—

CARBOLIC SMOKE BALL CO.,
27, Princes-street, Hanover-sq., London, W.

A Mrs. Carlill, of whom no personal details seem to have been handed down, bought a Carbolic Smoke Ball, used it as directed for two weeks, and contracted influenza. On her recovery she requested £100 from the manufacturers. When they declined to pay, she took them to court.

The defendants offered a variety of pleas. There was no contract, they said; or if there was a contract, it was void on the ground that a wager was involved, or that it was contrary to public policy. They also argued that a contract could not be binding unless it was made with a specific person. Queen's Counsel for the company was the future Lord Oxford and Asquith. He pleaded: 'The advertisement was a mere representation of what the advertisers intended to do in a certain event. The defendants did not, by issuing it, mean to impose upon themselves any obligation enforceable by law.' To this remarkable defence, Mr.

Justice Hawkins said '. . . It must be remembered that such advertisements do not appeal so much to the wise and thoughtful as to the credulous and weak portions of the community.' A vendor making a promise 'must not be surprised if occasionally he is held to his promise.' The Court of Appeal upheld this decision, saying that the promise by the Carbolic Smoke Ball Company had been 'as plain as words could make it.'

Mrs. Carlill collected her £100, to the envy, no doubt, of many who wished they had thought of the idea first. Today the case of Carlill *v.* The Carbolic Smoke Ball Company is a red light over the desk of the advertising copywriter. It was the first case of its kind and it should have been the last; but it was not.

In less sophisticated lands, the advertiser who made specific promises and attempted to go back on them sometimes received shorter shrift. In 1900 a New Orleans dealer sent a consignment of toothache drops to an agent in Chile. The drops were 'warranted to cure the worst case of toothache in ten minutes.' The first customer who tried the remedy did so on the spot; he took out his watch, and after ten minutes, finding that he still had toothache, had the agent arrested. The penalty imposed was a fine of one thousand dollars with three months' imprisonment. Only with great difficulty did the American consul succeed in having the jail sentence cancelled.

Then came 'Bubbles'

In the latter part of the nineteenth century the fly-posters were gradually squeezed out by the big contractors. The excesses of the free-lance banditti had been such that no one was prepared to shed tears over the eclipsing of the 'little man.' Jokes about fly-posting were slow to die, however. The Victorians took an innocent delight in the production of satirical prints showing enormous hoardings on which posters had been pasted, one partly over the other, in such a way as to produce 'messages' like: 'Funerals Conducted with Dignity and Decorum by FUNNY FOLKS EVERY WEDNESDAY with a Band and Chorus of 700 Performers in A. LYNES AND SONS' 13s. TROUSERS.' Or, perhaps: 'Mr. J. L. Toole will PUNCH EVERY WEDNESDAY the Rev. Dr. Parker.' The joke was played for all it was worth; sometimes no doubt juxtapositions little less farcical did appear on unregulated poster stations.

It is on record that by 1860 there were 'orderly and attractive'

hoardings in many English cities. Much of the credit goes to
Edward Sheldon, of Leeds, who rose from the scuffle and forced
the public and his rivals to respect his orderly, rented bill stations
(see Cyril Sheldon's *A History of Poster Advertising*). He was a
founder of the United Kingdom Billposters Association, which
took shape in Manchester in 1862. This assembly of hardy
individualists was often at loggerheads with itself and the world,
but it originated and enforced a rough code of ethics designed to
crowd out parasites. To begin with, it compiled a directory of
responsible bill-posters, all of whom could reasonably be relied
upon to paste up the bills with which they were entrusted instead
of burning them or tossing them over the nearest hedge. Unfortunately a rival bill-posting association was formed soon afterwards, and the two bodies jeered at each other unflaggingly until
1889, when they buried the hatchet and called themselves the
United Bill Posters Association. The more far-sighted members
could see trouble looming; public criticism was growing and there
were restrictive Bills to be filleted.

The new Association even began to consider voluntary censorship of the lurid theatrical posters which it put up on its
hoardings. For the members by now craved respectability. From
'external paper-hangers' they had degenerated, in mid-century,
to bill-stickers; slowly (as Cyril Sheldon points out) they had
struggled upwards to the status of bill-posters, and now they
were beginning to call themselves outdoor advertisement contractors. Such errors of taste as came up for judgment were
mostly infringements of the decencies. If the Association had been
qualified to censor artistic taste there would have been very few
posters to put up.

Though the poster industry in Britain got away to an early
start, it was not until colour lithography began to be perfected
in the 'eighties that the hoardings could be described, even play-
fully, as an art gallery. The first British poster of any artistic
merit is generally agreed to have been Fred Walker's classical
black-and-white woodcut advertising the stage version of Wilkie
Collins's *Woman in White*, in 1871—'a first attempt at what I
consider might develop into a most important branch of art,'
said Walker modestly. No such development was visible in Britain
until twenty years later, however.

The civilizing influence came from France, where Jules Cheret, having extended his lithographic knowledge in London, took the boulevards for his studio and covered them with vivid, sparkling posters in praise of everything from aperitifs to oil lamps, from ice-rinks to music-halls. Karl Huysmans in 1880 said that there was a thousand times more talent in the smallest poster by Cheret than in most of the canvases in the Paris salons. The public agreed; and very little criticism was heard of the high-spirited, frothy posters by the *Maître de l'Affiche*, whose output ran into four figures. A writer in the magazine *The Poster* said (1899):

Cheret has revived the traditions of Watteau; like Verlaine in dreamland gardens he brings his masks and pierrots; but true son of his time, he spices the eighteenth century, its 'Fêtes Galantes' and all graces of a past epoch with a striking note of modernism.

Cheret can make fair claim to have fathered the 'poster girl,' a creature always radiant, wholesome and eupeptic; of indeterminate age and of no recognizable social background; starry-eyed in her loyalty to her sponsor's toffee, purgative or—latterly—beer.

Less starry-eyed were the damosels portrayed by Toulouse-Lautrec, whose posters also lent colour and vigour to the boulevards. Lautrec's mordant compositions embarrassed the critic of *The Poster*, for was not this artist in the pay of the Moulin Rouge?

. . . just as the source of (Lautrec's) inspiration is unclean so is the outcome, not unclean of deliberate purpose but essentially and intrinsically unclean. It must not be supposed that Lautrec has sought to glorify the mean erotics of the home of the can-can; he depicts the frequenters of the place with terrible reality.

Yet (sighed this critic) how preferable, with all their occasional Gallic shortcomings, were the posters of Lautrec and Cheret, Steinlen and Manet, to the 'ferocious orgies of the colour-printers' hacks' in Britain!

Mr. James Laver has asserted that in France by the middle of the 'nineties 'the art of the poster was at the highest point it has ever reached, before or since. Magnificent designs were produced, so it seemed, as a matter of course. . . . It is a curious thing that so many arts come to their full stature immediately, and this is true of the poster. . . . No one will ever design better posters than Toulouse-Lautrec.[1] . . .'

[1] In a foreword to *Art For All: London Transport Posters* 1908–1949.

Certainly Toulouse-Lautrec showed an exemplary personal interest in the technique of poster printing. With his pockets stuffed full of old toothbrushes (for imparting delicate *crachis* to the lithographic stone) he would linger for hours in the workshop, experimenting and adding loving touches. He accepted at least one commission from an English advertiser, a confetti-maker of Charing Cross Road, London. Another poster, advertising a British bicycle chain, was abandoned.

It was a long time before British painters of repute could be persuaded to paint for, or to allow their works to appear on, the hoardings. Finally, they had to be tricked into it. Loud were the cries of 'degradation of art' which greeted the appearance of the famous 'Bubbles' poster, in 1887. Sir William Ingram had bought this work by Sir John Millais for the *Illustrated London News*; afterwards he disposed of it to the firm of Pears for the sum of 2,000 guineas. When Thomas J. Barratt called at the artist's studio with colour reproductions there was a considerable scene, but after the first explosion Millais seems to have been mollified by the excellence of the engraving. Less ready to forgive was Marie Corelli, who made a character in *The Sorrows of Satan* say:

I am one of those who think the fame of Millais as an artist was marred when he degraded himself to the level of painting the little green boy blowing bubbles of Pears' soap. *That was an advertisement*, and that very incident in his career, trifling as it seems, will prevent his ever standing on the dignified height of distinction with such masters in Art as Romney, Sir Peter Lely, Gainsborough and Reynolds.

Millais prevailed on Miss Corelli to expunge this passage from subsequent editions, after convincing her that he had not painted the picture specifically for Pears.

Two years later, it was W. P. Frith's turn. In a moment of rashness, he had painted a picture of a little girl holding up a white pinafore, with the title 'The New Frock.' The future Lord Leverhulme, who was not above following in the footsteps of Thomas J. Barratt, bought the picture and turned it into a poster entitled 'So Clean.' Frith made a show of anger, and the still-smouldering controversy flamed up anew. Millais by now had decided that he had no feelings one way or the other about advertising, though he said he would object if a reproduction were badly executed. (According to Barratt, Millais shortly before his death was about to undertake commissions for Pears.)

Lord Leverhulme is on record as saying that Sidney Gross, who commissioned leading artists for Sunlight, and Thomas J. Barratt did more than any other men in the world to infuse Art into advertising. Less generous critics have argued that Barratt did Sir John Millais a considerable disservice by causing him to be remembered, in the popular mind, by one of his worst pictures. The Art Critic of *The Times*[1] was one of the many to make the point that the 'Bubbles' poster 'hindered rather than helped the development of the poster by leading advertisers to bank on circumstantial interest instead of on the direct appeal of form, colour and rhythm.'

To those artists who still regarded the hoardings with abhorrence the future was a dismaying one. Yet what could they do, apart from choosing subjects which could not conceivably be used to further the sales of soap? If there was a falling-off in the number of nudes at the Royal Academy of 1890, the reason must be that artists were apprehensive lest their visions of Aphrodite be pasted up piecemeal on gable ends, before ribald mobs, with a legend 'So Clean.' Nor was the peril confined to pictures depicting or implying cleanliness. A study of fat kine might be snapped up by a meat extract firm. Any canvas expressing a mood of *joie de vivre* might appeal to a pill manufacturer. There was no end to it all. And one day the Old Guard saw, without surprise, that a picture by Sir Edwin Landseer was being used to advertise dog biscuits. Happily they did not live to see the day in the 1920's when a titled artist—Sir Reginald Blomfield—designed, not a poster, but a hoarding to carry posters.

Not all Royal Academicians waited to be tricked into advertising soap. After some persuasion by Thomas J. Barratt, Stacey Marks drew his picture of the two monks at their ablutions—'Cleanliness Is Next to Godliness.'[2] Barratt was equally prepared

---

[1] In 1928.

[2] Barratt wrung the utmost capital out of this saying. He told in a posthumously printed article in *The Strand Magazine*, September 1914, how, when visiting America, he decided he must have an inspiring testimonial for Pears' Soap from a man of the highest distinction. Ruling out President Grant, the Governor of New York, and various Civil War heroes, he marked down as quarry the eminent divine, Henry Ward Beecher. One evening he called unheralded at Beecher's home in Brooklyn, and found to his consternation a

to pay handsome fees to an 'unknown,' witness his purchase of the 'Dirty Boy' statuette which figured in a variety of Pears' advertisements. The sculptor was Focardi, an indigent Italian artist whose genius had begun to wilt in the uncongenial atmosphere of a boarding-house in Preston, Lancashire. One day when he rang for breakfast he received no answer, so he set off downstairs to find the landlady. Through a neighbour's open door he saw a rugged beldam scrubbing a dirty, howling boy. She was exclaiming, 'Drat the boy! Will he never come clean?' Here was Focardi's inspiration. Not without difficulty, he persuaded the old woman and the boy to pose for him. A suitable expression was maintained on the boy's face by pouring soapy water over his head at frequent intervals. For the resulting marble, Barratt paid the sculptor £500. What the boy received is not on record.

After Fred Walker, the first British poster artist of repute was probably Walter Crane. If the mantle of Cheret fell on anybody, it fell on Dudley Hardy, whose designs had a certain colourful ebullience, and whose posters were to be seen on the hoardings for many years to come. At the opposite pole were the brooding designs of Aubrey Beardsley, who was widely but not wisely imitated in America. (A poster of two enigmatic nymphs, hot from the Decameron, poised above their Barlock typewriters, may have done much to fill moralists with misgivings about the wisdom of employing women in offices.) The Beggarstaff Brothers (James Pryde and William Nicholson) developed a new technique of starkness and flatness, oddly powerful. The style was too flat and economical for some sponsors, however; it seemed hardly worth paying good money for such large expanses of white. When the Beggarstaff Brothers' design for the 1895 pantomime at Drury Lane was displayed on the stage of that theatre, Sir Augustus

party in progress. He shook hands all round ('perhaps they took me for a visiting English preacher or writer') and parried questions until the guests had gone. When Beecher learned that his visitor was soliciting a testimonial for soap, his face 'underwent a sudden change'; but as Barratt expatiated on the merits of the soap, the preacher checked him with a laugh, wheeled round in his chair and wrote on half a sheet of paper the soon-to-be-famous testimonial beginning, 'If cleanliness is next to godliness. . . .'

Like many celebrities who have given testimonials, Beecher apparently had little or no acquaintance with the product; but unlike many, he seems to have accepted no reward other than the advertiser's understandably 'hearty' thanks.

Harris disapproved heartily, and Dan Leno said the design looked as if someone had spilled a pot of paint down it. At that point Phil May entered the theatre. Quickly sizing up the situation, he congratulated Sir Augustus Harris on his taste in selecting such an admirable poster. After that there was nothing to do except send the design to the printer. It is only fair to say that the public at large did not always take kindly to the work of the Beggarstaff Brothers.

Gradually poster artists were learning the secrets of simplicity, the effectiveness of bold, simple humour. One of the most popular of Pears' posters was the reproduction of the Harry Furniss drawing from *Punch*, showing a tramp writing a testimonial—'Two years ago I used your soap—since then I have used no other.' Long in favour, too, was the picture of the baby stretching out of his bath to pick up a cake of Pears' soap—'He won't be happy till he gets it.' (Cartoonists freely adapted this poster, converting the baby into the Czar or the Kaiser, and the cake of soap into the disputed territory of the day.) Phil May produced posters bearing such *jeux d'esprit* as 'Apples make cider but Pears make soap.' Nestlé had their famous two cats on a wall, with Fat Cat saying to Thin Cat, 'Hullo! You *are* looking bad, old man—been feeding on skim milk, eh?' Bovril indulged in a good deal of simple humour, too. The advertiser's message, as a rule, was mercifully brief. Mere reiteration of name or slogan was usually enough.

Primitive though much of this wit now appears, it apparently sold goods. One of the most inescapable posters carried a picture of two spades spanned by the legend: 'Call a—a—and Branson's Coffee perfection.' When this design was first propounded, the manufacturer was dubious. 'They'll think we sell spades,' he said. It was hailed as such an effective poster that the printer who had dashed it off on an odd sheet of paper thought he might do worse than safeguard the idea; but he found that the manufacturer had beaten him to it. The slogan is still used to-day.

Occasionally there were unhappy dabblings in impressionism and symbolism. One poster showed a ship on a grassy ocean, surrounded by savage rocks, heading to a horizon where rose the sun, burdened with a brand-new typewriter. 'Dawn of a New Era' said the title; 'past praying for,' said the critic of *The Poster*. The same writer was unhappy about a poster showing Britannia,

astride a £5 bicycle, outdistancing Germany, France and the
United States.

The bicycle advertising of the period was gently guyed by
Jerome K. Jerome in *Three Men on the Bummel*. Jerome's man
George, pedalling painfully through the Rhineland, complains
that his bicycle is not like those advertised on the posters. On only
one poster has he seen the rider represented as doing any work,
and on that occasion a bull was pursuing him. The general purpose
of the artist was to convince the hesitant neophyte that bicycling
consisted of being wafted along by unseen heavenly powers.
Usually the rider was a lady, wearing the kind of costume which
might cause an old-fashioned landlady to refuse her lunch; she
would float effortless, with one foot on the saddle and the other
on the lamp, lighting a cigarette or waving a Chinese lantern.

Less often it is a mere male thing that rides the machine. He is not
so accomplished as is the lady; but simple tricks such as standing on
the saddle and waving flags, drinking beer or beef tea while riding he
can and does perform.

According to George, the only haggard-looking persons seen
riding bicycles, on the posters, were those who bestrode machines
of inferior make.

There was an attempt to represent cycling as the sport of
princes. 'The best I have ever used,' said Prince Ranjitsinhji of
the Dursley Pedersen cycle. Prince Henri of Bourbon was allowed
to praise the Bantam in his native language: '*Depuis plusieurs
mois je me sers presque tous les jours du 24 in. Bantam. Jamais
je n'a i eu de bicyclette plus agréable et j'ai complètement écarté
pour mon usage les autres machines.*'

But the girl in the saddle was a more potent sales force than
princes. The symbol of the age, she appeared in all kinds of
advertisements—for hats, clothes, health foods and toffees, much
as the sports girl was to appear a generation later, and the bathing
girl a generation after that.

As the century ended the cycling girl was temporarily eclipsed
—by the British soldier. The South African War might have been
won earlier, it would appear from the advertisements, if soldiers
had spent less time standing on *kopjes* waving packets of cigarettes
in the air, or marching up to exposed positions under enormous
Union Jacks superimposed with the names of meat extracts.

Advertisers quickly learned how to tie in patriotism with the product; for once, there was value in the testimonial of a humble warrior. One gallant soldier who suffered alike for King and Commerce was Baden-Powell, who was hailed as smoking somebody's cigarette. He was a non-smoker.

The poster of the cheaper theatrical show was as unregenerate then as the cinema poster is now. At any given time there were three or four hundred melodramas on the road in the British Isles and their posters were sensational and often immeasurably crude. When the United Bill Posters Association began to pass judgment on some of the offending sheets, censoring daggers, pools of blood, beds, female breasts and other inflammatory detail, loud protests were voiced by the theatrical companies. Nor were music-hall posters immune. In 1890 the National Vigilance Association opposed renewal of the London Aquarium's licence because of a 'suggestive' poster showing a woman acrobat in flesh-coloured tights. By modern standards the poster does not seem to have been very reprehensible.

Some excessively prudish criticisms of posters were voiced during this period. Cyril Sheldon records that even the Bovril bull was condemned by the town of Cork, for the reason that it was too obviously a bull. This is no subject for superior mirth, for in our own times prize bulls have been emasculated by the retouchers of Fleet Street.

Nothing Sacred

How, with this rage, shall Beauty hold a plea,
Whose action is no stronger than a flower?
William Shakespeare

In the last years of the nineteenth century outdoor advertisers sowed their wildest oats. And appropriately enough it was an oats-selling firm which achieved one of the less forgivable enormities: the erection of a monstrous signboard half-way up the white cliffs of Dover.

In November 1892 readers of *The Times* began to report advertising excesses which had been forced on their attention, not only in Britain but overseas. It was from the indignation aroused by this correspondence that the Society for the Checking of Abuses in Public Advertising (S.C.A.P.A.) was born in the succeeding year; its founder was Richardson Evans. Some of those who wrote to *The Times* were out to abolish advertising totally. One of them pointed out that 'the colossal and flourishing biscuit works at Reading have never advertised—a proof among many that "good wine needs no bush".' (This red rag proverb inspires in an advertising man the same reaction as 'The Lord will provide' in an insurance agent.) It was not long before Thomas J. Barratt joined in the correspondence to suggest that, instead of seeking to put down advertising, those whose feelings were harrowed would be better employed trying to improve its standards. That, in effect, became the policy of S.C.A.P.A. The Society did not urge its supporters to follow the example of Miss Frances Power Cobbe, the feminist, who took a pot of paint and a long-handled brush on her rural drives in order to deface defacements; and, whatever its secret sympathies, it offered no encouragement to those other vigilantes who believed that the best criticism of an offensive hoarding was to haul it down, by night, with a rope.

At this period, all over the world, beauty-spots were exercising a suicidal fascination over the outdoor advertiser. There was a stark simplicity about the advertiser's logic: the best announcements were those which were seen by the most people; more people were likely to visit beauty-spots than any other spots; therefore a progressive advertiser must be first in the beauty-spots. Seaside resorts were, in many ways, ideal, because a holiday-maker had a good deal of time on his hands and an unoccupied mind, and he was therefore more susceptible to persuasion than he was when going about his daily occasions.

Travellers returning to Britain told of outrages everywhere. A Gothenburg margarine factory had painted its slogans on the walls of the fiords, right up into the Arctic Circle. The rock faces of the Thousand Isles of the St. Lawrence were hideously daubed with slogans for stove polish and tooth powder. Out of the Mississippi rose letters twenty feet high testifying to the virtues of a chewing tobacco. Voyagers on the River Hudson at night were regaled, whether they liked it or not, by endless hoardings on the banks, picked out for their benefit by the ship's roving searchlight. Every other rock in the canyons of Nevada was disfigured. In one of the loveliest bends of the River Reuss a giant boulder had been painted brown, with a chocolate firm's name on it. High on the Rigi were enormous gilt letters advertising a hotel. Even the

H

remote hills of the Sudan carried slogans for soap. It was gratifying to find, however, that the Rock of Gibraltar—contrary to
all expectations—was not disfigured by the name of the Prudential
Insurance Company.

Those homing travellers who hoped to save Britain from similar
insult found that they were too late. Pollution was everywhere.
Indeed, there were many who held that Britain was far more
widely and provocatively vulgarized than the continents of Europe
or America. Rudyard Kipling was one of them; William Archer
was another.

The newly formed Society was encouraged by the fact that, here
and there, public opinion had achieved its victories over the
advertiser. In the 'eighties, as was well known, Niagara Falls had
been saved at the eleventh hour from being over-run by advertisers and jerrybuilders; though, unfortunately, from a strip of
unprotected territory an enormous hoarding still looked down on
the Falls.[1] The Cape Town authorities, despite tempting offers,
refused to lease Table Mountain as a hoarding. Holloway's name
was no longer to be read on the Pyramids. In 1890 a soap company
had been compelled, by public outcry, to remove from Ludgate
Hill the sky sign behind which it was seeking to conceal St.
Paul's; but, to offset this, at the rail approach to Durham an
advertiser had succeeded in shutting off the famous view of the
Cathedral and Castle.

In 1891 a bold attempt had been made by Sunderland Borough
Council to rout the bill-posting interests by proceeding against
the owners of a hoarding under the Public Health Act of 1875,
which allowed urban bodies to make their own bye-laws affecting
the structure of walls and buildings. The local justices had ruled
against the bill-posters, but the higher court had reversed this
decision.

The Society went into battle with a sonnet by Alfred Austin,
soon to be Poet Laureate:

> Is nothing sacred then? nor grove, nor mead,
> Nor silent pool, nor solitary lane,
> Where tender souls, world-weary, may obtain
> The peace they covet and the rest they need?

[1] When the writer visited Niagara in 1936, the Falls were dominated by
a large electric sign reading 'See Falls From Here.'

> Shall woodland aisle and flower-paved pasture plead
> For loving head and reverent touch in vain,
> But every unclean huckster may profane
> Heaven's sylvan shrines with sacrilegious greed?
> By lust of gain divorced from Nature's heart,
> And quitting primrose brake and babbling brook
> For sordid joys of meretricious mart,
> Now they return, invade each shady nook,
> Each fair seclusion, and with impious art
> Deface the innocent Beauty they forsook.

That summer, members of the Society heard themselves
described by speakers of the United Bill Posters Association as
'sickly,' 'maundering,' 'querulous,' and 'super-sensitive faddists.'
Said the leading orator: 'They talk about "destroying the appearance of our towns, ruining street architecture." These are but
empty phrases. Take London, for instance. How little there is of
street architecture worth approval!' The 'Society of Busybodies,'
if allowed their way, would put men out of employment. It was a
free world and there were endless opportunities in it. The speaker
said he would prefer to echo the words of another bard:

> Behold to what a goodly world we come,
> For us the spacious bounty of the air,
> The impregnable pavilion of the heavens,
> And silent muster of the disciplined stars. . . .

It was a quotation of unrealized and sinister aptness, for a
generation later advertisements were to be towed by day through
the spacious bounty of the air and projected at night against the
impregnable pavilion of the heavens.

That same year S.C.A.P.A. bloodied its nose in an unsuccessful
attempt to promote a Bill which would have given local authorities power to ban any outdoor advertisements they disliked. A
similar Bill brought forward by Mr. W. S. Caine to limit advertisements in rural districts made no progress. The bastion was not to
be destroyed by a single mine; much patient sapping was required.

Like all reforming bodies, S.C.A.P.A. suffered from the over-
enthusiasm of extremists, some of whom refused to admit that
even derelict building sites, strewn with garbage and dead cats,
were better screened off in orderly fashion behind a hoarding of
gay posters. Hoardings, it was pointed out, too easily became a

screen for immoral acts; and what about the innocent people who had been injured by falling hoardings in Hyde Park, in the great gale of 1891? Then, as now, there was much arguing at cross purposes. 'The posters are the nation's picture gallery, and there is no charge for admission,' proclaimed the bill-posters, pointing proudly to the Academy pictures of the soap kings. Or (on another level): 'Who but a curmudgeon would prefer to gaze at a blotched and dilapidated gable-end rather than at the head of a pretty girl?' The critics retorted that it was a strange sort of academy in which 90 per cent of the exhibits consisted of paintings of whisky bottles, jars of ointment and cocoa tins. 'Come to my window,' someone would say, 'and I will show you a once-decent gable-end bearing nothing whatever but the letters "——'s Pills" in ten-foot letters.' So it went on, neither side listening to the other's arguments. Here it is fair to say that the insistence of certain manufacturers on reproducing their tins and bottles a hundred times larger than life has created much of the prejudice against poster advertising. (One of the posters selected for favoured display near the Thames South Bank Exhibition of 1951 was a literal reproduction of a sauce bottle on a paper doyley.)

The year 1894 produced some ingenious examples of desecration. After dark on Trafalgar Day in London, advertisements for pills, blacking, and watches were projected on to the side of Nelson's Column by a magic lantern device, and also, for the sake of variety, on to the pillars of the National Gallery. S.C.A.P.A. took counsel's advice and were informed that 'the owners of the buildings affected by the advertisement can proceed for trespass or nuisance.' But, asked the Society, 'Cannot the County Council or the First Commissioner of Works do something for us at once?' A resourceful reader of *The Times* suggested 'jamming' the advertisements by a more powerful beam. Eventually the offenders desisted, after being informed that if they did not the necessary legislation would be sought.

That same year a leading pill company announced its scheme for a brighter Britain. It offered a free mainsail to every boatman and fisherman in the country, the sail to bear a slogan praising the firm's pills. In the face of criticism, this offer was represented by the company as a generous gesture to indigent fishermen. Eastbourne Council viewed the offer in a harsher light and prosecuted a local fisherman who had equipped his craft with one of the sails; the charge was 'disfiguring the foreshore.' At the Royal Academy banquet Lord Rosebery invited Royal Academicians to consider how the illustrious Turner, if he returned to life, would feel on seeing the luggers and the coasting ships which he had made so glorious in his paintings converted into a simple vehicle for the advertisement of pills.

On Lake Windermere the same pill company erected a large metal sign at Bowness. When local vigilantes threw it into the lake, the company retorted by advertising on the sails of a boat. Thereupon the vigilantes drilled a hole in the bottom of the boat and sank it, but by that time the company had fished out the sign and re-erected it. The battle might have gone on long enough, but surprisingly the pill company agreed to withdraw on being assured that a personal request for the removal of the sign had been received from John Ruskin. 'They are evidently very aesthetic people at Windermere,' a representative of the company told the Press.

While pill companies were seeking to raise the standard of living of fishermen, other advertisers were generously saving farmers from bankruptcy by hiring strips of their fields, alongside railways, on which to erect signboards. The practice inspired such comments as:

> Ill fares the land, to hastening ills a prey,
> Where posters flourish and where crops won't pay.

Carter's Pills offered, in 1894, to withdraw their rail-side advertising where satisfied that public taste was being offended. But advertisers dared not trust each other. Thomas Beecham said he would remove his advertisements from Scarborough bathing huts on condition that no other firm was allowed to advertise there. 'While they are open to be used in this way the decoration may as well be "Beecham's Pills" as any other,' he said.

The year 1894 also saw the consolidation of rules restricting sky signs in London. For some years advertisers had been setting up names and slogans above the roofs of buildings in such a way that the letters stood out tall and stark against the sky. The result was that the roofs of London presented a crazed alphabetic silhouette calculated to make any painter break his brushes. Even a single-storey building might boast a sky-sign reared sixty feet above it, on a metal gantry stayed with cables, like a tremendous gibbet. Nor was this the only kind of roof advertisement which had been gaining ground; those who drafted the Act found it desirable to impose a ban, also, on 'balloons, parachutes, or similar devices.' Soon afterwards by-laws were passed restricting the use of flashing electric signs, which had been blamed in coroners' courts for causing street accidents. In these forms of advertisement, Britain appears to have been ahead of America. William Archer, in his *America To-day* (1900), said that sky signs were unknown in New York, and so were 'the flashing out-and-in electric advertisements' which vulgarized 'the august spectacle of the Thames by night.' One Thames-side building favoured by electric sign advertisers was the old Waterloo Shot Tower (which in the festival year of 1951 suffered the indignity of having an anti-aircraft gun mounting hoisted to the top of it).

In 1896 a Royal Academician, W. B. Richmond, told S.C.A.P.A. of a startling new form of advertising:

I was in my garden and I heard sudden reports of artillery. Presently from the sky fell masses of green and red paper advertising a tooth powder. These fell all over my garden and I am not exaggerating when I tell you that these were spread over two acres at least. It took my gardener a week to collect all these pieces of paper which were blown out of guns into my garden.

Other members had reported that handbills were being flung into the air in such quantities as to make horses bolt; but advertising artillery seems to have been a solitary phenomenon.

Next year a piece of opportunism by an advertiser rebounded. Nelson's battleship *Foudroyant*, on exhibition at Blackpool, was driven by a storm from its anchorage and lay half-capsized. The local agent for one of the pill companies went out and blazoned the firm's name on the hull. For this enterprise, agent and principal were compelled to pay damages, but it all spelled extra publicity. (Sir Thomas Lipton once cashed in on a shipwreck, too. He was a passenger on a ship which was stranded in the Red Sea, and to the master's annoyance he stencilled 'Drink Lipton's Tea' on bales of cargo as they were jettisoned.)

So it went on. In 1897 a meat extract firm proposed to erect a giant advertisement along the open side of Princes' Street, Edinburgh, to the detriment of the view of the Castle. The city of

Edinburgh protested sharply, and the project was abandoned, but not before the firm had pointed out that, on an earlier occasion when it had given up a proposed site, a rival had stepped in and seized it. Taking no chances, the City of Edinburgh secured the passage of a protective Bill through Parliament.

The worst was still to be. On October 19, 1900, this letter to *The Times* from Richardson Evans, secretary of S.C.A.P.A., inaugurated a new battle:

Sir: Few Englishmen can have eyes so blind and souls so dull as to contemplate without an emotion of pleasure and of pride the novel panorama of the bay of Dover.

Many a home-returning traveller has felt that on all his wanderings he has found no scene richer in historical interest or natural beauty. For some time past the delight has been qualified, if not destroyed, by the intrusion of a colossal disfigurement. One of the American food companies has got some one to erect high up on the cliffs two monster boards on which the name of their product is painted in letters that dominate and degrade the whole prospect.

We ought perhaps to regard with a resentful sense of gratitude the feat of this remote Chicago firm in demonstrating to what lengths in the absence of rational restraint the instinct of vulgar competition can go in affronting the public eye.

But those who love Dover cannot afford to take this grimly philosophical view of the wrong that is being done to them. A memorial has been prepared for presentation to the Mayor and Town Council asking them to exercise such influence as a municipality possesses for procuring the removal of the eyesore. . . .

As soon as the people who resort to these barbarous modes of soliciting custom realise that the community is alive to its rights they will desist. It is a mere question of establishing an authoritative standard of decency.

There appears to have been rivalry between the oats firms at this time to make their names the first words decipherable wherever ships made landfall. There was a similar disfiguring sign over Southampton Water (which was removed as a result of action by the landowners). Another, by a different firm, dominated New York harbour.

Representatives of S.C.A.P.A. wrote to the London agents of the Chicago firm but received no reply. The Society also sent many letters to newspapers and enlisted much editorial support. Worried by the extent of the agitation, a deputation representing the London advertising trades tried to persuade the firm to pull down the sign, in the wider interests of the advertising business. They were met with a harsh refusal. 'A man sitting in a counting-house in Chicago has only to draw a cheque for so many thousands of dollars, and lo! the glory of an English harbour is destroyed!' exclaimed Richardson Evans.

But the municipality of Dover had not been idle. An Improvement Bill on the Edinburgh model was passed through Parliament, giving the town control over unsightly advertisements; and a year after the sign was erected it was pulled down, all eight tons of it. Thereafter many towns which felt themselves threatened by the advertiser promoted Bills to give them the same powers as Edinburgh and Dover.

Since those days America has been schooled to a suitable reverence for the white cliffs of Dover, though an urge to erect extravagant edifices there still persists. Immediately after World War Two an American business man expressed a keen desire to see built, on 'Hell Fire Corner,' a giant statue of Mr. Winston Churchill, with an ever-glowing cigar to serve as a beacon to mariners.

Street advertisers also had their setbacks during the 'nineties. A firm which packed the tops of London omnibuses with garishly dressed figures, all engaged in extravagant pantomime in praise of a brand of tobacco, found itself prosecuted. Seven men who were seen patrolling along Leadenhall Street to Aldgate pump and back, holding close to their noses copies of a certain newspaper, were each fined one shilling. This represented a major part of their day's income, for they were paid 1s. 6d. to patrol from ten in the morning until six in the evening.

The derelicts of the big cities were submitted to endless indignities in the name of advertising. In London a number of them were dressed in convicts' garb and made to patrol the streets clanking their chains. Much preferred to the uniform of Her Majesty's Gaols, however, were those of Her Majesty's Forces. In the early 'nineties it was no rare sight to see processions of seedy old men, dressed in the Queen's scarlet, trudging along the gutters of London, advertising the inevitable soap or pills. This was not a sight calculated to encourage the young man who had just accepted the Queen's shilling.

The scandal became such that a Uniforms Bill, designed to

prevent military and naval uniforms being worn by others than soldiers and sailors, was introduced into Parliament in 1894. On the second reading, Members told of abuses which had come to their personal notice. Colonel A. M. Brookfield had seen a procession of 'bluejackets' marshalled by an individual in the uniform of a naval officer, with cocked hat and sword. More recently he had emerged from Charing Cross Station to see a procession of men dressed as Royal Marine Light Infantry, with pith helmets. One contractor had dressed his men in the uniform of the Artists' Rifles, and when the adjutant of that regiment protested the agent 'heard him with the greatest good temper and urbanity and in answer to his representations clothed all his men in the uniform of another battalion.' The colonel reported that he had even seen a man dressed as a Staff officer standing on the kerb handing out leaflets; and he felt that even Staff officers deserved some protection.

Major F. C. Rasch assured the House that it was because of the way the Queen's uniform was degraded in the streets of London that officers were unwilling to wear uniform when off duty. Indeed, it was considered such a hardship among young officers to be seen in uniform that a refractory subaltern had recently been ordered by Field-Marshal the Duke of Cambridge to wear his uniform in public for a specified period as a punishment.

Another Member, Stuart Wortley, said that when he had served at the Home Office news had been received that an advertising contractor was proposing to dress up his sandwich-men as Napoleon's Old Guard. This had been felt to be most undesirable, and on private representations the plan was dropped. Yet Whitehall had not been stirred to take action to protect the uniforms of British regiments.

The Bill went through without much difficulty, though one or two Members feared that innocent persons might be arrested for wearing uniforms at fancy dress balls or on the stage.

Some advertisers who found these frustrations too much for them began to turn their eyes to Paris, where nobody greatly worried even if bills were pasted on churches or public monuments (if the posters were by Cheret, so much the better). On payment of a few francs bills might even be stuck on pillar boxes, police kiosks and *urinoirs*. There was a report, too, that a bill-posting machine had been devised in Paris capable of sticking posters on

An advertising contractor reviews his troops: by Paul Renouard (1884). *The Uniforms Bill of* 1894 *stopped the clothing of sandwich-men in military uniforms.*

sites fifty feet high. Yet, even as the new century dawned, France dashed the hopes of the enterprising by the forming of a *Société pour la Protection des Paysages*.

It is worth recording that the biggest eyesores of the period did not necessarily generate the greatest heat. Much bitterness was voiced during this period at minor advertising innovations which are now taken for granted. A reader of *The Times* protested in 1892 at the 'brutal vulgarity' of inserting advertisements through the text of magazines instead of segregating them at the end. A man who bought a volume of Pepys was incensed to find that it contained fifty-six pages of advertisements at the back, instead of an index. 'To tack advertisements of 1896 on to a diary of the seventeenth century is a gross impertinence,' he wrote. No sooner had the safety curtain been introduced into theatres in the 'nineties than angry theatregoers saw it degenerate into a bill-board which ruined the atmosphere and dignity of the auditorium. And Rudyard Kipling spoke for many (then and now) when he complained of the 'beplastering of railway platforms with every piece of information in the world except the name of the station.'

The public were spared other infringements of their liberties, however. An ungrateful Government declined a huge sum offered by Thomas J. Barratt for the right to advertise on postage stamps. It also rejected an offer to print all the census forms of 1891 for nothing, provided that the back of the form bore an incitement to use Pears' Soap. As it was, the Government clashed with Barratt over a publicity scheme which had involved importing a quarter of a million bronze 10-centime coins from France and stamping 'Pears' on them. At this period French 'pennies' were accepted as tender in England. Barratt issued the stamped coins, at fourteen to the shilling, for distribution all over the country. However, the Government failed to appreciate the beauty of the scheme. It bought up the coins and melted them down, and after that no more foreign money was suffered to circulate in Britain.

1800–1900

AMERICA: BARNUM AND THE BENNETTS

UNRESTRICTED by 'taxes on knowledge,' the American newspapers in the eighteenth century had expanded rapidly. In the early years of the nineteenth century they were devoting between one-half and three-quarters of their space to advertisements. The price of a newspaper was only three-halfpence, as against sevenpence in Britain.

In 1829, when there was only one newspaper to thirty-six inhabitants in Britain, Pennsylvania had one to four. The editor of *The Scotsman* computed that in one year twelve daily papers in New York had published 1,456,416 advertisements, while in the same year 400 newspapers in Britain had published 1,020,000 advertisements. The cost of a 20-line announcement, repeated every day for a year in a New York newspaper, was £6 18s. 8d.; in a London newspaper, £202 16s.

In content, the American advertisements were not vastly different from those in English newspapers: announcements of sailings, stage plays, books, freaks and patent medicines. But there was one conspicuous difference. Whereas the British upper classes had almost ceased to advertise their black boys for sale, American advertisers still trafficked in human flesh, often in outrageous terms.

Charles Dickens recorded a selection of advertisements for the recovery of runaway slaves in his *American Notes* (1842). The notices would appear under a bold black heading, 'CASH FOR NEGROES,' sometimes illustrated with a line block showing a manacled runaway cowering before a top-booted planter. Dickens quoted, among others:

RAN AWAY, a negro boy aged about 12 years old. Had round his neck a chain dog-collar with 'de Lampert' engraved on it.

RAN AWAY, a negro woman and two children; a few days before she went off I burnt her with a hot iron on the left side of her face. I tried to make the letter M.

RAN AWAY, a Negro named Arthur. Has a considerable scar across his breast and each arm, made by a knife; loves to talk much of the goodness of God.

RAN AWAY, the Negro Ham. Has a ring with iron on his left foot. Also Gresi, his wife, bearing a ring and chain on the left leg.

RAN AWAY, Sam. He was shot a short time since through the hand and has several shots in his left arm and side.

RAN AWAY, my man Fountain. Has holes in his ears, a scar on the right side of his forehead, has been shot in the hind parts of his legs and is marked on the back with a whip.

Whip marks hardly seem to have been a sufficient guide to identity, since many of the runaways were said to be 'much scarred' in this way. Others had 'a good many teeth missing'—the violent punching out of teeth was a popular way of marking a slave. Phrases like 'has lost all her toes except the large one,' 'the rim of his right ear has been bit or cut off,' and 'one of his ears cut off and his right hand cut with an axe' suggested the use of mutilation both as a punishment and as a means of identification.

As a rule, a negro lost his value when he ceased to be able-bodied; but there were exceptions, as for example the carefully preserved Joice Heth, whose frail body served as the first stepping-stone to fame of a young Connecticut Yankee, Phineas T. Barnum, that rogue elephant of advertising. In the *Philadelphia Inquirer* of July 15, 1835, appeared the following advertisement:

CURIOSITY: The citizens of Philadelphia and its vicinity have an opportunity of witnessing at the Masonic Hall one of the greatest natural curiosities ever witnessed: viz Joice Heth, a negress aged 161 years, who formerly belonged to the father of General Washington. She has been a member of the Baptist Church 116 years and can rehearse many hymns and sing them according to former custom. She was born near the Old Potomac River in Virginia and has for 90 or100 years lived in Paris, Kentucky with the Bowling family. All who have seen this extraordinary woman are satisfied of the truth of the account of her age. The evidence of the Bowling family, which is respectable, is strong, but the original bill of sale of Augustine Washington in his own handwriting, and other evidence which the proprietor has in his possession, will satisfy even the most incredulous.

At the suggestion of his friend Coley Bartram, Barnum bought the negress Heth for 1,000 dollars. She played her part well, being 'pert and sociable,' and suitably garrulous about 'dear little George.' Though she died the following year—not surprisingly, of old age—Barnum had seen that his future lay in showmanship. In 1841 he acquired the American Museum in New York, and ran a non-stop entertainment featuring educated dogs, industrious fleas, ventriloquists, living statues, albinos, giants, dwarfs, rope-dancers, glass-blowers and Red Indians. As well as advertising widely (and not always arrestingly) in the newspapers, Barnum put much of his effort into flaming posters and transparencies, handbills, flags, banners and bands. Over his museum he erected a gaslit sign which was as effective as many an 'electric spectacular' of the following century. He was an adept at engineering free publicity, which brought him into clashes with James Gordon Bennett, proprietor of the *New York Herald*. One day when a down-and-out begged for 'any kind of job' at a dollar a day, Barnum gave him a coin to buy breakfast and then presented him with five bricks. These he was instructed to lay one at a time on the sidewalk at busy points; then he was to march rapidly from one point to the other and change round the bricks; and at the end of every hour he was to pass through Barnum's Museum. The man said it was 'all one to him so long as he could earn a living.' Half an hour later 500 people were watching his move-ments. As instructed, he marched from point to point with military bearing, and refused to answer questions. Each time he entered the museum a dozen or more spectators would accompany him, out of curiosity. The game went on for days until the police complained. Such pranks as these, and the erection of the famous sign 'This Way to the Egress' (designed to speed the passage of laggard spectators through his zoo), earned Barnum more renown than columns of paid advertising could have done.

Barnum's triumphal tours with 'General' Tom Thumb (his London visit infuriated *The Times*) and his sponsoring of Jenny Lind made his name world-famous. Though there was much to criticize in many of his earlier exploits, he gave the public a run for its money.

Gradually Barnum formulated a philosophy of advertising which he set out in his autobiography, published in mid-century. 'You may advertise a spurious article and induce many people to call and buy it once, but they will gradually denounce you as an impostor,' he said. (Nevertheless, for generations to come, impostors were to make quick and gratifying 'killings' out of spurious articles.) Barnum was one of the first to pronounce that 'advertising is like learning—a little is a dangerous thing.' He quoted a French writer as saying: 'The reader of a newspaper does not see the first insertion of an ordinary advertisement; the second insertion he sees, but does not read; the third insertion he reads; the fourth insertion he looks at the price; the fifth insertion he speaks of it to his wife; the sixth insertion he is ready to purchase; and the seventh insertion he purchases.'

If a man has not the pluck to keep on advertising, said Barnum, all the money he has already spent is lost. As illustration, he told the story of the scrounger who asked a gentleman for ten cents, saying that he wanted to save himself a dollar. When the gentleman asked for an explanation, he said, 'I started out to get drunk but I have not quite succeeded, although I have spent a dollar. Another ten cents would suffice to make me drunk and thus save the dollar I have already expended.'

Barnum's advice (perhaps for no other reason than that it was Barnum's advice) was not fully believed by many business men fifty years later, and it still has to be reiterated to-day. Hamilton Basso, in *Mainstream*, says of Barnum: 'Out of a wedding of the circus and the New England commercial instinct was born a new and generic art which forever after was to be the most beguiling maidservant of business, teaching a nation to want things it did not need and throw away other things it could still use.'

In the same year that Barnum acquired the moribund body of Joice Heth—1835—James Gordon Bennett, a Scots immigrant, put out from a basement the first issues of his *New York Herald*, of which he was editor, publisher, and advertisement manager. This was the start of a new journalism. Built up on sensational stories of clashes with his rivals—'MR. JAMES GORDON BENNETT PUBLICLY HORSEWHIPPED,' 'MR. JAMES GORDON BENNETT HORSEWHIPPED A SECOND TIME!'—the *Herald* became in little more than ten years the leading advertising medium in America. At the height of his success Bennett was strong enough to be able to impose his own terms on advertisers. These were: cash down, all announcements in small type, no illustrations, and copy to be changed daily. The first of these restrictions was one which only the more prosperous publishers could impose; the less prosperous (as in Britain) were frequently forced to accept payment in kind, which meant anything from bottles of elixir to Vinegar Bitters.

Bennett at first allowed advertisers to use bigger type and double-column displays, but later he ruled out these experiments on the grounds that the smaller advertisers were overshadowed by the big ones. His *Herald* was to hold out stubbornly against display long after the battle was lost. The rule that advertisers must change their copy daily was a salutary one, both for the newspaper and its advertisers. Some firms were content to run the same advertisement for years on end. Bennett realized what many contemporary editors were reluctant to admit: that readers were often no less interested in the advertisements than in the editorial contents, and he went out of his way to proclaim 'Advertisements Renewed Every Day.'

It was not long before advertisers began to chafe at Bennett's rule that they could say whatever they liked so long as they said it in small type. Soon they showed much more resource in capitalising the restriction than their English counterparts. In the van of the attack was Robert Bonner, publisher of the *New York Ledger*. He had been impressed by the policy of repetition adopted by English advertisers in *The Times*, and decided to carry the idea a great deal farther. He began to lease entire pages in the *Herald*, then as many as four pages at a time, filling the columns with endlessly repeated sentences like 'Fanny Fern writes for the *Ledger*' or 'Read Mrs. Southwold's new story in the *Ledger*.' Tackled by Bennett, Bonner pointed out that there was no rule saying that advertisements must be changed *every line*. Eventually Bennett decided to humour him and take his money. The public also began to show a certain exasperation, and Bonner's friends, learning that he was spending as much as 2,000 dollars in a single issue, began to fear for his financial stability. 'What is the use of your taking the whole side of the *Herald* and repeating that statement a thousand times?' a critic asked him. 'I put it in,' replied Bonner, 'to attract your attention and make you ask that question.'

Publishers who leased space to Bonner now began to show considerable apprehension as to how he might use it. Sometimes he varied the policy of repetition by taking a page and leaving it almost blank except for a few small notices. Angry editors complained that he was disfiguring their sheets and holding them up to ridicule; to which Bonner was able to reply that he had used the type size stipulated, so where was the offence? At other times he filled pages of the *Herald* with the opening chapters of new serial stories which he was about to publish in the *Ledger*, cutting them off at an exciting point with some such notice as 'No more of this story will be published in the *Herald*. It will be continued in the *Ledger*.' On one occasion at least Bonner spent 25,000 dollars in a week on advertising; but wisely he refused to accept the credit terms which were offered him. Though he advertised lavishly and eccentrically in other newspapers, Bonner refused to have advertisements in the *Ledger*, seeking his revenue from a high circulation. He paid handsomely for literary contributions— $5,000 to Tennyson for a short poem, the same to Dickens for a short story.

When his premises were burned down in 1860 (a fate which monotonously befell publishers of his day), Bonner inserted in all the leading papers a notice: 'Unless we are burned out more than once a week the *New York Ledger* will be ready Monday mornings on all news stands of the United States, the Sandwich Isles, and New Jersey.' The circulation of his paper eventually rose to nearly half a million.

Because his policy of repetition was mocked in fashionable quarters, Bonner hatched an ingenious plot. *Harper's Magazine* was then being started in a blaze of respectability. To various publications Bonner sent advertisements which consisted of 'Buy *Harper's Magazine*' monotonously repeated. When these appeared the scoffers had to admit that there must be something to be said for Bonner's style of advertising, since *Harper's* were not above using it. *Harper's* took the prank in good part.

The only restrictions imposed by Bennett were typographical. His advertisers could make whatever claims they wished. To complaints that quacks abused his columns, he retorted: 'Business is business, money is money . . . we permit no blockhead to interfere with our business.' In this attitude he did not greatly differ from his rivals, who held that so long as the language of the announcement was decent, the publisher had no further responsibility. Even Horace Greeley's temperate *New York Tribune*, which

I

declined the more obnoxious quack advertisements, preached the doctrine of *caveat emptor*. This attitude was to persist almost until the end of the century.

During the Civil War American publishers had a brief taste of an inconvenience which Britain had at last shaken off: a tax of 3 per cent was imposed on advertisements. It does not seem to have caused much hardship. Editors were still strong enough to hold out advertisements on days when the war news was unusually exciting; and the war provided a useful excuse for putting news on the front page and relegating advertisements to the interior—a policy which was maintained in the years of peace.

One authority has attributed to the Civil War the proliferation of medicine men in the next two decades, contending that it was among the ill and disspirited survivors that rough-and-ready nostrums found ready acceptance. Certainly the patent medicine men now began to advertise across the continent on a prodigious scale. The name of Holloway already led all the rest, but he had formidable rivals. One of them was Dr. Benjamin Brandreth, born in Leeds, who had begun to sell his pills, a box at a time, in New York in 1835—three years before Holloway began his struggles in London. When he had sold enough boxes Brandreth put an advertisement in the *Sun*, and kept on using his profits in this way. In due course he was surprised to find that the druggists were selling more of Brandreth's Pills than he was making, and the next advertisements were strongly worded pleas to the public to avoid substitutes. At a critical time in the *Herald's* early history James Gordon Bennett made a lucrative advertising contract with Brandreth, whom he later denounced as a rogue. By 1870 Brandreth owned several blocks of real estate in New York, including 'a huge pile on Broadway worth its weight in gold,' and a big laboratory at Sing Sing. It was estimated that he spent two and a half million dollars on advertising.

Dr. Henry T. Hembold, 'Prince of Druggists,' specialised in 'fluid extracts.' His leading nostrum was 'Buchu,' a name which (as a writer admiringly testified in 1870) adorned 'every dead wall, fence, rock, and telegraph pole from the Atlantic to the Pacific.' Three million bottles of 'Buchu' were sold in 1868–69. Then there was Dr. Joseph H. Schenck, who acquired a mansion and 300 acres on the Delaware, and a fine yacht, from the

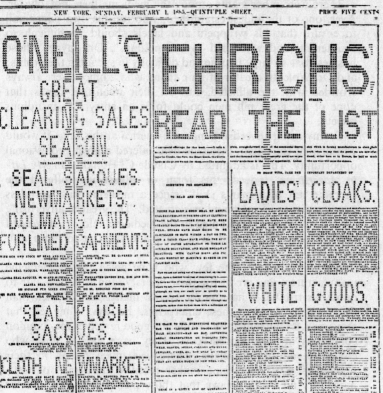

To defeat the editorial ban on large types, advertisers built up big letters from scores of smaller ones. The proprietor of the *New York Herald* refused to remove the vertical rules.

sale of his Seaweed Tonic (originally mixed in a barrel in a back yard), not to mention his Mandrake Pills and Pulmonic Syrup.

There were other giants among the medicine men, notably Dr. Ayer, one of the oldest established, who ran his own paper mill to ensure that his wrappers and labels should be difficult to counterfeit, and who died 'worth millions'; Dr. Jayne, whose business was so large that he had difficulty in spending the profits; and Dr. Wolcott, creator of Pain Paint, whose offices were always crowded with the afflicted. For all their wealth, it seems that none of the great pill men could force an entry into fastidious society.

To any rising advertising man in America at this time, it would appear that the patent medicine field offered a great professional opportunity. This is admitted by Claude C. Hopkins, in *My Life in Advertising*. Indeed, this form of advertising 'offered the supreme test of a man's skill,' since a medicine was worthless merchandise until a demand was created. 'The greatest advertising men of my day were schooled in the medicine field . . . it weeded out the incompetents and gave scope and prestige to those who survived.'

Hopkins is one of the few who have given patent medicine manufacturers any credit for their honesty, and it is only fair to quote his tribute. 'I have never known higher-minded men than those who engaged in these enterprises,' he says. 'They felt that they were serving humanity by offering good remedies for common conditions at very modest cost. They were aiding those who could not afford physicians. There was much reason in their arguments. Every medicine maker received thousands of testimonials. And I still believe that those medicine makers did far more good than harm.'

In the year that the Civil War ended a young freebooter, George P. Rowell, conceived a happy idea for diverting some of the riches of advertising into his own pocket. He was not the first advertising agent, by a long way. Many unscrupulous middlemen were already in business, their chief object being to extort the maximum commission from both sides, in return for the minimum of service (there was as yet no question of preparing the advertiser's copy for him). Secret fees were freely pocketed, secret rate adjustments were negotiated in taverns, and accounts shamelessly filched. Rowell's plan was to buy up advertising columns from country newspapers for a period of twelve months, and lease these to advertisers at one hundred dollars an inch, on the understanding that each advertisement would be inserted four times in 100 newspapers. Though this brought Rowell a spectacular profit, the country editors were well content; they were relieved of the worries of drumming up trade, and Rowell guaranteed prompt payment in cash, as distinct from bitters. Two years later, in 1867, Rowell opened an agency in New York. He did not disguise that he was in business for himself alone, owing allegiance neither to publisher nor to advertiser. In his eagerness for quick riches he decided to market his own patent medicine. But 'Ripans Tabules,' made of nothing but rhubarb and soda, and sold at a tremendous profit, failed to take on, despite all the arts of promotion lavished upon them. Whether or not as a result of this unfortunate venture, Rowell's views changed, and in later life the one-time freebooter did much to bring order, organization, and respectability to advertising.

Already, from 1869, the agency of N. W. Ayer and Son, of Pennsylvania, had shown that a policy of truth in advertising was not the reckless and disastrous course that it might appear to many. Though the Ayer agency handled patent medicine accounts at first, it shed this line of business ahead of its rivals. But the man who has been widely hailed as 'the father of honest advertising' was John E. Powers. He came to prominence in the 'eighties, when advertising agencies were beginning to assume responsibility for preparing their clients' advertisements. Powers wrote some of the early announcements for John Wanamaker's store and became a highly paid consultant to many firms, ranging from Castoria to Scott's Emulsion. Powers wrote in short, simple sentences, scorning the exaggeration which had hitherto been considered essential. Indeed, it is probable that Powers did as much to make advertising literate as to make it honest. He arrived during a period when many small town advertisers chose their slogans from handbooks containing 'suitable' phrases for all occasions, like 'Enormous slaughter in every department' (just as football reporters were once able to turn up handbooks to find phrases like 'rattled the upright' and 'nettled by this reverse').

John E. Powers had a partiality, which became a fetish, for

dressing up his advertisements in Caslon Old Style type. Rivals who imitated his make-up are said to have found great initial difficulty in telling a lie in Caslon Old Style.

Once, in Pittsburg, Powers was called in to advise a big store which was in financial straits. He told them (says Claude C. Hopkins) to publish a prominent advertisement saying something like this: 'We are bankrupt. We owe $125,000 more than we can pay and this announcement will bring our creditors down on our necks. But if you come and buy to-morrow we shall have the money to meet them. If not, we go to the wall.'

The hitherto unprecedented blend of truth and showmanship appealed to the public, who responded on such a scale that the store was saved.

With the Powers reign, the technique of repetition as popularized by Robert Bonner began to die out. Instead came the age of slogans, backed by 'reason why' copy. A slogan was an effective way of clinching the message. Kodak's 'You press the button, we do the rest' was one of the most admired. Cascarets proclaimed 'Works while you sleep.' Under the stimulus of Pears' Soap slogans (the British soap firms enjoyed the same flying start in America as the British pill makers) American soap manufacturers concocted their counter-slogans. Ivory Soap put out the triumphant boast 'It floats,' and claimed for their product that it was 99 44/100ths pure (though all others screamed 'absolutely pure'). Sapolio were more easily content; their slogan, and a ubiquitous one, was 'Use Sapolio.'

One of the leading writers of slogans, who has been credited with devising 'Safety First' and 'See America First' was G. Herb Palin, who was ready to turn out unlimited numbers at ten dollars a time.

The growth of big-store advertising was one of the most important features of the last thirty years of the century. To the agents it was a welcome development, respectable as well as profitable, enabling the more successful among them to unload their patent medicine accounts as gracefully as possible on to less prosperous firms. Among the pioneer big-store advertisers were Marshall Field, of Chicago, A. T. Stewart, Macy and John Wanamaker of New York. Their early advertisements showed no especial originality. John Wanamaker's 'new kind of store,' launched in 1877, got away to a shaky start. Mass production threatened to choke the many departments; a quick turn-over of goods was imperative. John Wanamaker knew that there was no solution in the old-fashioned publicity methods, in the deferential listings of taffetas and tulles. He scorned handbills; the type of person who accepted them was too poor to be interested in the kind of bargain he offered. Newspaper advertising, as he admitted, was his salvation.

The rival stores took advantage of the quickening competition in popular journalism to wring concessions in the way of display types. Even the jealously hidden black types were reluctantly produced in the 'eighties. Double-column displays came slowly, and when they were sanctioned the advertisers demanded three- and four-column displays. At least one advertiser in the *New York Tribune* in 1880 achieved the equivalent of a four-column display by tipping his proclamation on end, so that the paper had to be turned on one side to read it. The advertisement was still contained within the compass of a single column.

Soon Joseph Pulitzer's *New York World* was making heavy inroads into the circulation of the *Herald*, and it was in fact Pulitzer who relaxed many of the hitherto sanctified restraints— at a price. In 1887, armed with a dollar club, William Randoph Hearst began to beat his way into the popular newspaper field. But not until 1895 did the *Herald*, under the second James Gordon Bennett, lift its ban on display.

In a more dignified field, the struggling *New York Times* had been setting its face against the disreputable advertiser. By 1896, when Adolph S. Ochs secured control, the newspaper seemed doomed. Yet, in face of many tempting offers, Ochs extended his slogan 'All The News That's Fit To Print' to cover advertisements. Determined that no one should be able to accuse the *Times* of being influenced by advertisers, he turned down a big Tammany Hall contract, even though assured that no attempt would be made to pull strings if it were accepted. He also rejected lucrative advertisements advocating schemes which he regarded as a waste of public money.

American newspapers did not enjoy, and never have enjoyed, circulation over wide areas. No advertiser could insert his message in one given newspaper and know that it would reach the whole nation, as was the case in Britain. Popular magazines, however, did range across the continent, and for that reason their advertising revenue began to build up on an impressive scale in the latter part of the century. The volume and standard of advertising in such magazines as *Scribner's*, *Harper's*, *Munsey's*, *The Ladies' Home Journal*, and the *Saturday Evening Post* was noticeably higher than in any periodical publications in Britain. It was left largely to the magazines, moreover, to inaugurate the cleaning up of disreputable advertising. One of the pioneers was the *Farm Journal*, which announced in 1880 that it would make good any loss sustained by a reader as a result of buying an article advertised in its pages.

The last decade of the century saw much talk about the 'science' of advertising. There were several journals devoted to the subject, one of them being George P. Rowell's *Printer's Ink* (1888). In this organ, in 1895, appeared a significant sentence: 'Probably when we are a little more enlightened, the advertising writer, like the teacher, will study psychology.' There were numerous clubs at which advertising men met to talk shop, to convince each other that they were men with a mission, and to create a *mystique* of advertising. Already there existed schools, postal and otherwise, which undertook to teach advertising; and the subject was beginning to clamour for recognition in colleges and universities.

In one venerable New England college, so the story goes, a harsh surprise befell a Commemoration Day audience when a young prize-winning student, nominated to address the assembly, bowed and said with innocent amiability, 'Good morning! Have you used Pears' Soap?' After a harrowing pause, during which the Faculty writhed, the parents avoided each other's eyes, and even the students showed distress, the speaker went on: 'This is the advertisement that stares us in the face, turn where we will. Do you read the advertisements in the daily papers? You ought to.' He then went on to deliver an eloquent and well-informed address on the economics of advertising, and in the end was much applauded. It was a pity that Thomas J. Barratt could not have been present to hear this performance.

Many American advertisements of the nineteenth century, especially of the personal type, were marked by an engaging frankness of expression. Others oozed with idiosyncrasy, naïveté and homespun humour (conscious or otherwise), all in piquant contrast to the often-unctuous announcements to be found in many English newspapers. A good example is the following wedding notice which appeared in an American newspaper in 1877:

Millos–Fisher. On the 11th inst. by Rev. A. Vincent Group at his residence 136 Congress Street, Philadelphia, Mr. Frank Millos and Miss Julia Fisher. No cards. No cake. Nobody's business.

This form of humour often found expression in advertisements of the type beginning 'Whereas my wife has left my bed and board. . . .' These were as likely as not to begin 'Whereas my wife, thank God, has left my bed and board. . . .' A husband would publish at length his side of a domestic quarrel, blackening the character of his wife and mother-in-law and any other parties concerned; sometimes the wife would reply in similar vein. No thought of libel seems to have detained advertiser or publisher. Some of the examples which have been quoted elsewhere seem too good to be true, and it is hard to believe that they were not editorial concoctions designed to afford piquant reading.

The Barnum example was responsible for much cheerful irreverence in advertising. An English ecclesiastic, arriving in America to undertake a lecture tour, left the task of engineering publicity to an agent, not without misgivings. In due course he found himself being billed with great prominence as follows:

COME AND HEAR A

old

RARE English DEAN

The gentleman professed intense annoyance, but his lectures were packed.

There was a good deal of petty fraud, often of a good-humoured kind, in the advertising of the day. For instance, persons sending money for an advertised 'Potato Bug Eradicator' received two slivers of wood with the instructions, 'Place the potato bug between the two sticks of wood and press them together.' Telling this story in the *Atlantic Monthly* (1904), Macgregor Jenkins said that a victim's first reaction would be one of indignation, then of wry laughter; soon afterwards he would be urging all his friends to write to the advertiser. So it would go on, until the postal department, notoriously unable to see a joke, would step in. Commented Jenkins:

138 THE SHOCKING HISTORY OF ADVERTISING!

> The seeming indifference [to abuses] is due to a curious American toleration of a fraud or an injustice. . . . To be good-naturedly imposed upon is a positive pleasure, provided the cost of it is not too great.

A strangely censorious view of contemporary American advertisements is to be found in Henry Sampson's *History of Advertising*, which was published in 1874. With very few exceptions, said Sampson, the family papers arriving from the United States 'contain advertisements which would be rejected by the gutter journals of this country.' In course of time, he said, 'the American Press may adopt the plan now in use here . . . that of having an outward and visible show of decency in the advertisement columns, no matter what darkness or danger lurks beneath.' The great majority of American publishers, said Sampson, were too obsessed with making money to worry about what was said of their methods. 'Indeed there are many who exult in the notion of making capital by all kinds of advertisements, from the puff preliminary to the nauseating display of vile quackery or undisguised immorality, and vary this with agreeable little interludes in the way of blackmail.' Such blackmail, he indicated, consisted of publishing attacks on firms or corporations until they chose to take advertising space. Sampson was human enough to admit that the application of a stricter code of morality in American advertising would 'lead to a vast increase of dullness.' He said nothing about the disreputable advertisements of abortifacients and 'cures' for venereal disease which disfigured the British Press.

The type of 'immoral' advertisement which Sampson had in mind was that to be found in the notorious 'Personal' column of the *New York Herald*. Although the story of this column overlaps into the next century, it may as well be told here. The 'Personal' feature was at its spiciest on Sundays, when it covered the whole front page at a dollar a line and overflowed on to the next. From quite early days it had been a place for making simple assignations like 'Harry. In Town. ABC.' As the century reached its end the announcements became increasingly brazen. 'Jolly sports' began to advertise for 'witty, affectionate ladies'; 'young masseuses' offered 'special disciplinary treatment' to select clients; 'highly magnetic' Parisiennes promised 'very interesting conversation' in 'chic suites.' Many of these announcements,

For non-stop smoking
1898

couched in the *lingua franca* of vice, came from organizers of brothels who had been forced under cover as a result of purity drives. Here are a few typical items from issues of June 1905:

BRIGHT unencumbered woman, pleasing personality, seeks work afternoons, evenings by hour.—ADAPTABILITY.—236 Herald.

CONFIDENTIAL work for wealthy ladies by refined, discreet, well-appearing gentleman. EXCLUSIVE. Herald, Brooklyn.

COURTEOUS and discreet gentleman will oblige ladies in any confidential capacity.—'College-Bred.'

AN ADAPTABLE, handsome girl of Bohemian tastes can find exclusive board with liberal-minded woman. SMART WIDOW 324 Herald.

AFFABLE trained nurse would like patients; massage; baths. Alys, 42 West 66th.

ACCOMMODATIONS for refined parties in private flat, convenient to subway, reasonable. SELECT 135 Herald.

So it went on, column after column—unobtrusive service, absolute privacy, complete discretion. Occasionally the mixture was leavened by invitations to adopt twins, by offers to buy pawn tickets or to banish pimples.

The second James Gordon Bennett was warned of the risks he ran in publishing this column, but he said that it had always been a feature of the *Herald* and would continue to be so. It was, in any case, a lucrative source of revenue. Even when William Randolph Hearst began to crusade against the column, in 1899, Bennett refused to alter his decision.

The 'personals' might have gone on indefinitely had not Bennett in 1906 ordered the *Herald* to oppose the candidacy of Hearst as Governor of New York. Hearst held Bennett responsible for his defeat and had little difficulty in devising his revenge. His investigators rented a postal box under assumed names and readily established the true nature of the traffic for which the front page of the *Herald* was being used. Before a New York court Bennett pleaded guilty to using the mails to circulate improper reading matter and was fined $25,000. The firm was ordered to pay $5,000 and the advertising manager $1,000. A *Herald* employee who had come to court suitably prepared peeled the notes from a fat wad. Thereafter Bennett rarely visited New York and Hearst's name was excluded from the *Herald* for many years.

It is on record that before the sentence a Hearst executive had boasted, 'This will cost Bennett $250,000 a year.' Significantly, the Sunday circulation of the *Herald*, which had been the highest in New York, now dropped to third place.

1890–1914

THE PACE QUICKENS

BY the 'nineties, the spectre of over-production (*alias* under-consumption) was beginning to grimace at the factory windows. In this decade, the scale of advertising expanded, the tempo quickened. It was the period when modern advertising began.

In 1892, it will be recalled, a hostile critic of advertising wrote to *The Times* to point out (rightly or wrongly) that 'the colossal and flourishing biscuit works at Reading have never advertised.' At the turn of the century it was less easy to find a colossal and flourishing firm which did not trumpet its wares. Unless a manufacturer had a monopoly of some essential product, or enjoyed the perennial and indestructible goodwill of a specialized public, he had to fight for a market.

In 1890 Richardson Evans, founder of S.C.A.P.A, asserted in the *National Review* that of all those who assailed the public by advertisement, few were willing offenders. 'One pushing tradesman begins, and the rest, to the ruin, not to the advantage of the industry, are forced in self-defence to follow.' (To this, the advocates of advertising could retort: 'Has the cocoa industry been ruined?')

Evans then advanced this analogy:

Suppose a dozen people are in a small room. Two begin to talk to each other at the top of their voices. The others must either give up conversation or shout also. The result is that no one hears as well as before and that comfort is at an end. So it is with advertising. . . .

There is evidence that many firms did, in fact, embark on advertising with the deepest reluctance and misgivings. They feared that, to their business associates, an advertisement would be interpreted as a flag of distress, and the bigger the flag the graver the distress. Hence, possibly, the determination of these firms to spend no more than they could help on the preparation of their announcements. There is also evidence that the heads of some businesses secretly sighed for a ban to be imposed on advertising, especially out of doors, to save the drain on their purses.

Henceforth, said the cynics, the country would see the survival of the loudest. Probably the fiercest competition was in soap. Surely (it was argued) no soap manufacturer could hope to persuade the public to use more soap (the Englishman's passion for washing himself was already a joke in many parts of the world). All he could do was induce people to buy more of his soap at the expense of somebody else's. Many of the public had began to wonder whether soap might not be cheaper if it were not so wastefully advertised. They were never entirely reassured when told that it was advertising which made their tablet of soap as cheap as it was, by enabling raw materials to be bought in bulk. In fact, there is little doubt that the soap war *was* wasteful. Lord Leverhulme's purpose (or one of his purposes) in bringing about mergers of soap firms in the early years of the twentieth century was to reduce the costs of competitive advertising; an aim which inspired the savage attacks on his enterprises by the Northcliffe newspapers in 1906 (for which Lord Northcliffe had to pay damages of £141,000).

Those manufacturers to whom advertising was a faith rather than a vulgar necessity refused to believe that they were nearing the bottom of the public purse. They accepted that, in the new conditions, the mere manufacture of an article was only the tenth part of success; the selling of it was the task that would call for the sharpest brains and a heavy budget. There were, after all, encouraging signs. Newnes, Pearson, and Northcliffe were widening the reading public, and hence the buying public. If readers of the popular sheets were uncovetous of material goods, then they must be made covetous. If supply really was treading on the heels of demand, then demand must be stimulated. From this conclusion was to evolve, by slow degrees, the next stage in advertising: the stage of persuasion, as distinct from proclamation or iteration. Lord Leverhulme was one of the first to see that whereas it had once been enough for an advertisement to be 'pithy, bright, original and humorous' the public now needed 'logical and considered arguments.' More and more there was a vogue for 'reason why' copy. Even Thomas J. Barratt had begun to explain *why* Pears Soap was the best. By the turn of the century the cocoa firms had discovered that their product had other virtues besides purity. A Cadbury's advertisement said:

For the INFANT it is a delight and a support; for the YOUNG GIRL a source of healthy vigour; for the YOUNG MISS in her teens a valuable aid to development; for the YOUNG WOMAN a reliable and always beneficial influence; for the WIFE a solace and a stay; for the MOTHER a beverage that gives endurance; and for the ELDERLY DAME a never-failing help to the enjoyment of a vigorous old age.

There was even a Sunlight advertisement which foreshadowed the fashion of proclaiming, not the intrinsic functions of a product, but its possibilities as a generator and guardian of marital bliss. The illustration showed a harassed wife perspiring over the wash-tub, with an offended husband, newly returned home, in the background. 'Don't let steam and suds be your husband's welcome on wash days,' said the heading. To-day this would probably be criticized as showing the 'negative' side of the picture; far better to show a pert-bosomed, carefree, *soignée* wife (all her washing completed hours before) greeting her husband with a radiant smile.

Luckily, a large section of the public was quite willing to be stimulated into adding to its material possessions, a process variously described as raising the standard of living and keeping up with the Joneses. To the manufacturer it did not matter what the process was called so long as the household with a pound or two to spare opened its maw and allowed it to be stuffed with encyclopedias and sewing machines.

So the advertising campaigns went on, and instead of one firm stealing the market from the others it frequently happened, to everyone's surprise, that after a more than usually frenzied battle all the participating firms sold more, even though the market was supposed to be saturated. Sometimes a small firm benefited from the advertising of its big competitors, just as a 'flea pit' cinema sometimes takes in the shillings of the persons unable to gain admittance to the over-advertised attraction at the luxury cinema across the street. All too often, however, the little firms which did not advertise were squeezed out, or bought out.

There was still the other function of advertising: the introduction and popularizing of new inventions. In the 'nineties the first motor-car advertisements began to appear. Because of the 'red flag' law the British industry got away to a late start, but the lyricist who drew up the advertisements of the Great Horseless Carriage Company in 1896 did his best to force the pace. 'Vehicle Revolution! A New Industry!' he cried, and stressed the need for a parent company to take up, work, and develop 'this immense industry.' In the prospectus were quoted Press opinions. *The Engineer* had said: 'It seems that a great sale is found in France for the vehicles to country doctors, who are able to do from 40 to 50 miles a day, and in some cases the Motor has taken the place of four Horses, which had to be kept previously in order to obtain a satisfactory service.' The *Glasgow Evening News* thought the life of the draught horse not worth thirty years' purchase. And the *Freeman's Journal* said: 'Carlyle's method of testing respectability by the keeping of a gig will disappear when every man has his motor-car in his backyard and has only to light his petroleum lamp when he wishes to go out for a drive.'

The Great Horseless Carriage Company was ahead of its time and disappointed its promoters. Development in the motor-car field was strictly individual and competitive. There is much fascination in the early car advertisements. For instance, the Daimler Company in 1901 said:

> Kindly write to us, stating your requirements, and let us know:
> 1st. At what speed you wish to travel.
> 2nd. Number of persons to be carried.
> 3rd. Whether your district is flat or hilly.

In the popular newspapers and magazines, however, motor-car advertisements were infrequent until Henry Ford began to attack the British market. (The first Ford was driven to the top of Ben Nevis in 1911; a year later the Morris-Oxfords began to stream on the roads.)

*   *   *

The new century brought an extension of the rule: 'Advertise or go under.' Not only must a firm advertise for its own salvation,

K

but British firms collectively must advertise overseas, for their country's salvation. Already the emissaries of more energetic countries—notably the Germans—were peddling their wares under palm and pine, while British salesmen slumbered. His Majesty's consuls complained of the 'take it or leave it' way in which British goods were offered; often there was no attempt to adapt a product for local needs, or even to translate the instructions that went with it. In 1901 the Prince of Wales (later King George V) made this point, modestly enough, in a speech at the Guildhall:

> To the distinguished representatives of the commercial interests of the Empire, whom I have had the pleasure of meeting here, I venture to allude to the impression which seems generally to prevail among their brethren across the seas, that the Old Country must wake up if she intends to maintain her old position of pre-eminence in her Colonial trade against foreign competitors.

To the Prince's surprise, this solitary, diffident sentence caused the speech to be loudly hailed as a 'Wake up, England!' call. In succeeding years, the Prince pressed home the charge whenever possible, urging British firms to display their wares arrestingly at international exhibitions. This, he said, was in accord with the principle of advertising which they already accepted. They knew that if a firm ceased to advertise its sales fell away. What if Britain herself ceased to advertise?

The 'Wake up, England!' speech came as a timely rallying-cry for one group of manufacturers who were fighting a stern battle against foreign rivals—on British soil. Leading cigarette firms had long been trying to frustrate a skilful and determined invasion from the other side of the Atlantic. The American Tobacco Company, selling in particular Richmond Gem and Sweet Caporal, took half-pages in the newspapers to proclaim 'Genuine Imported Cigarettes at Popular Prices.' Usually these advertisements were followed, and sometimes accompanied, by sneering announcements from British manufacturers. Ogdens' cried:

> Don't be gulled by Yankee Bluff.
> Support John Bull with every puff!

and to press the point home, a large picture of a gull was incorporated in the advertisement, with sportsman John Bull discharging both barrels at it. Godfrey Phillips showed Uncle Sam plunging a dagger into the back of John Bull. The same firm had a picture of the British lion crouched defensively over a display of the firm's Guinea Gold cigarettes, and snarling at a top-hatted and star-spangled octopus which had swum up with some notion of giving battle. In the background was the Statue of Liberty, with the sinister word 'TRUSTS' radiating across the sky like the Aurora Borealis. In common with most of the British firms' advertisements, it was indifferently drawn and badly laid out. By contrast, the American advertisements, though there was more than a touch of billposting about them, were intelligently displayed and showed some regard for the rules of typography.

In the London evening newspapers, at the end of the year 1901, the rivalry culminated in a frenzy of knockabout, which delighted the public no less than the advertising managers. Ogdens printed a large drawing of their factory, which was said to employ 3,000 British workers. Then, perhaps because the sight of rows of roofs lacked emotional appeal, they printed an interior picture showing the 3,000 workers whose happiness was in the hands of the British smoker. The American companies retaliated with drawings of healthy, upstanding workers in plantations, nobly dedicated to the task of selecting the best of the leaf for Britain. Steadily, the American advertisements grew bigger, and the British firms were goaded to new heights of patriotism. By now Ogdens were running an ambitious project whereby they undertook to buy every month from members of the public 10,000 albums filled with the firm's cigarette cards, at 10s. an album. One day in November 1901 they took more than four pages of the London *Evening News* (ordinarily only a four-page paper) to print, in small type, the names of those to whom they had paid ten shillings. The collecting of cigarette cards was already something of a craze, though one firm of tobacconists regularly advertised, 'Don't Waste Our Unique Cigarette Pictures (Beauties of All Nations)! We Buy Them Back!' One manufacturer at least despised the issuing of cards; he boasted '12 for 3d. and No Pictures.'

Godfrey Phillips also had a four-page advertisement—in *The Star*. 'We offered a fabulous sum for the entire eight pages of *The Star*,' said the announcement, 'but the proprietors decided otherwise.'

American competition stimulated this British tobacco firm into taking four pages in The Star *on November 12, 1901. This was page one.* The Times *had already carried a four-page advertisement on December 29, 1834.*

The pace was too hot for individual firms. On December 2 leading newspapers carried a full-page advertisement dressed up in the arresting type reserved for portentous news. It was the first announcement of the banding together of several leading firms as The Imperial Tobacco Company (see page 151).

The immediate upshot of this advertising war was the now familiar one: both sides prospered. Whether the rush of orders received by British firms was inspired by patriotism will never be known. Little or no attempt was made during the campaign to tell people why they ought to smoke, or what benefits they might expect to derive from so doing. Like the cocoa firms, the tobacco lords contented themselves with stressing the purity of their products. The ridiculous claims for which modern tobacco advertising was to become notorious did not come along until the 'twenties and 'thirties.

The early years of this century saw many other well-planned and determined advertising campaigns launched in Britain by foreign countries anxious to dispose of surplus foods. The Greeks unloaded their unwanted currants in this way. Then the State of São Paulo, Brazil, faced with serious over-production of coffee, launched a big campaign on behalf of 'Fazenda' coffee. At that time Britain consumed only half a pound of coffee per head against ten pounds consumed in many other countries. There was obviously progress to be made here, and the State of São Paulo made it.

How could Britain counter-attack? Only by means of better-planned advertising campaigns overseas, said the leading agents; and they pointed to their specialized knowledge of foreign markets, foreign tastes, foreign wiles.

Flattered, perhaps, by cordial words from the royal house, some of the advertising agents were seeking to band together in order to improve the status of their calling. Already the word 'ethics' was being used in conjunction with advertising, but no ethical code could be set up until there was some measure of co-operation among advertisers, who for the most part were cut-throat individualists. The young firms were willing to go to any lengths to outshine the old ones; respectability was a thing which could come with riches. Nevertheless, the year 1900 saw the formation of the Advertisers' Protection Society (later the Incorporated Society of British Advertisers). The enemies of advertising were not only the sworn abolitionists. Increasing vexation was caused by the furtiveness with which all but the most triumphant publications concealed their net sales. By their own rough tests, agents could discover that certain publications brought better results than others, but much wasteful trial and error was necessary. To the newspapers, these demands for circulation figures were only the newest of a long list of impertinences.

It is time to trace briefly the rise of the new popular papers and periodicals in which advertisers were to be allowed much greater liberties than ever before. Sir George Newnes, Sir Arthur Pearson, and Lord Northcliffe, who had been so quick to extend their sway over the new Board School generation, were themselves advertisers and 'stunt' men of no mean order. Sir George Newnes, who launched *Tit-Bits* in 1881, was the first to offer the bait of free insurance against railway accidents, a form of bribe which was to lead his later imitators into deep waters. At one time he offered to pay £10,000 to hospitals if his readers would lift the circulation of his paper to a million; after much exhortation they raised it to 850,000 and he made a gift in proportion. Sir George Newnes' proudest publication was *The Strand Magazine* (1890), which in its heyday carried 100 pages of advertisements.

Lord Northcliffe (Alfred Harmsworth) started *Answers* in 1888. The trick which brought him prosperity was the famous contest in which readers were invited to earn £1 a week for life by guessing the total amount of gold and silver in the Bank of England on December 4, 1889. Each entry had to have five supporting signatures, and there were more than 700,000 entries. Originally Northcliffe had hoped to run *Answers* without advertisements, but he rapidly changed his mind. Many of the other publications which he founded in the 'nineties were boys' papers, which could never hope to carry more than a few announcements about stamps and stink bombs (certainly this was not the medium in which to advertise soap). In 1896 he launched his most ambitious venture: *The Daily Mail*, which was to be the pace-setter in newspaper advertising for the next generation.

The third member of the trio, Sir Arthur Pearson, started his *Pearson's Weekly* in 1890 (he had earlier won a prize of a £100-a-year post on *Tit-Bits*). He, too, showed himself a fertile stunt-monger. Once he had the entire issue of his paper soaked in

On December 2, 1901, full-page advertisements in many newspapers told of the formation of the Imperial Tobacco Company—to fight intense American competition.

eucalyptus during an influenza epidemic; any copy, if waved about sufficiently, was supposed to ward off germs. Pearson and Northcliffe also sponsored contests which involved such monumental futilities as counting how many times a certain letter occurred in a given book of the Bible, or in supplying missing words in poems. Some competitions were so much of a gamble that the law intervened.

These frivolous, yet undeniably lucrative stunts, went on year after year. One which rocked the country, and which is worth recalling at length, was the treasure hunt organized by the Northcliffe *Weekly Dispatch* in 1904. It was not an original idea, for *Tit-Bits* had already run a similar contest. Tokens representing various amounts in cash were buried up and down the country, and clues to their whereabouts printed in the newspaper; the whole scheme was then vigorously publicized in the *Daily Mail* and the *Daily Mirror*. There is no doubt that the results exceeded the dizziest dreams of the promoters.

Soon the *Weekly Dispatch* was obliged to print this warning in bold type:

> It cannot be too clearly understood that *the treasure is only to be sought in public places*, none of it having been hidden in private grounds. . . . Some over-enthusiastic treasure hunters have sought the medallions in flower beds, under paving stones, in chinks of walls and in such-like places, but they have in every case been altogether off the track. *Persons who trespass or who do injury to private property may rest assured that they do not stand the slightest chance of finding the buried treasure. . . .*
> No spades or pickaxes are required.

Gloatingly, each week the *Dispatch's* reporters described the activities of the treasure hunters. Hundreds were seen digging in 'the most extraordinary places' in Islington and Holloway. Because one clue had indicated that a token was concealed near a spot 'where people went against their will,' ten constables had to clear destructive crowds from the vicinity of Pentonville Prison and a nearby fever hospital. 'This was not the fault of the *Weekly Dispatch*, the too energetic seekers having altogether mistaken the published clue.' In Lower Clapton was to be seen 'a vast crowd of men and boys digging up every soft piece of ground in the road . . .' A stretch of waste land in Canning Town was being turned over by 'hundreds of men and boys using knives, shovels, sticks, pick-axes, iron bars, and every imaginable implement.' In this area a man believed to have unearthed treasure was chased by the mob. Elsewhere a joker who planted misleading discs of his own manufacture had to flee for his life. In their excitement women fell into rivers. On Sunday mornings the newspaper offices were invested by such large crowds eager for clues that the wholesalers could not be supplied. In the provinces hundreds waited at the railway stations for the arrival of the newspaper trains. After six weeks, during which the equivalent of £3,790 was buried and £2,935 paid out, the contest was called off because of the heavy volume of complaints, presumably from angry property owners. The contest had served to raise the circulation of the *Weekly Dispatch* from a modest total to nearly a million.

In appearance the *Daily Mail* did not greatly differ from its more sedate contemporaries when it first appeared. But standards were fast changing. At long last the advertisers had successfully raided the big black type. In 1897 a writer in the *Nineteenth Century* had much to say about the 'typographical impropriety' of the advertiser.

Today *The Times* itself is ready, subject to certain conditions, to clothe advertisements in type which three years ago would have been considered fit only for the street hoardings, while even that once intolerable monstrosity, the picture block, is now cheerfully accepted by journals of the highest standing to emphasise a full-page advertisement.

The debauching of *The Times* evidently caused much distress among the priesthood of Printing House Square. According to the advertising journal *Fame* in 1892 'one man in the office was struck dumb and another had his hair turn grey in an hour when the proposal was made to put a block into the sacred pages.' This illustration was nothing more than a map illustrating a railway prospectus. Another decade was to pass before *The Times* suffered illustrations to appear regularly in its advertising columns. Even then readers rebelled. Surely there should be one sheet in which the eye was not confronted with the hirsute head of George R. Sims, 'donor' and popularizer of the hair tonic 'Tatcho.'[1]

[1] No mention is made in Sims' obituary notices of his association with 'Tatcho,' but to the masses he was as well known for the vigour of his hair as for the vigour of his Sunday writings.

Like its rivals, the *Daily Mail* at the outset leaned heavily on classified advertisements. Then the day came when Northcliffe decided that advertisements were news. Peremptorily he sent for his £3-a-week advertising manager, a young man called Smith, who had begun to call himself Wareham Smith. The dialogue, as recorded in the latter's *Spilt Ink*, went like this:

Your name is Smith, isn't it?
Yes, sir.
You are in charge of the advertising department?
Yes, sir.
When are you going to start thinking? When are you going to *do* something? The advertisement columns all look alike. They are the same today as in the first issue. I want to see something different. Start thinking. I'm busy now. Good day.

Northcliffe had only himself to blame for what followed. Wareham Smith was a young man of ambition and hardly needed this stimulus to action. Soon the rider who had so callously applied the goad was tugging madly on the reins.

Wareham Smith had noted that there was no such thing as creative advertising. His fellow-advertising managers merely perused the rival sheets, clipped out advertisements which did not appear in their own, and asked the advertisers, 'Why did you not send this to us?'

It seemed to Wareham Smith that the big stores were the greatest source of advertising riches, as yet not properly tapped. Only within quite recent years had the stores been persuaded (or permitted) to take extensive advertising space. It was the life-long rule of William Whiteley, founder of London's first department store, never to advertise in the newspapers, though he went out of his way to engineer free editorial publicity. Old and respectable stores had long cherished a hallowed advertising formula. This began with an expression of thanks to all patrons who had so liberally supported the establishment in the past, followed by a deeply respectful invitation to inspect (not to buy) a new range of calicos, bombasines, silks and taffetas (all unpriced). The less respectable firms also had their time-honoured formula; this was to placard their shop fronts with concussive posters, 'AWFUL SACRIFICE!' 'SOLD AT FEARFUL LOSS!' and so on. Hardly a window but held (allegedly) the fruits of bankruptcy, mergers, shipwreck, inundation, and fire (sometimes goods were specially singed).

After a hundred years or so this joke had begun to wear thin, though it was an unconscionable time a-dying (and is not extinct yet).

Those stores which took space in the Press had concentrated their advertising in the latter part of the week. Under the prodding of the *Daily Mail* they consented to insert their announcements also on Monday, Tuesday, and Wednesday. In return they demanded concessions in the use of ever-bolder type and illustrations, to the open wrath of Northcliffe. Wareham Smith tells in his autobiography how the 'Chief' denounced the *Daily Mail's* advertising displays as 'bludgeoning,' 'shocking,' and 'disgraceful,' assured him, 'You are a damn nuisance to everyone who is trying to produce a good-looking paper,' and persuaded the rest of the staff to 'freeze' him. And yet, comments Wareham Smith, 'he plastered the sides of houses and railway bridges and the sky with hideous advertisements of the *Daily Mail*.'

There were other pitfalls in the way of progress. One of the early drapery advertisements showed a woman in combinations, and from valley and plain 'a howl of execration went up.' Northcliffe told his advertising manager: 'You are ruining the paper with your vulgar advertisements. Stop it at once.' Wareham Smith argued that drapers could not illustrate combinations properly without putting a woman's body inside them, and that 'millions sterling' were involved in the principle.

Alfred bullied. I urged a fight with the reader. We compromised. 'Give combinations a rest.' I did for a time and then let them through gradually. But it was a near thing.

At this period and for long afterwards the big drapers seemed to have only one idea: to pack the front page of the *Daily Mail* with as many drawings as possible of simpering women in unerotic undress. How morals could conceivably have been imperilled by these studies of bosomless matrons posed in forbidding knickers and shroud-like nightdresses, all as sexless as the heroines in schoolgirl stories, is difficult to conceive. Day after day the advertising pages of the *Daily Mail* and other newspapers showed parades of crudely drawn female figures in row after row, like monstrous parodies of classical figures on a Grecian urn. Some of the distaste which the *Daily Mail* aroused in politer breasts may well have stemmed from the first glimpse of its front page, as disfigured by drapers. How much more seemly, by contrast, the front page of *The Times*!

No one who turns through the files of the *Daily Mail* for the early years of this century will deny that Northcliffe at times suffered grave provocation from his advertisers. It had not yet occurred to the big stores—or indeed to any but a handful of advertisers—to spend money on effective lay-out. Too many of the store advertisements, as the *Advertising World* pointed out, looked like the work of office boys. The new half-tone blocks which came into general use in the newspapers from 1904 onwards did not always make for a more elegant appearance; often the subjects of them were barely recognizable.

A shake-up came in the spring of 1909, when a retired American businessman, H. Gordon Selfridge, opened his new store in Oxford Street. Selfridge was no stranger to the ways of advertising. He once told how in his youth, as a space seller, he had tried to collect the price of an advertisement from a hard-up dentist, and finally had allowed one of his teeth to be pulled out in settlement. His London venture was supposedly inspired by Blücher's verdict on London: 'What a city to sack!' It was a great gamble. If this new store, at the end of seven days, was not accepted by the public as of equal status with any other big store, then (said Selfridge) he was lost.

Preliminary announcements were couched in the then unfamiliar prose of High Commerce, with many capital letters:

The Great Principles upon which we will build this Business are as everlasting as the Pyramids. These Principles are Integrity, Truthfulness, Value-giving, Progressiveness, Dignity, Liberality, Courtesy, Originality, a daily presentation of what is New, coupled with a determination to Satisfy.

As the day of the opening neared, the old-established stores responded in a way which must have warmed the Wareham Smiths. Harrods opportunely discovered that their diamond jubilee coincided with the Selfridge opening week, and planned to celebrate it with grand afternoon concerts, floral galas, and special fashion displays. Waring's announced that they had redecorated all their model houses; Derry and Toms took full pages to boast of a special display of hats; D. H. Evans cried 'Paris in London!' Through it all the Selfridge trumpet sounded portentous and daily louder. 'We have issued 600,000 personal invitations to the opening,' said one advertisement, 'but if you haven't received one, come anyway.' On the night before the opening, hotels in London were heavily booked; in the morning enormous shopping crowds descended on Oxford Street from suburbs and provinces. At the stated hour a bugle blew and the curtains on the windows were pulled back like stage curtains. Sixty police were called out to control the crowds in the store.

In six days Selfridge filled ninety-seven newspaper pages with advertising. He had hired a number of artists to draw 'cartoons,' in which bearded or bosomy classical figures represented Courtesy, Liberality, Integrity, and so on. These appeared as full-page advertisements in all London daily newspapers (with one exception) every day for a week, and also in certain provincial and overseas papers. The scale of this advertising was so overwhelming that it became news, whether editors liked it or not, and Selfridge became a household word quicker than he dared to hope.

Critics were not lacking. The *Advertising World* congratulated Selfridge on infusing new vitality into the columns of the Press, and noted that the responses of rival stores were 'like the feeble attempts of a few small boys to arrest the legions of an invading army.' But it complained that the announcements contained much 'high-falutin' nonsense,' not to mention bad English. There was 'an apparent attempt to be more British than the British themselves.' Nobody held it against Selfridge that he was an American, hence 'the pouring out of a soothing balm for the cure of a quite unwounded national susceptibility was as graceless as it was unnecessary.'

Selfridge paid no attention to these objections and continued to sprinkle capital letters through his rich prose. On top of it all, he hired 'Callisthenes' to laud the commercial virtues in a daily half-column in the more serious papers. (John Wanamaker's store in New York had long been famous for its daily talks.) Those advertising agents who had shaken their heads at the extravagance of the opening campaign were now quick to use the Selfridge example as a stick to beat their pinch-penny clients.

Advertising had reached the stage at which writers were beginning to discuss not only its ethics but its psychology, its economics, and its value, if any, to the community. Clarence Moran, author of *The Business of Advertising* (1905), noted that much successful advertising merely resulted in pulling trade away from a rival. He summed up: 'To the extent that the general volume of production is increased by advertising there is a gain to the State, provided that the increase exceeds the cost of advertising.'

The leading writer on psychology in advertising (which was taken rather more seriously in America) was Professor Walter Dill Scott, Director of the Psychological Laboratory at Northwestern University, Chicago. His book, *The Psychology of Advertising*, was issued in Britain in 1909.

In the previous century psychology had been an abstract study, couched in intimidating jargon. In order that practical use might be made of its conclusions, 'psychological laboratories' like the one at Northwestern University had been set up, and those psychologists who could pass on their knowledge in simple terms had begun to address advertising clubs. Many of the truths they announced had been discovered, empirically, generations ago. It is open to argument whether the psychologist gave the advertiser new ideas, or whether he merely told the advertiser which of his ideas were good ones (which the advertiser probably knew already).

Through familiarity, many of Professor Scott's maxims now seem elementary enough. One of them was the principle of 'association': an advertisement should be presented in such a way that a reader would associate it with his own experience, which was best done by appealing to his ruling interests and motives. These included the desire to be healthy, to hoard, to possess, to wear smart clothes, to get something for nothing, to be like the more privileged and successful classes. The instincts were there to be played on. A picture of a mother dosing a child would appeal to the 'maternal instinct'—but scores of advertisers knew that already. (In 1843 the *Edinburgh Review* had noted how Atkinson's Infant Preservative was 'forced on the public attention by the portrait of a female, far gone in the family way, in the act of pouring the anti-Malthusian fluid down the throat of a struggling baby with a spoon.')

Professor Scott stressed the need for cheerful advertisements. Patent medicine manufacturers were fond of portraying ugly, consumptive-looking women coughing their heads off or sneezing in the reader's face. While these pictures made an appeal, possibly, to consumptive women they frightened away healthy readers from the neighbouring advertisements. It was better to draw pictures of men and women in sparkling health. (Even to-day advertisers still debate the relative virtues of the negative and positive approaches.)

The Professor criticized those advertisers who linked their products, even in jest, with bulls, pigs, frogs, squids, and even less engaging creatures. It was also a bad mistake, he pointed out, to associate the product (even in jest) with tramps or other unprosperous-looking characters; the rule was to portray it in the households of the wealthy and distinguished. So literally was this advice taken that manufacturers of cheap bagatelle tables showed their product being enjoyed by aristocratic young men in evening dress, with lovely patrician women looking on.

Professor Scott distrusted humour. 'Advertising is a serious business and unless the advertisement is extremely clever it is unwise to attempt to present the humorous side of life, although it is highly valuable when well done.'

Among other recommendations were these: do not appeal to men when selling goods (like boys' stockings) which are bought by women; do not caution the public against substitutes—write the advertisement in such a way that it will not occur to the reader that there can possibly be a rival product.

A few of the criticisms voiced seem a little baffling at this remove, but no more baffling than some of the criticisms of advertisements to be found in professional journals to-day. For instance, he criticized a Packard advertisement on the grounds that it did not contain 'directions for securing the product.' It might be thought that anyone successful enough to be able to afford a luxury limousine would know how to set about buying one.

As a period piece, the article on advertising in the eleventh edition of the *Encyclopedia Britannica* (1910) is not without interest. The writer of it holds his subject at arm's length but is quite willing to theorize about it. He enunciates what he calls 'a curious and obscure principle' at the back of advertising: 'The average man or woman who goes into a shop is more or less affected by a vague sense of antagonism towards the seller,' he says. The potential buyer entertains a powerful suspicion that the shopkeeper is out to give him the worst of the bargain. The customer, however, can rapidly disarm the shopkeeper if he asks for the article he wants by its trade name, 'not because he has any reason to believe it to be better or cheaper than others, but simply because he baffles the shopkeeper and assumes an authoritative attitude by asking for some specific brand.'

If shoppers ever thought along those lines, they would appear to have ceased to do so to-day; for the modern shopper has now cheerfully and unthinkingly swallowed the proposition that if an article is advertised widely enough, it must be a good one, or at least a reliable one. Probably more citizens enter a shop in a mood of diffidence and indecision than in a state of antagonism.

The writer in the *Encyclopedia Britannica* forebore to touch on one interesting aspect of his subject: the attacks which for some years had been levelled by Socialists at advertising. To the Marxist, the advertiser was one of the more pernicious lackeys of capitalism. His role was to persuade the public to mis-spend money on inessentials instead of on goods or services produced by common agreement for the common good. The advertiser, it was argued, should serve the community, not the rapacious elements in that community.

In 1914 Sidney Webb elaborated the Socialist attitude to advertising in an introduction which he wrote to G. W. Goodall's *Advertising: A Study of a Modern Business Power*. (In that year Britain was spending as much on advertising—£10,000,000—as on her Army and Navy combined.) Was it in the public's best interest, asked Webb, that rival capitalists should go on spending huge sums on advertising until the weaker went to the wall? Did the three million pounds which the late Thomas J. Barratt had spent on the advertising of soap represent 'the value of the wrecks to which the competition of this giant soap manufacturer has reduced so many old-fashioned soap boilers'?

When each branch of industry falls into the hands of a single monopolistic trust, these cannot pretend to effect any further economies in the cost of production by further increasing their business. The cost of advertising would then represent their struggle one with another for the largest share of the consumer's income.

How much more alluring, thought Sidney Webb, to consider the way in which advertising might be employed in a 'co-operative commonwealth.' There was no question of eliminating advertising

completely, only of eliminating motives of personal self-interest.
He was willing to concede that even a Socialist State might 'find
it convenient to publish a catalogue of its productions, so as to
allow the customers freedom of choice in the outlay of the incomes
received by them in cash.' He recognized the value of advertising
as an educational force—'however great may be the common
improvement in intelligence, farmers, we may presume, will
continue to be relatively slow to move.' The United States
Department of Agriculture had been bombarding farmers with
good advice, and that, Webb noted, 'may be the type of much
advertising of the future.' He also admitted: 'Unless our freedom
of choice is to be a mockery all novelties must up to a certain
point be actually forced on our attention. This means advertising.'
    What kind of advertising would the co-operative State adopt?
Webb explained:

Even when all our various manufactories and stores have become
public services, and when no capitalist levies a toll upon our supplies,
we can easily imagine the various public health departments advertising
their baths and other hygienic opportunities; the educational authorities
importuning every young man and maiden to try their attractive lecture
courses and organised games; the municipalities of the various pleasure
resorts commending their holiday attractions; the national railway
and steamship administration tempting us to enlarge our minds by
travel; the State Insurance Department urging us all to insure for
allowances in old age or sickness, supplementary to the common
provision; in short no end of advertising intended to influence our
decision as to how to spend our incomes in the ways that the 'general
will' of the community felt to be good.

    This was written in May 1914. The next four years were to see
enormous developments in State advertising, but on very different
lines from those envisaged by Sidney Webb.

America: 'Truth' is Suggested

    In America, at the turn of the nineteenth century, the technique
of advertising was being studied with great seriousness, more so
than in Britain. The jargon was being enlarged every year, and
agencies boasted of their files packed with arcane wisdom gained
during twenty years or more of advertising research. In the early
years of this century perhaps the most widely publicized postal

courses were those saying 'write advertisements—earn $100 a week.'

Research by Professor Walter Dill Scott showed that, as one century merged into the other, the dabblers in advertising, the experimentalists, the dilettantes were being squeezed out. Analysis of a popular magazine showed that the total advertising space was almost the same in 1907 as it was in 1890, but that there was a 60 per cent decrease in the number of firms advertising. The average amount of space taken by those still in the running had increased by 150 per cent.

One of the most spectacular campaigns at the beginning of the century was the promotion of the cereal Force, with its buoyant character 'Sunny Jim.' Edward Ellsworth worked up immense popularity for his product with the aid of a series of jingles, the first and best-known being:

> Jim Dumps was a most unfriendly man,
> Who lived his life on the hermit plan.
> In his gloomy way he'd gone through life
> And made the most of woe and strife,
> Till Force one day was served to him.
> Since then they've called him Sunny Jim.

Verses like these were breakfast reading for hundreds of thousands of children, to whom Sunny Jim was a better-known character than Hiawatha or Robinson Crusoe. Sunny Jim began to appear at fancy dress balls, on the stage, in newspaper cartoons. The name of the food also helped to inspire free publicity of this kind:

I can't coax my husband to eat any breakfast.
Have you tried Force?
Madam, you don't know my husband.

An over-ambitious programme of 'empire building' brought Ellsworth into financial difficulties, but his Sunny Jim lived on.

The cereal wars of this period were aggressively fought. Quaker Oats and Hornby's Oats had disputed the market in the late nineteenth century. Then came the products which originated in the Battle Creek Sanitarium, formerly a health reform institute run by Seventh Day Adventists. Here John Kellogg devised flaked cereals for his patients, one of whom, C. W. Post, saw commercial possibilities in them. Post Toasties were only one result. In 1899 W. K. Kellogg, brother of John, entered the field himself and in due time made a fortune of $50,000,000 out of Kellogg's Corn Flakes, Rice Krispies and other foods.

Odd were the wiles by which some of these breakfast foods were later sold. "It pops! It snaps! It crackles!' was the cry on behalf of Rice Krispies. Claude C. Hopkins has told[1] how he invented the slogan 'Foods shot from guns' to describe Puffed Wheat and Puffed Rice. 'The idea roused ridicule and one of the greatest food advertisers in the country wrote an article about it. He said that of all follies evolved in food advertising this certainly was the worst. But the phrase was such a curiosity rouser that it proved itself the most successful campaign ever conducted in cereals.' There was never meant to be anything humorous in the idea of 'food shot from guns.' Hopkins' maxim was 'Never seek to amuse. People do not buy from clowns.'

America was ahead in the car race. In 1901 Ransom E. Olds was turning out four hundred cars a year, which put him ahead of all rivals, anywhere in the world. But in 1903 selected American magazines carried the announcement of a Fordmobile:

It is positively the most perfect machine on the market, having overcome all drawbacks such as smell, noise, jolt etc. common to all other makes of Auto Carriages. It is so simple that a boy of 15 can run it.

Nevertheless, Henry Ford continued to perfect perfection. By 1906, when he was building 10,000 cars yearly, he began to enunciate his mass-production economics:

Such quantities were never heard of before. If we made as a profit one-fifth as much on each car as is usually figured as a proper profit, we would make as large a gross profit as a manufacturer who builds 2000 cars.

Ford did not encourage the romantic, adventurous note in his advertising (though in later days his copy-writers grew lyrical enough). He left it to other manufacturers, like Jordan, to hint at the joys of roaming the wide open spaces. To Ford, at this stage, a motor-car was a means of transportation, not a subject for transports. One early advertisement read:

[1] *My Life in Advertising.*

Our purpose is to construct and market an automobile specially designed for everyday wear and tear—business, professional and family use; an automobile which will attain to a sufficient speed to satisfy the average person without acquiring any of those breakneck velocities which are so universally condemned.

Later, however, a Ford announcement said that a person could either drive slowly 'or press down the foot lever until all the scenery looks alike to you and you have to keep your eyes skinned to count the milestones as they pass.'

'We never bothered with a sporting car,' said Ford in *My Life and Work*; but he entered Fords in many races and reliability trials. In 1909 he decided that perfection had again been reached. There would now be only one car: the Model T, or 'Tin Lizzie.' And he proclaimed: 'Any customer can have a car painted any colour he wants so long as it is black.' Nor did he abandon his stand until eighteen years and 15,000,000 cars later.

The vogue for 'Tin Lizzie' jokes was encouraged by Ford himself, against the earnest advice of his executives. An old lady was supposed to have sent a consignment of tin cans to Detroit; by return she received a Ford car and a letter saying that a few tins were left over and these would be credited to her. It did not matter how silly the stories were, so long as Ford became a household word. As will be seen in a later chapter, a vogue for 'ribbing the product' developed in advertising on the radio, but in Ford's early days few manufacturers were willing to laugh at a joke against themselves. (In 1904 the comedian Courtice Pounds, appearing in *The Cherry Girl* in London, said of some hypothetical horses, 'Alas, they are Bovril now!' He received a peremptory demand for a public apology by the Bovril Company.)

There was no slackening in the pace of invention, and each new device brought its advertising opportunities. A young American, H. Cecil Booth, watched a railway cleaner blowing the dirt out of a carriage with compressed air. How much tidier, he thought, to reverse the process, and suck in the dirt. His first vacuum cleaner was considerably larger than a heavily laden railway trolley, and ugly to a degree. Even when it was reduced to more comely proportions, the housewives of two hemispheres needed a good deal of persuasion to try it.

Then came the safety razor boom. Another young American,

ambitious for fame, whose name was King C. Gillette, had been advised by one of his employers to invent 'something that can be used and thrown away.' One morning, so the story goes, he gazed disgustedly at the dull blade of his 'cut-throat' razor. It was a lump of expensive steel, of which only a tiny sliver did any useful work. Why not manufacture just that sliver of steel, to be thrown away when blunted? Experts said that wafer-thin metal could not be given an effective cutting edge. Gillette's idea, which 'changed the face of the world,' was perfected only after many disappointments. From the advertising point of view it was not enough to persuade men to turn to safety razors; it was necessary to persuade them to turn to razors. For years the J. B. Williams Company, manufacturers of shaving soap, had been trying to make the nation clean-shaven by such appeals as 'Adam was created without a beard. Shaggy, unkempt beards were common among fallen barbarous nations until the time of the Emperor Julian, who was the first to denounce them. . . .'

Gillette joined in the 'back to Adam' movement. Perhaps his assurance that his safety razor could be used as freely as a knife and fork was not the happiest of inducements. Nevertheless, the idea caught on. Rival manufacturers saw in Gillette's five-dollar razor a target to be shot down with all speed. Soon there were two-dollar and one-dollar razors on the market; then razors at fifty cents and at twenty-five cents; and finally came the ten-cent razor, complete with blades. Gillette opened a British factory in Leicester in 1905, pricing his British model at a guinea, and again rivals brought the price down with a rush.

Another American whose name figured largely in the advertising of this period was Robert H. Ingersoll, the man who put a watch in the pocket of millions of schoolboys. Obstinately convinced that a sound watch could be marketed at a dollar, Ingersoll wore down opposition and made his fortune. After many years' success in America, he began to advertise his five-shilling watch in Britain, in 1905. Jewellers were hostile. Why sell a five-shilling watch with a year's guarantee, when a bigger profit could be made on the sale of a non-guaranteed watch, with lucrative repairs to be charged over and above? But Ingersoll advertised his watch to such good purpose that the jewellers *had* to stock it, if only to keep the cheap watch trade out of the hands of drapers and newsagents. Not for the first time, or for the last, advertising was used as flail to break down, not the consumer, but the retailer.

Occasionally British firms were to be found counter-attacking with vigour in the American Press. The face of John Mackintosh looked out from many a printed page, with variations of this message:

I AM THE TOFFEE KING

I have given to England a great national candy and I am now offering to America the same toffee that has made me famous abroad. Does America propose to welcome me—to welcome a candy that is so pure that any mother can recommend it to her child? The answer is 'Yes, by all means.'

John Mackintosh's advertising owed rather more to Barnum than it did to Professor Walter Dill Scott. It is possible to do much research in American newspapers and magazines of this period and find very little evidence of the 'psychological attack' which the pundits were advocating; this did not become a wide-spread weapon until the 'twenties. It is true that American canned meat firms now refrained from showing bulls and carcasses, and were illustrating their advertisements with plates of succulent slices of meat, tastefully arrayed, and carried by pretty girls—the first move towards the mouth-watering appeal so chromatically cultivated today. In view of Upton Sinclair's disclosures in *The Jungle* (1906) it was undoubtedly good policy to overlook the animal origin of meat.

An interesting early example of 'scare' selling was an advertise-ment by a school of memory training. It showed a railway signal-man clapping his hand to his brow, and exclaiming 'I forgot!'; in a 'balloon' above his head two express trains were crashing, magnificently, head-on. The advertisement continued: 'How much is expressed in those two words "I forgot!" Thousands of human lives and millions of dollars worth of property have been sacrificed to a faulty memory.'

This was an exception, however. In an American magazine chosen at random—the October 1905 issue of *Munsey's*, a Strand-type magazine with 138 pages of advertisements—very few announcements attempt psychological warfare. First in the magazine, inevitably, was Pears Soap, with a challenging sentence attributed to Bacon:

Cleanliness of body was ever esteemed to proceed from a due reverence to God, to society and to ourselves.

Sapolio's variation on this theme was: 'You can't be healthy, or pretty, or even good, unless you are clean.'

The issue contained four advertisements for revolvers, a reminder that the West was still the West. One of these announcements began: 'The Baleful Green of the big cat's angry eyes has no terror for the cougar hunter armed with a Smith and Wesson.' A full-page advertisement by Otis Elevators showed a grandmother sitting confidently in a lift while her grand-daughter, aged about two, pressed the appropriate button, just as confidently. 'Now Grandma, no more stair climbing,' said the caption. The advertisement of the Victor Talking Machine Company cried 'Loud enough for dancing!' It incorporated the picture of the dog listening to 'his master's voice'—a trade mark which was to inspire a change of name by the firm. The Columbia Phonograph Company proclaimed that their new model was 'sixteen times louder than all other talking machines.' Electric broughams were still competing with petrol-driven cars. 'Coca-Cola' was content with a mere quarter-page. A notable feature of the issue was the number of firms anxious to sell diamonds on credit. But the prize went to the advertiser who offered 'ball-bearing garters' for men—'assures ease of movement.'

In this issue of *Munsey's* almost the only unillustrated advertisement was by Kodak. Yet it was during this decade that the Kodak girl laid the foundations of her considerable popularity, rivalling even Sunny Jim and Johnnie Walker. The public regarded her as a 'nice girl' and were concerned that she should remain so. Her striped skirt is said to have had its influence on popular fashion.

One thing that American advertisers had learned—whether from the psychologists or from each other—was the positive approach. This tendency of the day was remarked by the *New York Evening Post* in 1909:

The hypothetical and somewhat overworked visitor from Mars who should pick up a copy of one of our magazines could not help being struck at the difference in spirit between the literary and advertising sections. If he concludes that the earth is inhabited by two races of men, a race of stumbling, bungling, unhappy failures and pessimists, and a race of vigorous, successful, radiant optimists we can scarcely blame him. In the literary pages the world is the worst of all possible worlds; in the advertising supplement it is the best of all conceivable worlds. In the magazine proper everything goes askew. The rail-roads cheat us and kill us. The food manufacturers poison us. The liquor dealers destroy our moral fibre. The army is depleted. The navy has its armour belt in the wrong place. Workmen go about without work. Lack of sanitation kills its thousands. Automobiles do their share—the list is endless. But what a reconstructed world of heart's desire begins with the first-page advertisement. Here no breakfast food fails to build up a man's brain and muscle. No phono records fail to amuse. No roof paint cracks under cold or melts under the sun. No razor cuts the face or leaves it sore. Illness and death are banished by patent medicines and hygienic shoes. Worry flies before the model fountain pen. Employers shower wealth upon efficient employees. Insurance companies pay what they promise. Trains always get to Chicago on time. Babies never cry; whether it's soap or cereal, or camera or talcum, babies always laugh in the advertising supplement. A happy world indeed, my masters!

In 1911 the visionaries who were striving for a code of ethics in advertising scored their first success. They persuaded the Associated Advertising Clubs of the World, meeting in America, to adopt the slogan, if not the policy, of 'Truth in Advertising.' It was, and is, an almost impossible goal; if it were necessary to proclaim 'the truth, the whole truth and nothing but the truth' advertising would stop abruptly. Some advertisers did try, honourably, to live up to the ideal. Many others were content with an unvoiced slogan of 'Half-Truth in Advertising.'

War on the Quacks

On both sides of the Atlantic, the period 1890–1914 saw the mounting of vigorous attacks on the more presumptuous of the medicine men. If advertising were to be made respectable it was necessary to dissipate two centuries of distrust created by cure-mongers. Today the advertising world claims to have cleaned up the major abuses by its own efforts and on its own initiative; which is by no means wholly true.

Certainly a powerful motive for reform was that, until late in the nineteenth century, reputable (and rich) firms refused to advertise in the same columns as the medicine vendors. Not only did the quacks' advertisements create an atmosphere of mendacity, but their pictures of warty women and consumptive adolescents were so repellent that the healthy reader's eye forebore to linger in their vicinity.

Already it has been seen that certain leading agencies in America dropped their patent medicine accounts as soon as they could afford to do so. It required moral courage to give up a contract worth hundreds of thousands of dollars a year in the knowledge that it would forthwith be transferred to a rival agency, which would not even attempt to discourage the impudent claims of the client. Sometimes an agency was in the position of the girl who, finding that her fine dress was leading her to perdition, gave it to her young sister.

In America it was the *Ladies' Home Journal*, under the militant Edward Bok, which made one of the first stands against patent medicine advertising. In 1892 it refused to carry any medicinal announcements whatever. By contrast, some of its contemporaries continued to publish announcements which would have aroused suspicion even in the *Spectator* of 1711. One of them, in a popular magazine of 1895, read:

BE BRILLIANT AND EMINENT. The new physiological discovery Memory Restorative Tablets quickly and permanently increase the memory two or ten-fold and greatly augment intellectual power; difficult studies etc. easily mastered; truly marvelous; highly endorsed. Price $1.00 post-paid. Send for circular. MEMORY TABLET COMPANY, 114 Fifth Avenue, New York.

In 1904 the *Ladies' Home Journal* opened a vigorous campaign, extending over two years, exposing dishonesty and chicanery by the medicine men. *Collier's* joined in the attack in 1905, Samuel Hopkins Adams conducting scathing exposures under the title 'The Great American Scandal.' The public learned for the first time that its favourite catarrh powders contained cocaine, that the soothing syrups with which it dosed its children were composed of laudanum and morphine. The Women's Christian Temperance Union was invited to take note of the fact that some medicines were 40 per cent alcohol (it was unlawful to sell a certain widely advertised pick-me-up to Red Indians, for this reason). One article by Adams began with a list of names and addresses of persons who had died from the effects of a named medicine. Numerous scare advertisements were reproduced, of the kind which listed common, trifling ailments and represented them as the symptoms of grave disease. One of them read:

Does Your Back Ache?
Thousands of men and women have kidney disease and do not know until it has developed into Bladder Trouble, Rheumatism, Diabetes or Bright's Disease, which will prove fatal if not attended to at once.
IT'S YOUR KIDNEYS!

The advertisement was accompanied by a picture of a man turning over in bed, holding his hand to his back in pain.

Another advertiser who said 'I will give $1,000 if I fail to cure any cancer or tumour' proclaimed in black type:

ANY LUMP IN WOMAN'S BREAST IS CANCER.

Readers were told how the medicine firms handled those confiding letters beginning 'Dear Doctor . . .' which they received in shoals by every post. The letters were rough-sorted by clerks according to whether the symptoms seemed to indicate tuberculosis or cancer, and an appropriate routine letter was sent in return. If there was some unusually intimate passage in a letter, it was handed round so that a good laugh might be enjoyed by all. When the replies had been sent out and the medicines passed off on to the victims, their letters were sold for five cents each to other firms seeking an outlet for their rubbish.

'Unsolicited testimonials' to medicines could be obtained from a bureau in Washington which existed solely to supply them. Nor was that the only source. Adams told how the representative of a celery compound firm called on the editor of a Chicago newspaper, flourishing a proof of a full-page advertisement for his firm's product. It contained some blank squares. 'We want a few testimonials to fill out with,' explained the representative. When the editor replied, 'You can get all of those you want, can't you?' the representative slapped the proof and said, 'Show me four or five strong ones from local politicians, and you get the advertisement.'

Some newspapers, it appeared, were coerced into signing agreements to the effect that the advertising contract was void if the editor published any material hostile to patent medicines. But newspapers were not always the innocent victims; there were

Taking in Oxygen: 1898

instances in which firms were blackmailed into advertising by threat of exposure if they did not.

These campaigns in *Collier's* and the *Ladies' Home Journal* were first-class journalism. As a result many publications, usually the more prosperous ones, were persuaded to ban, or to censor, patent medicine copy. More important, the attacks inspired the passing of stringent food and drug regulations which greatly discouraged the more flagrant offenders.

In Britain, H. G. Wells (who in his apprentice days had rolled many a pill) published in 1908 his novel *Tono-Bungay*, in which that ambitious humbug, Uncle Ponderevo, debauches the population with his 'mischievous trash' at 2s. 6d. a bottle. The plot is not extravagant by comparison with the success stories of real-life Ponderevos of that day. Wells sums up neatly the philosophy of quackery. One of his characters has the idea that it would be profitable to adulterate mustard with horse radish, but baulks at the thought of adulteration. He is assured that adulteration is unnecessary. Far better to concoct a mixture, three-quarters horse radish and one-quarter mustard, give it a fancy name and sell it at twice the price of mustard. Then the question is frivolously raised: Could cinders be turned into biscuit? 'Why not?' argues the Devil's advocate. 'You might advertise 'Why are birds so bright? Because they digest their food so perfectly.

A Heroine of the Home. Mrs. George Fuller put Antidipso in her husband's tea and coffee when he wasn't looking, and completely cured him of drunkenness. c. 1905

Why do they digest their food perfectly? Because they have a gizzard! Why hasn't man a gizzard? Because he can buy Ponderevo's Ashpit Triturating Friable Biscuit—which is better.'

Tono-Bungay let some much-needed light into the underworld of patent medicines. A more calculated attack, deadly and skilful, was loosed by the British Medical Association, which published two pamphlets *Secret Remedies* (1909) and *More Secret Remedies* (1912). These contained laboratory analyses of some of the most widely advertised specifics of the day; analyses which made it all too clear that the public were paying heavily for rubbish. The first pamphlet had much of the effect on the medicine-mongers that Samuel Plimsoll's *Our Seamen* had on the shipowners. There were attempts to impugn the motives of the British Medical Association, and even to put the pamphlets out of circulation; some newspapers refused to carry advertisements of them. At least one action was brought against the Association, only to fail. There is no doubt that these pamphlets prepared the way for the House of Commons' Select Committee on Patent Medicines, which sat from 1912 to 1914.

The Report of this body inspired Lord Bledisloe to say: 'Never has such a tissue of fraud and falsehood been disclosed to any Parliamentary Committee in either House.' Undoubtedly the Report of the Committee is one of the most disillusioned documents of the century. It contains enough criminal plots to last a novelist a lifetime. Since it mentions the products of several firms which enjoy high eminence today, and which have lived down their pasts, it must be quoted with a certain reserve.

In one heavy-laden but devastating sentence the Committee summed up their conclusions:

For all practical purposes, British law is powerless to prevent any person from procuring any drug or making any mixture, whether potent or without any therapeutical activity whatever (so long as it does not contain a scheduled poison), advertising it in any decent terms as a cure for any disease or ailment, recommending it by bogus testimonials and the invented opinions and facsimile signatures of fictitious persons, and selling it under any name he chooses on the payment of a small stamp duty for any price he can persuade the credulous public to pay.

It was possible, the Report pointed out, for a single drug to be sold under an infinite number of trade marks. For example, phenolphthalein appeared under the following names: Aperione, Laxans, Laxatin, Laxatol, Laxatoline, Laxiconfect, Laxoin, Laxophen, Paraphthalein, Phenolax, Proliclin, Purgen, Purgo, Purgolade, Purgella and Purgylum. There were firms which did nothing else but buy well-known chemical substances, invent fancy names for them, and advertise them as remedies for freckles, falling hair or spots before the eyes.

For generations it had been the custom to proclaim that the recipes of medicines had been secretly handed down by Old Mother This or Nurse That, in romantic and implausible circumstances. The Committee set out to trace the origins of an American soothing syrup, the makers of which boasted having sold ten million bottles. Originally these bottles had borne a legend telling how 'an old woman . . . on her last legs with dyspepsia, was given up by her relatives and was allowed to wander in the lanes about her native village in Germany. One day she chewed a leaf of a herb only found in those parts and found immediate relief.' In the course of 1,607 questions, the firm's representative admitted that this story was a piece of fiction. Another product was 'composed of the active principles of certain rare plants which flourish in the valleys situated on the southern slopes of the Himalaya, between the immense gorge separating Nepaul from Bhutan on the East and Almorah on the Bhangulpore, India. . . .' Any rival manufacturer seeking to raid these happy valleys would have been frustrated at the start by being unable to find the word Bhangulpore in the gazetteer. A certain purge was said to have been inspired by Captain Cook, who had seen the beneficent results obtained by natives after eating the local vegetation. A drug to ease childbirth had been devised 'as a result of patient investigation of a minister of religion . . . profoundly impressed by the death of a young wife.'

As in America, there was a brisk traffic in nominal rolls of sufferers:

We were informed that there exist today agencies, one in Leeds which advertises frequently, and one or two in America, selling lists of names of sufferers from various diseases at so much per thousand. That is, a person about to put on the market a 'constipation cure' or a 'rupture cure' or a 'cancer cure' can buy a list of a thousand persons suffering from tuberculosis or rupture or cancer, these lists containing the names of persons who have at some time answered advertisements regarding those diseases, and whose names and addresses thus possess a monetary value.

Lists of sufferers from consumption were more highly priced, according to one witness, because this class was regarded as the most profitable.

The Report named various individuals—some of them well-known—who had exploited one class of sufferer after another, changing their names when they judged credulity to be exhausted. '——, a well-known swindler, is believed to have spent £20,000 a year in advertising an "alcohol cure"—at his death he left £80,000.'

From this disreputable trade, the country derived an appreciable revenue in the shape of stamp duty. Often, to the innocent, the presence on a bottle of a Government stamp appeared to be an endorsement of integrity. Some manufacturers even went so far as to indicate on their labels, and in their advertisements, that the stamp was a guarantee of excellence. The regulations were riddled with loopholes, and a manufacturer could avoid paying tax altogether on his 'cough mixture' if he renamed it 'chest mixture.'

Manufacturers of 'tonic wines' were heavily raked by the Committee. Many of these wines—including one which claimed a testimonial from the Pope—were 'about twice as intoxicating as ordinary claret.' There was no doubt, the Report said, that many persons acquired the drink habit from taking these wines, 'either knowing that they are alcoholic, since they can be purchased and consumed without giving rise to the charge of drinking, or in ignorance that they are highly intoxicating liquors.' One wine firm was said to have obtained the signatures of six thousand doctors by offering to send a free bottle to any person the doctor cared to name. The president of the British Medical Association said that the profession had since learned its lesson.

Some newspapers, the Committee noted, exercised their own censorship over patent medicine advertisements, but it was probable that a number of small provincial papers would be unable to exist without them. The 'so-called religious Press'— which had been criticised by the jury in the Chrimes case— showed wide hospitality to quack announcements, especially 'in the sexual class.' Dr. Alfred Cox, of the British Medical Association, quoted the Association journal as saying: 'It is a fact that quack medicines have more vogue among Nonconformists than among sects of a different theological shade.' Apparently contempt for the established clerical order was extended to include the established medical order.

Cheap 'home' papers were said to contain many advertisements of 'a grossly improper nature.' A single issue of a Sunday newspaper carried nineteen announcements of drugs intended to be used as abortifacients. (One prosperous witness, who showed resentment when asked how many tons of soap he used annually in his pills, tried to convince the Committee that the phrase 'for any unusual delay' employed in his advertisements was directed at the costive; but by this time the Committee were incurably sceptical.)

As unscrupulous as any of the medicine men were the makers of useless appliances, which ranged from electric belts to artificial ear-drums. The assistant editor of *Truth*, G. Sidney Paternoster, who had exposed many frauds in his journal, told of the curious principle of 'gas pipe therapy' as displayed in a device of American make. 'It consists of a piece of tubing which may have some charcoal or something else inside to which two pipes are attached, and discs. You are supposed to put the piece of pipe in a bucket of water and attach the discs to your ankle, and by this means your blood becomes oxygenated and you are cured of anything that is the matter with you.' The device, which was 'merely a piece of pipe nicely polished and got up,' sold at between £3 and £5. An American 'sight restorer' consisted of a cap fitted over the eye; by squeezing a rubber ball, the victim gave himself 'a mechanical massage with air pressure.'

At any given moment, up and down the country deluded citizens were sitting down in the privacy of their homes seeking to woo back the faded senses with the aid of preposterous engines, expensively bought. It was a grim jest played by the New World on the Old. Before sailing for Britain, some of these adventurers secured flattering headlines in their own towns. 'Anti-Fat Missionaries to Reduce London' had run a headline in the *Denver Post*.

The Assistant Director of Prosecutions told the Committee some of his difficulties. As the law stood, manufacturers could say what they liked in their advertisements so long as they avoided gross impropriety. It was hard to find witnesses to testify against a product, and in any case the manufacturers could always produce a string of witnesses, many of them voluntary, to say the medicine had saved them from an untimely grave. Besides, it was almost impossible to persuade a woman who had bought an abortifacient, or a man who had been trying out a cure for sexual weakness, to go into the witness-box.

The Committee made many obvious and sensible recommendations, among them that all manufacturers and their products should be registered. It suggested that the sale and advertisement of cures for cancer, consumption, deafness, diabetes, paralysis, fits, locomotor ataxy, Bright's disease, and abortifacients should be banned—a recommendation which did not become law until twenty-seven years later.

Not the least reason for the Government failing to follow up the recommendations of this Select Committee was that the Report—by a grim coincidence—was issued on August 4, 1914. Even so, it sold out rapidly. It has been alleged that those whose activities were described in its pages bought up copies by the hundred.

1914-1939

THE TECHNIQUE CHANGES

DURING the First World War, the technique of advertising ripened under fierce stimulants. It fell to the Government to initiate, or at all events to endorse, the outright appeal to the emotions—to pride, to shame, to fear, to vengeance.

The detailed story of the great recruiting campaigns need not be told here, but it is important to see how the psychological attack—which was to be followed up, nervously at first, in commercial advertising after the war—was sharpened in the days of peril.

In 1914 the Government had planned to pull in 35,000 Army recruits by advertising. Then Kitchener asked for 100,000. Sir Hedley le Bas, who was concerned with the ensuing publicity campaign, has told how Kitchener was 'sometimes startled,' as indeed many were, by popular appeals which 'departed so drastically from traditions he had respected all his life.' The appeals were of a brutal simplicity. One of them was the famous 'Five Questions to Men Who Have Not Enlisted':

1. If you are physically fit and between 19 and 38 years of age, are you really satisfied with what you are doing today?
2. Do you feel happy as you walk along the streets and see *other* men wearing the King's uniform?
3. What will you say in years to come when people ask you—'Where did *you* serve?' in the Great War?
4. What will you answer when your children grow up, and say, 'Father, why weren't you a soldier, too?'
5. What would happen to the Empire if every man stayed at home *like you*?'

Your King and Country Need You
ENLIST TODAY
God Save the King

M

This was only one of a series of posters on similar lines. There were five questions to those employing male servants:

1. Have you a Butler, Groom, Chauffeur, Gardener or Gamekeeper serving *you* who at this moment should be serving your King and Country?
2. Have you a man serving at your table who should be serving a gun?
3. Have you a man digging your garden who should be digging trenches?
4. Have you a man driving your car who should be driving a transport wagon?
5. Have you a man preserving your game who should be helping to preserve your country?

A great responsibility rests on you. Will you sacrifice your personal convenience for your Country's need?

Ask your men to enlist TO-DAY

Hence the sonnet by Siegfried Sassoon which begins 'Squire nagged and bullied till I went to fight. . . .' Certainly many employers needed to be jolted into a sense of reality. An advertisement by a provincial firm of drapers on August 29, 1914, began: 'The War and the Drapery Trade. The present problem of the moment to all employers, particularly those in the Drapery Trade, is how to keep their assistants fully employed . . . we shall endeavour to retain our entire staff. . . .'

There was a third line of attack. The women of England were asked, *inter alia*:

When the war is over and your husband or your son is asked, 'What did you do in the great War?' is he to hang his head because *you* would not let him go?

It was also hinted that a man who let down his country, by not volunteering, was the sort of man to let down his sweetheart or wife.

The advertisements of commercial firms in the early months of the war showed ingenuity in giving the product a patriotic glow—an art already practised in the South African War. 'British eau-de-cologne for British people,' cried Boots. 'The Pianola piano enables you to play the national anthems of all the leading nations,' cried another headline. 'If you owned a Pianola Piano you could render the Marseillaise with all the fire and vigour that

Daddy, what did YOU do in the Great War?

Psychological warfare: this famous poster of World War One pointed the way to commercial advertisers.

has made it famous.' A fountain pen firm exposed a rival which (it asserted) had 99 per cent of its shares owned by Germans. 'Would you not like to talk to the wounded Belgians in their own language?' asked the proprietor of a French course. A clothing firm promised that if a person bought three pairs of socks it would send a fourth pair, free, to the Belgians. Nurses were called upon to use Palmolive—'they know that hard rough skins would irritate and often cause pain to the sufferers whom they have to tend and care for.' The Y.M.C.A. took full pages (well laid out) to proclaim: 'Queen Alexandra herself gives a building. Will you also give one?'

As the war progressed the commercial advertisers sobered down. Lord Northcliffe at one stage had his qualms about the corset displays which his newspapers were accepting. Might not the paper control condemn this as a frivolous use of paper in war time? His underlings were able to assure him that corsets were now regarded as an essential for women.

During the war entirely new feminine garments began to be marketed: the brassière, dating from about 1916, and cami-knickers, shortly afterwards. The brassière of those days was designed to flatten rather than to flatter, and it bore no visible resemblance to the uplifting, bifurcating garment which was to dominate the advertising pages a generation later. The war also stimulated the fashion of pyjamas for women. Those who had been shocked by pictures of families romping in their combinations now turned the pages shuddering.

One long-notorious type of advertiser encountered a permanent setback during the war: the quack peddler of 'cures' for venereal disease. In 1917, according to a Government spokesman, there were 5,000 men calling themselves herbalists who offered treatments, and who prospered only because victims of the disease—which, through wartime laxity, was rapidly spreading—were afraid to go to their doctors. The Venereal Diseases Bill putting the quacks out of business was not passed without the expression of fears that the liberty of the subject was being jeopardized. One Member pointed out that 'a quack may be, and very often is, a man who has definitely studied this disease and is an honest, straightforward and an honourable man.' So, under pressure of national emergency, ended a type of advertising which had disfigured newspapers for more than three centuries.

By the war's end leading advertising men who had been called on to spend millions of the taxpayer's money felt that they had done their bit; and the subsequent award of a knighthood to Charles Higham, who had been associated with most of the big wartime campaigns, was considered no more than his due.

The 'buy bonds' campaigns ended on an unhappy note. Some tens of thousands of patriotic citizens had risen to the lure seductively offered by Horatio Bottomley, who invited the public to buy one-fifth portions of the £5 Victory shares, with the prospect of winning £20,000. 'The British Empire is your security. You cannot possibly lose your money,' said Bottomley. But they did, and Bottomley went to serve seven years' penal servitude.

In 1920, to mark an international advertising exhibition at the White City, an advertising procession a mile and a half long wound through the streets of London. The public were invited to applaud 'Bubbles,' the Kodak girl, the Michelin man, the Monkey Brand monkey and other characters from the advertisers' mythology. The biggest exhibit possibly aroused the least fervour in the public's breast; it was a banner reading 'Advertisers Demand Net Sales.' This cry was now being raised ever more loudly. As Britain was spending a yearly sum estimated at £100,000,000 on advertising, and as advertisers of eminence were admitting that half of every appropriation was wasted (but which half?), it seemed only reasonable that obvious steps should be taken to cut out the waste. The Advertisers' Protection Society had drawn up its own estimates of newspapers' circulation and usefulness, for the benefit of its members. This enterprise brought upon the Society a writ for libel by Lord Northcliffe, who complained that the Society's assessment of the *Observer* had done that newspaper less than justice. Lord Northcliffe, however, lost his case.

Even Whitehall was now advertisement-minded. Some indignation was aroused when the Postmaster-General, in 1922, proposed to lease the backs of stamps for advertising. 'A great shock,' said a reader of *The Times*. 'I wince at advertisements on stamps as much as I should wince at an advertisement on a cathedral or on my wife's forehead.' That same year there were complaints that income-tax forms (on which Thomas J. Barratt had once sought to advertise) carried offers of plots of land in Canberra.

In the newspaper field, the *Daily Mail* was still the pace-maker, but its competitors, notably the *Daily Express* under Lord Beaverbrook, were beginning to press hard. Still protesting about bludgeoning headlines, Lord Northcliffe in 1921 took a step which some regarded as just another sign of increasing unbalance, though others have since wondered whether the 'Chief' was perhaps saner than they thought. One day, out of the blue, he summoned his head hall porter, Robert Glover, to Carlton House Terrace and told him that henceforth he would be censor of advertisements. Glover was a forthright, sensible and level-headed man, as befitted a head hall porter, and Northcliffe's idea was that Glover should bring the judgment of the average man to the subject of advertisements. For three hours or so Northcliffe briefed his censor in the rudiments of typographical decency. Then he sent for his advertising staff and instructed Glover to lay down the law, first pointing out that Glover weighed 18 stone and had a reach as long as Jack Dempsey. Glover appears to have risen to the occasion commendably, smoking a cigar at the same time. Daily thereafter until Northcliffe's death in 1922, he submitted a report on the appearance of the day's advertisements, earning an extra £2 a week for so doing.

A periodical feature of the *Daily Mail's* pages was the composite advertisement, in which perhaps a dozen firms were persuaded to band together. One of the more ambitious of these was a full-page advertisement on June 1, 1922, entitled 'A Page of Robey.' It had twelve pictures, in each of which Mr. George Robey was intimately involved—drinking health salts, shaving, flying to Paris, pumping up his motor tyre, buying batteries for his radio, listening to the gramophone and so on. The practice of endorsing goods could not go much farther than this.

As before the war, Britain once again became a dump for overseas food growers, who were willing to spend huge sums on advertising in order to rid themselves of their surplus crops. California led the attack. Over a span of five years the Walnut Growers Association of that state increased their sales in Britain by 200 per cent, and the British public, instead of cracking walnuts in only two months of the year, were cracking them in six.

Even more successful were the Sun-Maid Raisin Growers, also of California. Although they had taken energetic steps to increase their sales at home, they nevertheless found themselves in 1920 with an immense glut of raisins. On their behalf, Stanley Q. Grady spent half a million dollars advertising Sun-Maid Raisins in Britain. He 'won the British market in one of the quickest campaigns ever held in England,' defeating vested interests which had maintained a bulk market for eighty years. Grady claimed that he saved the growers between seven and eight million dollars. He achieved his results by full-page newspaper advertisements and a big poster barrage. Consumption was stimulated by the popularizing of raisin bread, and by drawing attention to the iron content of raisins—'Have you had your iron today?' Three years later a critic of advertising complained: 'People have stopped eating raisins because they are good and now eat them because they are fatigued at three o'clock in the afternoon.'

If the British public could be driven to eat raisins in such prodigious quantities, why not apples, pears, lemons, grapes? Late in 1923 the British Fruit Trades Federation launched their 'Eat More Fruit' campaign, a well-mounted broadside levelled at 12,000,000 people daily. Shippers and brokers contributed funds—many of them sceptically—at the rate of one farthing per package. More than one hundred different advertisements were put out, with slogans stressing the enjoyment and good health to be derived from eating fruit. Fortuitously, an influenza epidemic broke out, enabling the promoters to point out how fruit fortified the human frame against illness. A diet of fruit, it appeared from the advertisements, would make children sparkling eyed, good-tempered and even clean-kneed, and girls eupeptic, graceful and enchanting. The mixture of reasoning and 'charm' had gratifying results, and the fruit trade were left in no doubt whether to repeat the campaign. Thus the way was paved for rival 'eat more' and 'drink more' campaigns, of which the public eventually tired. There was a limit to its stomach capacity as well as to its purse.

America's assaults on the British market were not invariably successful. A big campaign to popularize chewing gum in Britain soon after the war made poor progress; but failures, on the whole, were few, and Britain acquired more and more American tastes and customs. By way of counter-attack, Sir Charles Higham tried hard to make America a nation of tea-drinkers.

Sir Charles Higham at this time was a powerful advocate of

collective advertising.[1] It had been shown time and again, he argued, that when many firms selling the same product advertised competitively, the result was that the sales of all of them increased. If firms adopted schemes for group publicity, the result would be to ripen the market for competitive advertisements. Moreover, a group could afford to buy full pages where a firm could rise only to a quarter of a column. 'It does not matter which firm gets the most orders,' he wrote, 'so long as all the firms composing that industry or service get more orders than are customary.'

Sir Charles's writings also suggested that he had accepted the teachings of American advertising pundits—never appeal to the conscious, only to the subconscious; never give the customer a chance to marshal rational objections. He argued that it was bad psychology for a manufacturer of cosmetics to hold out the lure of beauty, because most women knew they were plain; the association would only bring about reasoned resistance in a woman's mind. It was better, he said, to present the idea of improvement, of increased attractiveness. This ingenious advice seems to have been widely disregarded.

In the year 1924 came a reaffirmation of the ideal of 'Truth in Advertising.' A Code of Ethics adopted by the International Advertising Convention at Wembley ran:

We pledge ourselves:
1. To dedicate our efforts to the cause of better business and social service.
2. To seek the truth and to live it.
3. To tell the Advertising story simply and without exaggeration and to avoid even a tendency to mislead.
4. To refrain from unfair competitive criticism.
5. To promote a better international understanding based upon a recognition of our mutual responsibility and our interdependence.
6. To conserve for ourselves and for posterity ideals of conduct and standards of Advertising practice born of the belief that truthful advertising builds both character and good business.

In the emotional fervour of a big convention it was easy to make resolutions like these. It was more difficult for a manufacturer to adhere to them when a competitor was seen to be stealing a march by making questionable claims; and it was

[1] *Advertising: Its Use and Abuse.*

difficult for an agency to refuse to make reckless claims on behalf of a client's product, knowing that refusal would simply mean the loss of a valuable contract. In any event, the man at grips with his conscience would ask himself, what is truth in advertising? Nobody complained because Beecham's Pills were proclaimed to be 'worth a guinea a box,' a statement never intended to be taken literally.

Slowly, however, the advertising industry began to put its house in order. That International Advertising Convention of 1924 had been promoted by the Associated Advertising Clubs of the World, on which the British representation was a very modest one, cloaked by the title 'District 14.' After the convention District 14 expanded rapidly, and in the following year established a vigilance committee to examine questionable advertising. At the end of that year the Advertising Association was formed, with the object of raising professional standards and efficiency.

The year 1924 is still remembered in advertising circles as the year the *Daily Mail* made its sensational attack on the patent preparation 'Yadil.' Full-page advertisements of this product, which was not without value in the treatment of certain minor conditions, had been appearing in a number of newspapers and 'Yadil' was already a household name. On July 22, 1924, out of a clear sky, the *Daily Mail* published a long article entitled 'YADIL': 'An exposure by Sir William J. Pope, K.B.E., F.R.S., M.A., D.Sc., LL.D., Professor of Chemistry in the University of Cambridge.' Sir William said he would set out to show that 'Yadil' was not 'trimethenal allylic carbide' as it professed to be, but a dilute solution of a well-known substance; that it was sold at a price some sixty times the actual cost of the materials used; and that no valid evidence had been produced to show that it had any efficacy in curing the maladies listed in its advertisements —namely, consumption, cancer, bronchitis, pleurisy, pneumonia, malaria, scarlet fever, measles, diphtheria, pernicious anaemia and others. To the layman, the evidence in Sir William Pope's article seemed disturbing enough. The proprietors of 'Yadil' flew to court in an effort to restrain publication of further attacks; they were unsuccessful. Sir William Pope's article was followed by another broadside from Professor W. E. Dixon, Reader in Pharmacology at Cambridge. The *Daily Mail* also printed names of directors of the firm and of its associated printing company, many of them men of distinction. Within a very brief period, the preparation which had been hailed as 'the antiseptic sought by Lister' was off the market, rejected by the chemists.

To say that the 'Yadil' case fluttered the advertising world would be like saying that Pearl Harbour fluttered America. If one firm of such eminence could be put out of business as easily and swiftly, what of the others? Some advertising agents were worried by a sentence in Sir William Pope's exposure. He had said:

That the selling price is 60 times the actual cost of the materials should cause no surprise when it is remembered that the product is sold largely through the agency of full-page advertisements in the daily press.

Had it not been proclaimed for years that advertising reduced the cost to the consumer, that the cost of it was more than offset by the reduction in overheads? There were cautious attempts to correct any unfortunate misapprehension which might have been inspired by Sir William Pope's statement.

The 'Yadil' exposure, which would have cost the *Daily Mail* a vast sum if the charges had been contested and disproved, turned out to be a solitary incident. The man in the street may have suspected that other widely-advertised commodities were no less vulnerable than 'Yadil,' but if they were, it appeared that no other newspaper was prepared to take the risk, or court the honour, of destroying them. According to H. G. Wells in *The Work, Wealth and Happiness of Mankind*, 'No newspaper . . . has any interest in the exposure of fraudulent or adulterated commodities, unless such an exposure will frighten or flatter the owners of competing articles, to its profit.'

The man in the street soon forgot about 'Yadil.' It was a day when the public mind was easily distracted; the day of jazz and cocktails, of face-lifting, of long-distance flights (in themselves an elaborate form of advertising), of Ethel M. Dell, of 'It,' of 'baby' cars, of '£1,000 Must Be Won!' For the first time, silk stockings and rayon brought sex appeal to the advertising pages; the large photographs of pretty models in the new scanty underwear swiftly changed the dress habits of women.

The 'never, never' system was making rapid headway, but it was not yet wholly respectable. Unless it could be made to appear so the outflow from the factories—particularly the furniture factories—would be arrested. The man who did much to break down the prejudice was the benevolent Mr. Drage, whose immaculate courtesies bestowed on Mr. and Mrs. Everyman were inescapable in the newspapers of the late 'twenties. His rivals were, or should have been, grateful to him. Here he is in 1926:

Mr. Everyman: Your new Drage Way of furnishing appeals to self-respecting people.

Mr. Drage: I am glad to hear it. They are the very folk I aim at —independent-minded men who want fair treatment without patronage, and to furnish out of income with absolute security. . . .

Mr. Everyman: Well, my wife's chosen £90 worth of your furniture.

Mrs. Everyman: I should like to have chosen a lot more, for your furniture is so beautiful, Mr. Drage.

Mr. Drage: There is nothing to prevent you choosing more, Mrs. Everyman, only we make it a rule never to press our subscribers to buy.

Mr. Everyman: I should like to pay £8 now and 45s. a month on our £90 order.

To his credit, Mr. Drage never lapsed into unction or familiarity, but he had a heart of gold:

Mrs. Everyman: How you love children, Mr. Drage!

Mr. Drage: Well, it's second nature to me—a builder of homes can't help it. Now what can I do for this happy family today?

If Mr. Everyman nervously suggested producing references, Mr. Drage would say, 'I am offered references fifty times a day and I always decline even to look at them. The Drage Way would cease to be confidential if we asked our customers' friends or employers about them.'

A rival to Mr. Drage in the field of bespectacled benevolence was Mr. Barratt, who was always ready to listen to any suburban housewife limping into his shoe shop with a 'George loves walking, Mr. Barratt—but I don't.' Mr. Barratt, in fact, has stayed the course from the late 'twenties to the present day. Among those hard-pushed to defend advertising it has been argued that advertisements like those of Mr. Drage and Mr. Barratt set a public example of courtesy which cannot fail to have a good effect on the firms' employees, inspiring them to unusual civility and solicitude; a pleasing thought.

The year 1926 saw the founding of the Empire Marketing

Board, empowered to spend £1,000,000 a year on improving trade with the Commonwealth. Sir Stephen Tallents was its secretary, and he had the help of W. S. (later Sir William) Crawford and Frank Pick. The result was another assault on the housewife:

This Can't be You!

There is a woman who finds shopping dull—just a weary round of small change and parcels, day in, day out.

And yet—every food shop is a little living map of the world brought into her street. All the Empire fruits just tumbling off the shelves in their eagerness to tell their story of good quality and good fellowship.

But *she* can't hear.

Every shop window invites her to ask where it all comes from, to remember she is British—to *think*.

And she won't.

But of course she is not you?

Even if this appeal did not inspire women shoppers to pace the streets bright-eyed, eager and inquisitive, there is no gainsaying that the seven years' propaganda of the Empire Marketing Board did have the effect of awakening interest in Empire produce.

Many people today, if asked to name the advertising campaign which most took their fancy in the 'twenties, would give their vote to the Mustard Club. This was a lively, knockabout series devised by Colman's. Leading members of the Club, which all were invited to join, were the Baron de Beef and Miss Di Gester (from whom a lapel badge of membership might be obtained). There was also Herbert, who roused much anxiety by vanishing mysteriousl .

A typical Mustard Club advertisement showed the Baron de Beef, attired as a barrister, lying in an empty bath in a court of law. 'What is a Bath? Baron de Beef appeals to the House of Lords,' ran the heading. The Baron's case was that the bath was not big enough to wallow in, and for a mustard bath it was essential to wallow.

'Now the value of a Mustard bath is complete and comfortable submersion. In that way you get a feeling of absolute rest and peace and the mustard and water flowing all over the body opens the pores of the skin and enables one to sweat colds and influenza out of the system. A lively tingling sensation comes over you, all your muscles grow supple ——'

'That's enough,' said his Lordship. 'We don't want any advertising.'

The ruling was that the bath was a bath *in esse* but not *in posse* as it could not contain the complete *corpus*.

By such painless methods the public was persuaded to use mustard at breakfast as well as at dinner, to throw away the unused mustard at the end of every day and to pour mustard in its bath. The usual influenza epidemic arrived opportunely to give the promoters of the Mustard Club new opportunities.

So far the standard of copywriting, with a few exceptions, was indifferent to poor. There was no sign of any fulfilment of the prophecy made in 1923 at Atlantic City by H. Dennis Bradley: 'The copy of tomorrow will be written by men of genius—representatives of literature, and with the help of great painters there will be born a new great public garden of art.' It was the American copy-writers assaulting the British market who penned the more imaginative prose. In 1926 the firm of Pears, once the *enfant terrible* of advertising, in announcing a new soap, merely discoursed on the qualities, not the possibilities, of that soap. By contrast, the American firm of Palmolive had a full front page, simply and forcefully laid out, showing a girl with a dreamy love-light in her eyes speaking on the telephone, with the query in big letters: 'Will his eyes confirm what his lips are saying?' The copy which followed began: 'The kindly candles of last night, the tell-tale revealments of noon! Do you fear the contrast they may offer?'

Although the First World War had shown the effectiveness of the psychological attack, many British advertisers, many agents too, were still nervous about employing it. Was it (they asked themselves) the decent thing to do? Might not a policy of appealing to greed, fear and snobbishness rebound eventually on the advertiser? The American public, notoriously, were conditioned to crudities. Besides, their mass-production machine was geared to such a tremendous output that drastic measures had to be employed to keep it going. The British public was different. . . .

But was it? As the 'thirties neared, more and more voices were heard proclaiming that the only hope for Britain was to model her salesmanship increasingly on the American pattern. Support for this view came from an unexpected quarter: Mr. Beverley Nichols. In his book *The Star-Spangled Manner* (1928) Mr.

Nichols, taking the slogans of soap-makers for his text, said that in his 'riotous youth' he was comforted through 'numberless orgies' only by the conviction that if he used a certain soap he would retain his schoolboy complexion. 'It did not matter how much I drank or smoked, how many nameless and exquisite sins I enjoyed—they would all be washed out in the morning by that magic soap. . . . I bought it merely because years ago a bright young American sat down in an office on the other side of the Atlantic and thought of a slogan to sell soap. And he certainly sold it.'

Petulantly, Mr. Nichols then attacked that historic slogan which was still to be seen on British railway stations: 'Good morning—Have you used Pears Soap?' He asked: 'Of what conceivable interest is that question? Has it a single "selling point"?' The slogan ought to say something *about* the soap, or about its possibilities.

Advertising, said the Empire-minded Mr. Nichols, was as important to England as was ammunition during the war—'yet we still seem to think that advertisement is a sort of parasitical growth upon industry.' His considered view was that 'children should be brought up at their mother's knee to believe that if they eat any but Australian bottled gooseberries they will choke.'

Many had been saying the same sort of thing in less excitable language; many more were to say it. The Board of Education set up Committees on Education for Salesmanship, in 1929 and 1931, and these, in their reports, blamed the British for 'a detached and insular attitude and unscientific practice, relics of the time long past when we enjoyed a virtual monopoly of the world's markets for manufactured goods.'

It was a painfully long time before copy-writers rose above pedestrian exposition or hackneyed superlatives. But the *avant garde* were already dabbling in what later came to be known, derisively, as 'word magic.' Some of it was deft and nimble enough, cunningly poised between poetry and bathos. The peril of fine writing in advertising is that the higher-flown the imagery and language, the more abysmal the anti-climax when the product comes to be mentioned.

One copy-writer, T. C. Steel, thought so highly of the style of some of his contemporaries that he published a diverting anthology —probably the first of its kind—in 1931, called *Prose of Persuasion*

Among lyricists quoted were the copy-writer for the Buoyant mattress—'adds to sleep the bloom which is the very bloom of the grape'; and for Johnson's Baby Powder—'Happy is the baby born in a world made beneficial and bland by the soft caressing touch of——'

But the most fascinating period specimens enshrined in *Prose of Persuasion* are the *tours de force* by the Jaeger copy-writer, written in the language of the Bright Young People.

My lovelies, with Paris and Berlin doing the most *angular* things with concrete, glass and metal—*so* stimulating—one does heave the old bosom just once to find mahoganised, diluvian London shedding the mildew at last. I mean, on the new floor at Jaeger's positively *all* the fungus has died in the night.

My dears, they've gone *completely* chromium! Tubey chairs, vulcanite tables, glass walls, plus-ultra pictures and *wholly* immediate carpets. A simply *gladdening* spot, darlings. Utterly 1930 and corpse reviving! The cerebral background, of course, for the *stupefying* smartness of the new Jaeger clothes.

After praising the 'slenderizing' quality of the clothes, 'cut with lethal precision but touched with the *coyest* inconsequence,' the writer ended: 'And so, my quinces, to see the pride of the Place Vendôme look *perfectly* paleolithic, one canters round to Jaeger's.' A variant of this was: 'If you want to see Paris look like a suburb of Gath. . . .'

Jaeger's clothes were only 'for the most *compatible* people,' or 'the most congenial and *lucid* people'; in other words, the cocktail, sports car, bridge and point-to-point set. One advertisement discoursed on how consoling it was, after losing on the race-course all the money one had won at cards, to 'drift along and *petrify* the paddock with some Elysian *ensemble*, don't you *utterly* concur?' Life had no more to offer than the 'trim festooning of the old carcase' with '*eupeptic* frocks' which were 'the wildest thrill since the zip-fastener.' Of one garment it was said: 'Bundle it into the dickey, treat it with the most *secular* indifference—it will still emerge trim and uncreased, still fall into *sculptured* lines with simply *monastic* good humour.'

A few other firms were trying out the humorous-sophisticated approach, notably Fortnum and Mason. Austin Reed told of the comical crises from which they had rescued their men-about-the-world. But in many of the national papers the standard of copy-writing, judged from a literary standpoint, was still indifferent.

There was sporadic debate then, as there still is today, about what constitutes a good slogan. Those which were in vogue between the wars were not necessarily the wittiest nor the most original—'That Kruschen Feeling,' 'Friday Night is Amami Night,' '*Daily Mail* Million Sale' (though the latter was admired for its scansion). The wiseacres said a slogan was no use unless (like those just cited) it mentioned the product. A motor-car firm advertised 'Safety Fast'—but which firm? A whisky firm boasted 'Equal to a Fine Liqueur'—but again, which? True, everyone knew the products referred to in the slogans 'Worth a Guinea a Box' and 'Born 1820—Still Going Strong,' but that was only because of the enormous sums unremittingly spent on popularizing these slogans over a generation and more. The lesson seemed to be that the wittiest slogan was no use unless the firm was prepared to use it constantly, year in, year out. By sheer weight of expenditure and repetition even an indifferent slogan could be made a household phrase.

As in America, the depression of the early 'thirties tended to strengthen the advertiser's appeal to the emotions. Goods *must* be sold, otherwise unemployment would grow steadily worse and worse. Some advertisers who had long been crying 'Buy British!' grew tired of appealing to the public's better nature. On March 27, 1930, the motor trade addressed this sharp reproof, in heavy black type, to readers of *The Times*:

Do You Know That

nearly £10,000,000 was spent last year
by our own people in these Islands for
FOREIGN MOTOR PRODUCTS?
A colossal loss to British trade and British workers.
No Government can cure unemployment
if this sort of thing goes on.
Do you realise this? You should.

Other industries tried the appeal to patriotism, with varying results. It was a black interlude. The shipping industry contrived to save much from the wreck by popularizing the notion of cruises. In the mournful winter of 1931 an advertising agency suggested to the newspapers that a little less gloom might stimulate

Christmas trade; not, perhaps, a very grave attempt to interfere with the liberty of the Press.

How the manufacturers of a tonic wine met the challenge of the depression was described, with unusual candour, to the *Advertiser's Weekly* by a representative of the firm in January 1931:

Rising unemployment figures, it seemed, were inevitably reducing our market; yet we refused to be intimidated by this. Consideration of the matter showed that even those who drew unemployment benefit represented a potential market and one likely to be productive enough if approached in the right way. So instead of neglecting the unemployed we visualised them as a prospective market of 2,500,000 people.

As a result of this visionary change of policy sales of the wine increased spectacularly.

Even before the depression the drink trade had been spending £2,000,000 a year on advertising. Licensing policy was to satisfy, but not to create, demand for intoxicants; but advertising gave the 'Trade' a chance 'to capture the younger generation growing up' (in the words of the *Brewers' Journal*). Disapproval of these tactics was expressed by the Royal Commission on Licensing 1929–1931:

We are unable to accept the contention that the effect [of liquor advertising] is merely to transfer demand from unadvertised to advertised beverages. That admittedly is one of the results, but all advertising experience establishes that the advertisement of goods of any particular brand tends to swell the total demand for all goods of that kind. Support for this view may be found in the strong advocacy by leading 'Trade' journals of bulk advertisement of intoxicants.

The Commission also complained that many liquor advertisements contained palpable scientific untruths, and deplored the use made of anonymous medical testimonials. It thought the flow of advertisements was 'almost a public nuisance,' but could think of no way of limitation which would not be open to substantial objection.

Through the depression, the popular newspapers still battled for the elusive prize of a two-million circulation. Ever more bountiful had become the sums which registered readers could earn by getting themselves killed on the railways—eventually the figure exceeded £10,000. Sums in proportion were awarded to those maimed in domestic explosions. But there were prizes to be won without being killed or mutilated. Bribes offered to new readers ranged from cameras to flannel trousers, saucepans to vacuum cleaners. Some 50,000 canvassers tramped the streets, persuading housewives who already took in more than one paper to take another, even if only for the duration of the latest free offer. Some households changed their allegiance according as the needs of the kitchen varied. On top of all this there were 'mammoth' contests calling for the minimum of skill, in which many thousands of pounds were given away.

By 1931 the pace had become too hot even for Fleet Street. Besides, advertisers were growing angry. Although newspapers were at last revealing their audited net sales (the Audit Bureau of Circulations was established in 1931) it was obvious that circulations built on bribery were useless; the public did not read half the newspapers it took in. Further, there were complaints of unfair competition in the distribution of goods (though many big firms were also giving away kettles and pairs of flannel trousers in tens of thousands). An armistice of sorts was declared in 1932. Just over a year later, on March 6, 1933, the *Daily Herald* invited its readers to turn to page four of the next day's issue in order to read of 'A Stupendous Attraction.' Those who did so had their expectations dashed when they found a small paragraph reading 'Owing to unforeseen circumstances the announcement of the Stupendous Attraction referred to yesterday is postponed.' Six days later, however, the unforeseen circumstances had evidently been mastered and the 'Stupendous Attraction' had become a 'Stupendous Sensation.' In a full-page announcement the *Daily Herald* said that it had decided to present its readers with 'a wonderful souvenir to celebrate the Third Birthday under its present management and also its unparalleled progress towards the two millions.' The souvenir was a 16-volume set of the works of Charles Dickens, of 'a rare, exquisite beauty,' bound in 'lustrous silk-grained cloth, tooled and decorated in real 22-carat gold,' each volume protected by 'glassine.' Any comparable set bought elsewhere would cost at least £4 4s., yet *Herald* readers could obtain this set for 11s. Production was costing £100,000 and was giving employment to thousands of British workpeople. 'A complete set of Dickens is the rightful heritage of every English home,' said the announcement; and in an afterthought: 'Needless to say no advertising matter of any kind appears in any volume in the set.'

After twelve giftless months it seemed too good an offer to miss, and the public rose to the bait. Intense exasperation was created in the camps of the *Daily Mail*, the *Daily Express* and the *News-Chronicle*, which quickly warned their readers that, if they were contemplating changing their allegiance to a certain other newspaper, 'it has been ascertained that the cost of production and delivery of the books in question is *less than the* 11s. *they are being asked to pay*.' ('A Dickens of a Bargain' was the *News-Chronicle's* heading.) At last, dog had rounded on dog.

Nor was that all. After the lapse of only a very few days the *Daily Mail*, the *Daily Express* and the *News-Chronicle* all offered sets of Dickens's works for ten shillings—at an undoubted loss. The *Mail*, though it had belittled the *Herald's* offer, was not prepared to belittle Dickens. 'No one can turn to this library in vain,' it said. 'It offers the delights of unrivalled comedy, the stimulus of the drama, the inspiration of many emotions.' Soon the country was in danger of foundering beneath a dead-weight of Dickens; millions of sets were distributed. For the most part unread, they still ornament the shelves of countless homes up and down Britain. Both the *Daily Herald* and *Daily Express* achieved their two-million circulation. Lord Beaverbrook was candid enough to admit that during the later stages of the gift wars he was buying 'readers' by the hundred thousand at a cost of 8s. 3d. each.

The presentation of free gifts, whether by newspapers or meat extract firms, was often represented as a social service, an act of dedication to the common weal. On March 7, 1933, the *Daily Herald* carried this advertisement under a bold heading:

AN OPEN LETTER TO THE RIGHT HON. GEORGE LANSBURY, PC MP

Sir, you have always given prime consideration to developments that will improve the social life of the people. This prompts us to call your attention to a plan directed towards a similar aim—the Kensitas Greater Service Plan.

We, along with other cigarette manufacturers, have given cards and inserts in the packets which were of little or no value. But today we give instead FIVE CERTIFICATES in EVERY PACKET OF 20 CIGARETTES—

certificates of real definite worth, exchangeable for articles of finest craftsmanship. . . .

There were two kinds of unemployment, 'normal' and seasonal. In 1933 a one-man drive was started with the object of reducing the latter kind. A larger than usual heading read, 'I dare not write home to Madge and tell her I've lost my job!' Something about the lay-out suggested that this was not just another cry from an errant young husband who had been sacked for not slicking back his hair with the correct dressing. It was in fact an advertisement by the pipe-smoking Mr. Murphy, who made radio sets. The advertisement went on:

I did not make that up. It is from a letter one of our 'hands' wrote when he got a week's notice recently. He was a good man. Why was he discharged? Why? Because you don't need wireless sets in the summer. Because you'd rather wait for the autumn. And that is why hundreds of good men from every radio factory in the country get the sack during the spring and summer.

Who says you don't want wireless sets in the summer? Do you know anyone with a wireless set who shuts it off from April to September?

Why do you wait for the Exhibition? Are you expecting some marvellous new inventions? Well, you've seen some of them in the last few years. This 'marvellous invention' business is claptrap—and nobody knows it better than the wireless manufacturer.

Mr. Murphy kept up the attack throughout the summer. 'We are going to spend thousands of pounds on advertising at the time when it produces the least results. If anyone says this is a stunt to sell Murphy sets then he is an ass.' Half of his readers, Murphy pointed out, paid for their sets all the year round, so they might as well take delivery of them all the year round. In this way they would get better and cheaper sets, and give work-people permanent employment.

The public had often been reminded that if they did not buy British they would put their fellow Britons out of work. Murphy put a specific, concrete case to them. Evidently he made enough people squirm at the thought of workers being dismissed that people did, in fact, begin to buy radios in the spring and summer.

The advertisers whose ascendancy began in the depression were the manufacturers of patent foods and medicines, vitamin pills and nerve tonics. On them is to be blamed the frenetic, frightened look of so much of the newspaper advertising in the middle 'thirties. Some of these products were useful and filled a need; it was the method by which they were publicized that called for condemnation. Fierceness of competition no doubt led firms into making claims they would rather not have made. It must be embarrassing for the directors of these companies today to look back at their cuttings books of fifteen or twenty years ago. These crudities overshadowed the newspaper advertising of the 'thirties. It is important to remember that there were sensible, intelligent, stimulating advertisements of worth-while goods in this decade, but they had to struggle hard for attention.

One half of the world, it appeared, was under-nourished and the other half was trying to slim. The most improbable commodities were advertised as being ideal for building up tissue; beer, for instance. Equally improbable commodities were proclaimed as ideal for stripping off 'ugly fat.' A cartoonist could have drawn (and possibly did) a picture of a board of directors watching a coin-tossing ceremony: 'Heads we say it puts on weight, tails we say it takes off fat.' Everywhere were coarse pictures of fat women in one-piece bathing costumes; only slim, pretty women were portrayed in modern two-piece suits.

The world was further divided into those who were trying to grow hair and those who were trying to remove it. No other decade can have produced so many 'amazing hair discoveries' as this. No less revolting than the pictures of fat women in bathing costumes were those of completely bald women, sometimes loosely identified by name, who were said to have grown luxuriant hair after a lapse of anything up to twenty years.

Many a page had a grim completeness of its own. At the top, news headlines told of Hitler and Mussolini, of Armageddon round the corner. At the bottom and sides were offers of aspirin and nerve tonics and vitamin pills, illustrated often by pictures of women with vibrating heads and suicidal looks in their eyes ('She didn't care whether she lived or not'). Not only were daughters implored to buy tonics for their depressed mothers, and mothers to coax yeast into their ailing daughters, but all classes were ordered to push pills down the throats of their dogs and cats and thereafter give them the 'vitaminized' foods without which they could not hope to survive in this strident century.

In 'the golden morning of the world,' according to one advertiser, it had all been very different. People had been vital, buoyant, carefree. (Sceptics wanted to know how the firm knew this.) Now the world was full of men and women tired out at thirty, suffering not only from the old primal diseases but from Incomplete Elimination, Summer Sluggishness, Enlarged Pores, Middle-Aged Spread, Cosmetic Skin, Body Odour, Iron Starvation, Tell-Tale Tongue, Smoker's Fur, Itching Scalp and a score of other afflictions.

According to the makers of tonic wines, Britain was a nation of nagging homes. One firm recommended its wine 'to put an end to those bickerings when your eyes get moist and your husband doesn't notice . . . those evenings when there seems to be nothing to do but turn on the radio . . . to make your lips red without lipstick and your eyes bright without tears and you and your husband lovers again.' A rival wine had a similar promise under a screaming headline: 'I'm fed up with your eternal nag, nag, nag!'

One advertiser—Horlick's—had discovered that what people were suffering from was 'night starvation' ('right through the night you've been burning up reserves of energy without food to replace it. Breathing alone takes twenty thousand muscular efforts every night'). It was a daunting thought; few had supposed that sleeping could be so strenuous a pastime. Other advertisers were blaming the malaise of civilization on uric acid, showing magnified pictures of bits of shrapnel in fantastic shapes which were said to be 'acid daggers' in the human veins.

So it went on. . . . 'Ted just sits and reads the paper,' 'Bill says it's just too hot to dance.' . . . 'He stopped holding hands and it was her fault.' . . . 'George says he'll be late—it's that blonde again, I'm sure.' . . . 'It's not only active people who get B.O.' . . . 'My feet are cold and wet and I'm all shivery. . . . My feet are wet too, but it makes no difference because I'm wearing Iodine Socks.' . . .

Even the Postmaster-General joined in the nerve war. 'Fears and doubts thrive well in the home where the telephone is not,' he said, below a picture of a husband worrying because his wife had not returned home from visiting friends. One of the Post Office advertisements was harshly criticized in 1936 in Parliament (and probably also at teachers' conferences of that year). It suggested that the telephone could be used by anxious parents to ring up school to enquire whether their children were on the way home or had been kept in. (One use of the telephone which the Postmaster-General did not advocate was as a means of advertising—a practice which caused some exasperation between the wars. Insurance agents, among others, hit on the idea of ringing up prospective customers and delivering a brisk, cheery sales talk. *The Times* warned on March 10, 1927, that any extension of the idea would make the telephone service unpopular.)

Occasionally, even the least curious member of the public must have wondered what evidence an advertiser could produce, if challenged, to support his claims. No doubt it was true, as one advertisement said, that 'the acid in your stomach would burn a hole in the carpet.' It was not the sort of experiment of which the average man would seek personal proof. But what about the advertiser who said 'Tests show . . . users have ONE-THIRD EXTRA energy at their command.' How were these tests conducted? How was human energy measured? Were a hundred men and women segregated from their fellows, half of them given the appropriate night food and the others not, and then the whole lot set to work in separate treadmills, while 'scientists' took observations? Other advertisements quoted doctors as saying that a certain soap gave one in three women lovelier skins over a given period. How did the doctors contrive a laboratory test for assessing loveliness? A face powder manufacturer cried: 'Women, Here's a Contract! . . . Try this new mystifying complexion secret. Be popular with men tonight or your money refunded. This powder has been thoroughly tested by scientists and guaranteed to be definitely lectro-static.' How many women took up this challenge? How many scientists could have defined 'lectro-static?'

Yet perhaps this way of selling cosmetics was no worse than that recorded by Robert Sinclair in *Metropolitan Man*: 'Manufacturers of cosmetics have now taken to advertising their wares by claiming that they were successfully used by harlots to seduce diseased Bourbon princes.'

Occasionally, but very occasionally, an advertiser tripped up, as the manufacturers of the Carbolic Smoke Ball had tripped up. In 1932 a firm manufacturing 'Letrik' electric combs found itself taken to court. Its advertisements had run:

What is your trouble?
Is it grey hair? In ten days not a grey hair left. £500 Guarantee.

Is it a bald patch? Covered with new hair in 72 hours. £500 Guarantee.

Is it straight and lifeless? Permanent wave starts the first day. Becomes full and natural colour in 48 hours. £500 Guarantee.

Is it falling out? Roots are strengthened and falling out stops in 18 hours. £500 Guarantee.

Is it dandruff? Definitely stopped same day. Scalp clear in three days. £500 Guarantee.

It was explained that electricity flowed from the battery in the comb 'down the hair stems and through the roots—waking them up, bringing them to life, like pouring life-giving water on parched soil.'

The plaintiff, who was a director of an advertising company, paid 3s. 6d. for a comb, used it for ten days as directed and found that his hair was still grey. He said the only result was that the comb 'scratched his head and made him very uncomfortable.' He therefore claimed £500.

The case inspired a certain amount of judicial humour, Mr. Justice Rowlatt being anxious to know whether the comb would turn his ermine black. The plaintiff was asked:

Which would you rather have—your hair black again or £500?—My hair black.

A director of the defending company said that a million of the combs had been sold, and only four claims made. The guarantee of £500 was 'a mere flourish.' Mr. Justice Rowlatt awarded £500 against the company—'rather a windfall for the plaintiff.' He had said, earlier, that he was not in favour of this kind of action; leaving it to be presumed that he was not in favour of this type of advertisement.

For humour and light-heartedness in the advertising columns in this decade the reader had to rely on the petrol companies, notably Shell and British-Petroleum, and the brewers, especially Bass, Worthington and Guinness. (The last-mentioned firm did not begin to advertise extensively until 1929.) For romance, the reader had to turn to the advertisements of the chocolate makers and cruise lines.

Sex appeal was now used to sell other things besides rayon. One of Mr. Drage's rivals had a curious advertisement of this kind in the *Daily Herald* (and doubtless elsewhere) in November

1933. An attractive lady in undress, sitting at her dressing-table, hears a knock and calls out 'Who's that? You can't come in yet!'

The caller is insistent, so without bothering to put on a dressing-gown, the lady half-opens the door of her bedroom, and exclaims: 'Good heavens, Rob! What's bitten you? You look all washed up!'

It emerges in due course that Rob is the lady's brother, and that she is a married woman, though it does not emerge how he gained admission into the house. While she stands with a shapely leg displayed in the doorway, her brother tells his story:

I'm back again in circulation! Carol's given me the air—says I'm wasting her life—Ought to have a home for her by now—that I'm a flat tyre—AND SOME! You know I can't afford to sink all my savings on furniture.

M'm. That's so. But it's 'Easier to pay ——'s four-year way.' Wouldn't a home like this suit you both?'

Gosh, that's an idea. Carol says this place always looks simply swagger. I'd forgotten you went to ——'s.

Carol's right—you need gingering up. Why keep her waiting with ——'s ready to do the waiting for you?

The conversation goes on in this vein, while the reader waits apprehensively for Rob's brother-in-law to return suddenly. But Rob eventually goes away to order some furniture on credit and his sister goes away to put on some clothes.

Social historians of the future must make what they can of advertisements like that; and also of dialogues like this (of the same period):

ELEANOR: Whoever is that handsome young man who has just come into the room? I have never seen him before. He has all the room looking at him. How bronzed and healthy he looks!

HER FRIEND: Oh, that's Jack Mordaunt. He is just home from the East. He's been excavating and you call him a young man, why, he is older than I am, and I'm 48. While he was in the East he put on his dinner jacket every night. He let the Arabs know that he was civilised and he swears by —— Cream. . . . Many a time he has shaved without water. You have often to do those things in the East, as water is so scarce.

ELEANOR: How interesting! I want to be the first girl to be introduced.

In 1935 the drink trade survived an attempt in the House of Lords to curb its methods of advertising. Lord Arnold quoted

some of the brewers' slogans of the day, which included 'For an
A1 Nation Beer is Best' and 'Rich Nourishment in Every Glass.'
There was as much nourishment in a glass of beer, he said, as
in three-fifths of an ounce of bread; and for the same outlay a
man could buy twenty-two times as much nourishment in the
form of milk. 'I see but little difference between some of these
advertisements and getting money by false pretences,' said Lord
Arnold. The indoctrination of the young generation had now
reached the stage at which school children were wearing lapel
badges in praise of stout.

The 'Trade' did not lack defenders in the House. This excerpt
from *Hansard* of March 28, speaks for itself:

> Lord Rhayader: I see advertisements all over the place 'Guinness is
> good for you'——
> The Earl of Iveagh: It is true.
> Lord Rhayader: It is a matter of opinion, perhaps.
> The Earl of Iveagh: My word is as good as yours.
> Lord Rhayader: I am told that if I put up 'Guinness is bad for
> you'——
> The Earl of Iveagh: It would be untrue.

The Earl of Rhayader was trying to say that if he did as he
said, he would presumably be sued for libel. Collective propaganda
on the lines of 'Beer is best' could be challenged less expensively.
Temperance propagandists answered that particular boast with
'Beer is best left alone'—a reminder that the ideal slogan is one
which cannot readily be perverted by the hostile or the humorous.

The Press at large does not seem to have queried the claims
of the brewers, though a few publications, like *Punch* and the
Observer, rejected liquor advertisements altogether. Most newspapers and magazines, however, maintained their own black lists
of advertisers, their own lists of banned phrases. In the former
category came firms who ignored customers' complaints or who
had not the distributive machinery to fulfil their promises; manufacturers of nostrums known to contain actively dangerous drugs;
firms engaging in 'snowball' enterprises; firms peddling land
overseas; firms with directors of proved or strongly suspected
dishonesty; companies with too-boastful prospectuses. Some
newspapers refused to take moneylenders' advertisements or
adoption appeals. Most of them 'vetted' with great care the

advertisements of massage establishments, private dancing classes and such.

The Advertising Association, having failed to bring about a general agreement among newspapers and advertisers to clean up medicinal advertising, began to press for legislation. In 1936 a Bill which had been four years in the framing, and which was approved by the Pharmaceutical Society and even by some of the proprietary medicine firms, was presented to Parliament. It proposed to ban the advertising of cures for cancer, tuberculosis and the other intractable illnesses which had been listed by the Select Committee of 1914. Unfortunately the Bill came up in the House of Commons on a day when the minds of all right-thinking Englishmen were focused on a point more than two hundred miles from Westminster: at Aintree. Nevertheless the initial attendance in the Commons on March 27, 1936, was such as to inspire one speaker to congratulate the Bill's chief pilot on 'such a good house on this grand national occasion.' Mr. A. Duckworth, who moved the second reading, went to perhaps unnecessary pains to point out that the Bill attempted to do much less than had been recommended by the Select Committee in 1914. Even if passed, 'it would still leave open an enormous field for the swindler and the cheapjack.' Also, it was milder in its provisions than legislation which had been passed in the Dominions. These were not the most cogent arguments in the Bill's favour, and its critics—notably Sir Arnold Wilson—attacked it on the grounds that it did not go far enough. Why did it not also ban the advertising of cures for asthma, rheumatism, the common cold and even baldness? Others thought that the Bill was more likely to safeguard the interests of the doctors than of the public. There had been a great deal of lobbying by those whose activities stood to be curtailed; one Member had received 1,350 letters on behalf of a single advertiser. Much eloquence was expended for and against the Bill, but at sixteen minutes after one o'clock it was found that there were not forty members present. The House was counted out.

That year £2,500,000 was spent on Press advertising of proprietary medicines.

Next year the Government was inspired to run its own slogan 'Use Your Health Services,' but the amount spent on this campaign was only what a private manufacturer would have spent on a single laxative. In its *Report on the British Health Service*, published in 1937, P.E.P. (Political and Economic Planning) said:

It is particularly disturbing to observe how official and scientific pronouncements and advice on health matters are promptly seized by the commercial interests to make capital for products the consumption of which is often irrelevant to, and may even be directly opposed to, the straightforward following of the advice quoted.

P.E.P. also deplored that the spreading of distorted notions by the makers of proprietary medicines had made it necessary to mount costly campaigns on behalf of elementary products such as milk and basic services which ought to be widely known. Besides the 'Drink More Milk' campaign of the Milk Marketing Board, there was an eat-more-bread campaign by the Millers Mutual Association, a herring-for-health campaign by the Herring Industry Board and an eat-more-bananas campaign by the firm of Fyffe. Simple foods for disordered times. . . . It was indeed a humiliation that such campaigns should be necessary.

That 'Drink More Milk' campaign led to a keen controversy in January 1938, when the British Medical Association asked newspapers to insert an advertisement headed: 'Is ALL MILK Safe to Drink?' (the contention being that milk ought to be tested for tuberculosis). Leading newspapers turned down this advertisement on the grounds that it 'knocked' the 'Drink More Milk' campaign and, furthermore, was a 'scare' advertisement. As the newspapers were already full of scare advertisements this sudden solicitude puzzled many. However, the British Medical Association modified its copy to read 'Drink Safe Milk' and most of the newspapers published it. The *Daily Express* still declined, arguing that the effect of the advertisement was still to persuade the public that only pasteurized milk was safe.

Lord Horder was the next to enter the lists against the medicine firms. Vexed that these interests had been excluded from the provisions of the Food and Drugs Act, he rose in the Lords on July 26, 1938, to call for a curtailment of their operations. Each year, he said, they bled the country of between £25,000,000 and £30,000,000 which was nearly equal to the total budget of the hospitals. In the long run, doctors had more patients, not fewer, through the activities of the proprietary medicine trade; 'ultimately the undertaker benefits sooner and oftener than he might.'

On the one hand the Government had launched a campaign to improve the national physique; on the other was the campaign by the makers of medicines and foods, a campaign 'led by very subtle and skilled generals bent on maintaining national ill-health, moral and physical, in order to have a ready market for their goods. For every £100 that the Government spends on making people health-conscious, quack medicine mongers spent £1,000 in making them disease-conscious.'[1] The Government derived £1,000,000 out of the sorry business, which was less than it could have derived if it had enforced the law strictly. As it was, cough mixtures and pills for backache were taxed, but chest mixtures and kidney pills were not.

Lord Horder mentioned that a famous group of patent medicine vendors (whose speciality was nervous and digestive troubles) had budgeted to spend £1,000,000 on Press advertising that year. The group controlled sixteen preparations, 'excluding shampoos and dog and cat medicines,' and the profits on its deferred shares had risen from £40,000 to £280,000 in the past six years. In 1931 its five shilling shares had stood at 5s. 7d.; now they had risen to more than £3.

He criticized various types of advertising, in all of which there was the appeal to fear. 'Much of this trade is in fact a huge form of blackmail. . . . The wretched man who does not take a laxative begins to wonder if he can possibly be well without it.' It was an eloquent indictment, but no Parliamentary action resulted. As will be seen, the country had to wait until it was neck-high in another World War before the appropriate Act reached the Statute Book.

The 'debunking' of advertising which was so popular in America in the early 'thirties (see next chapter) had its echoes in Britain. In 1933 Miss Dorothy L. Sayers, who had herself worked in an advertising agency, let out some of the secrets in her detective story *Murder Must Advertise*. The novice in this story had to learn 'that the word "pure" was dangerous, because, if lightly used, it laid the client open to prosecution by Government inspectors, whereas the words "highest quality," "finest ingredients," "packed under the best conditions" had no legal meaning and were therefore safe . . . that the *Morning Star* would

---

[1] In 1937 the heaviest expenditure on advertising was by manufacturers of proprietary medicines; then followed toilet goods, cigarettes, drink, soap.

not accept any advertisements containing the word "cure" though there was no objection to such expressions as "relieve" or "ameliorate" . . . that if, by the most far-fetched stretch of ingenuity, an indecent meaning could be read into a headline, that was the meaning that the great British Public would infallibly read into it. . . .'[1]

Lord Peter Wimsey's dictum on 'Truth in Advertising' was that 'It is like leaven . . . it provides a suitable quantity of yeast with which to blow out a mass of crude misrepresentation into a form that the public can swallow.'

Miss Sayers discoursed further on the subject of advertisers' double-talk in an article in the *Spectator* of November 19, 1937. 'Plain lies are dangerous,' she said. 'The only weapons left [to the copywriter] are the *suggestio falsi* and the *suppressio veri*, and his use even of these would be very much more circumscribed if one person in ten had ever been taught how to read.' Her conclusion was that 'we have the kind of advertising we deserve,' and that 'those who prefer their English sloppy have only themselves to thank if the advertising writer uses his mastery of vocabulary and syntax to mislead their minds.' This pleased neither advertisers nor their critics. Surely, it was argued, the ill-educated were entitled to some protection? Surely the reading of an advertisement need not be a battle of wits?

There were some who argued that the swollen newspapers of the 'thirties, which had to be sustained by such dubious means, were in any case an uneconomic proposition. To this advertisers said, 'What about the American newspapers, three and four times the size?' The reply was, 'Yes, but the public would not stand for a newspaper of which three-quarters was advertisements.' And the advertisers' retort was: 'Which is the better bargain: the *Chicago Daily News*, with 216 columns of advertising and 168 columns of text for three-halfpence or the London *Evening Standard* with 35 columns of advertisements and 61 columns of text for one penny?'

It was noticeable that the most impudent advertisements of the 'thirties were often badly laid out, badly illustrated and badly written. It was a fair deduction that they were not prepared by reputable agents. However, they were lucrative enough, and in

[1] Both the British and American publics are also adept at detecting the omission of wedding rings in pictures of mothers holding children.

the stress of competition they were accepted by advertising managers against their better judgment.

Strong though newspaper competition was, there is little real evidence that advertisers took advantage of their position to try to influence editorial policy. Many allegations have been thrown about, few have been proved. One or two glaring attempts recoiled on those who made them. In 1933 Sir Edgar Sanders, of the Brewers Society, launching a £130,000 publicity drive, said:

If we begin advertising in the Press we shall see that the continuation of our advertising is contingent upon the fact that we get editorial support as well in the same newspapers. In that way it is wonderful how you can educate public opinion, and generally without making it too obvious that there is a publicity campaign behind it.

These rash words brought a smart rebuff from the newspaper proprietors, and also from the Archbishop of Canterbury.

The PEP Report on the Press, published in 1938, said:

There is undoubtedly a tendency to tone down or suppress minor items of news or features if they seem likely to annoy advertisers or potential advertisers, and an even more serious tendency to prevent problems, emphasis on which would be inconvenient to advertisers, from securing widespread discussion if possible. Nevertheless if a big issue burst into prominence no newspaper would dare to jeopardise its circulation by suppressing it or even making too little of it to please its advertisers.

The Report considered that 'if the advertising manager (of a newspaper) wants a policy toned down in case advertisers should be offended it is more likely to be done than if the advertisers themselves actively complained.' Many cuts were made voluntarily by sub-editors, in order not to offend advertisers.

A famous editor went so far as to tell the Empire Press Union, on one occasion, that newspapers ought to avoid the 'needless folly' of placing reports of traffic accidents next to motor-car advertisements. He might have added, 'or of putting paragraphs about drunken drivers next to advertisements of beers which claimed to "stimulate the faculties." '

1914–1939

AMERICA: GIVING 'GINKS' A GOAL

IN 1916, before America entered the First World War, the publisher of the *New York Times*, Adolph S. Ochs, addressed the Associated Advertising Clubs of the World, who five years earlier had pledged themselves to a policy of 'Truth in Advertising.' He said:

> It may startle you if I say that I doubt if there is any business in the world in which there is so much waste of time, money and energy as in advertising and its correlative instrumentalities. It may be rank heresy for me to say this, yet I affirm that more than fifty per cent of money spent on advertising is squandered and is a sheer waste of printer's ink, because little thought and less intelligence are applied, and ordinary common-sense is entirely lacking; too frequently the dishonesty stamped on its face is about all the intelligent reader discerns.

These were harsh words, but the advertising men bore them bravely. Ochs had always been quick to find fault with the advertising offered him, and he had rejected millions of dollars worth—a policy which had paid handsomely. Now his paper was offering 100 dollars for information leading to the conviction of anyone inserting a false or misleading advertisement in the newspaper. A few other papers were cleaning up their advertising columns too, and claiming great virtue thereby, even boasting how much their honesty was costing them.

All too soon the American advertising men were to have an opportunity (like their opposite numbers in England) of proving their skill, high-mindedness and patriotism by promoting fervent campaigns on behalf of the Red Cross and Liberty Bonds. Against all their professional instincts they appealed to the public *not* to spend money. One Boston paper, presumably under pressure of the big stores, declined to print an advertisement urging the public to buy only necessities, and had to pay 500 dollars for breach of contract. Notwithstanding such backslidings, the Liberty Bonds campaign was triumphantly successful. For every dollar spent on advertising, some 1,500 dollars were coaxed into savings. Surely not even Adolph S. Ochs could argue that 50 per cent of *that* appropriation had been wasted?

With the end of the war all shackles on output were snapped. Now came the rush to capture the new fields of commerce. War profits which the tax collector might otherwise have garnered were thrown into vast advertising campaigns. Among those climbing over each other on the hill of riches, few listened to the Government recruiting advertisements of 1919, offering 'the chance of a lifetime to see the battlefields of France and the Rhine . . . you go to shows, dances, movies, you meet agreeable people in the hostess houses, you get acquainted with nice girls, in fact you have a better time than most civilians.'

Soon the factories were pouring out a stream of highly covetable but expensive commodities which somehow had to be absorbed into the American way of life—cars by the hundred thousand, vastly more reliable, and cheaper; new-fangled radio sets (the great boom began in 1922); ice-boxes and refrigerators, automatic furnaces, washing machines, more glittering water-closets, plushier coffins. On his bathroom alone a man was expected to spend six months' salary, in order to bring it up to Hollywood standards. 'From a mere utility the modern bathroom has developed into a spacious shrine of cleanliness and health,' said an advertisement of the house of Crane in 1925, and the shrine in the picture was of an arrogant magnificence. It contained, among other things, a 'dental lavatory of vitreous china, twice fired.'

People had to be taught to want these things, to feel ashamed of not having them. The volume of production grew terrifyingly. Soon it was not enough for a man merely to buy a new car, a new radio, a new washing machine. He must buy the latest model every year, and discard the old one, whether it functioned efficiently or not. Otherwise factories would close from the Atlantic to the Pacific and the golden century would come down in ruins. It was an American's patriotic duty to 'buy till it hurts,' in peace no less than in war. To plead lack of money was no excuse, when he could gain almost anything he wanted by making

o

a down payment. The man who was contented with his lot was a traitor to the community, un-American.

The twin pillars of this civilization were the copy writer and the salesman (though there were some who called them caterpillars). In *Only Yesterday*, Frederick Lewis Allen wrote:

> The public generally speaking could be relied upon to regard with complacence the most flagrant assaults upon its credulity by the advertiser and the most outrageous invasions of its privacy by the salesman; for the public was in a mood to forgive every sin committed in the holy name of business.

The torch-bearers, the trail-blazers of advertising gathered at Atlantic City[1] in 1923, and delivered themselves of such aphorisms as 'Appeal to reason in your advertising, and you appeal to about 4 per cent of the human race.' They noted with pleasure that 'thanks to modern education, teaching today includes matters of practical use and swings the gateway to the child mind wide open for the entrance of the advertising message' (nevertheless they discussed how best to break down the sales resistance of Boy Scouts). One speaker who was applauded as much for his enterprise as his sense of humour was J. H. Mowbray, vice-president of a Pennsylvania firm. He opened his speech as follows:

> Our ultimate consumer never re-orders, yet we manufacture 500 articles, and are in first place by so wide a margin that we have no near competitors. We never get a second shot at our man. This may seem strange but there are a million and a third deaths in the United States each year, and our principal product is embalming fluid.

Some of the methods by which the American nation was cozened and coerced into embalming its dead will be familiar to those who have read Cedric Belfrage's scarifying *Abide With Me*. To the average person in Britain, content that his body should rot 'to flowers and fruit with Adam and all mankind,' the advertisements of the American casket and vault manufacturers, with their promises of bodily immortality, were oddly shocking. Here are excerpts from an announcement which appeared in a family magazine, the *Saturday Evening Post*, on February 12, 1927:

> How often we find cause only for regret in our memories of the manner in which we disposed of the remains of our loved ones!

[1] Their deliberations are recorded in *Advertising and Selling*, edited by Noble T. Praigg.

We were thoughtless, perhaps. It might have been that at the time we didn't know. It would have been so easy to provide adequate protection against the elements.

However, it is idle to dwell on things past. Let us look into the future calmly and follow the example of thousands of families who rely upon the Clark Grave Vault to defeat Nature's destructive forces.

For never yet has this vault failed to protect its precious contents from the hurtful elements of the earth. . . .

On a cruder level, as Belfrage describes, the manufacturers of preposterous caskets instructed funeral directors how to bully the bereaved—'This is the last tribute you will ever be able to pay to your dear mother (father, wife, sister, husband, etc.). *How can anything be too good?*' So the worst racket of all was built up: the embalming, or 'preparing,' of the 'loved one,' the painting with cosmetics, the replacing of damaged ears and noses by 'new,' the dressing up in expensive new clothes; the lying in state in dim, tapestried pavilions, traversed by theatrical shafts of light; the perpetual organ music, the paintings, the statues; the final reluctant interment in Gardens of Rest, Vales of Sleep. Death was a cunning and greedy advertiser. He even demanded silver- and gold-plated coffins for his elect. And on their last resting-places he stipulated a Greek-pillared mausoleum of immemorial granite, or at the least a perdurable headstone styled by the Rock of Ages Corporation (*see* almost any issue of the *National Geographic Magazine* in the middle-'twenties). Who, with the power to invest in such funerary splendours, would lend an ear to the cry of the low-price mortician, with his 'Repose-Room Free, and Use of Twenty Palms'?

The delegates to that convention of 1923 talked at some length about church advertising. Joseph A. Richards, president of a New York advertising agency, said that if he were consulted in his professional capacity by a group of churchmen, he would first ensure that their church was a worthwhile, going concern. He would say to them:

It may be that you have the reputation of having stale goods; maybe you are foolishly stressing the side lines. It may be the first assistant sales manager, the pastor, is out of harmony with the Sales Manager, the Holy Spirit, and therefore all the salesmen, the members, are demoralised and don't know what they are selling; or have quit their job, and are just hanging around, blaming the preacher and their fellow members for the fact that the church does not 'go.'

Once assured that the church had 'something to sell worth having,' however, the agency would throw all its efforts into the campaign. 'I would make my church advertising prayed-over advertising,' the speaker promised. 'I would no more expect to put out an announcement of any kind which had not been individually submitted to the Sales Manager in prayer than I would expect to preach a sermon or lead a prayer meeting without so doing.'

The integration of the Holy Trinity with the advertising business was carried a stage further by Bruce Barton, author of the best-seller *The Man Nobody Knows* (1925). From this it appeared that Jesus 'would be a national advertiser today . . . as he was the great advertiser of his own day.' He had always been 'the most popular dinner guest in Jerusalem.' Of his enterprise, sufficient to say that 'he picked up twelve men from the bottom ranks of business and forged them into an organization that conquered the world.' Jesus, according to Barton, 'recognized the basic principle that all good advertising is news.' And, as a copywriter, he was without equal. 'Take any one of the parables, no matter which—you will find that it exemplifies all the principles on which advertising text books are written. Always a picture in the first sentence; crisp, graphic language and a message so clear that even the dullest cannot escape it.'

It was inspirational stuff this, for the copywriter who had begun to doubt the dignity of his calling, who had been sulking because Thorstein Veblen had described his job as the administering of 'shock effects, tropismatic reactions, animal orientations, forced movements, fixation of ideas, verbal intoxication . . . a trading on the range of human infirmities which blossom in devout observances and bear fruit in the psychopathic wards.'[1]

Half-way through the 'twenties 'consumer resistance' must have been stiffening, for there was a campaign to advertise advertising. Examples are to be found in the pages of *Life* in 1925. One full-page announcement shows a meek, hard-driven husband wincing as his wife looks up from a magazine to say, 'Andy, I want one of these electric washing machines.' Andy begins to blow off steam; he is even allowed to say, 'Sometimes I get mighty mad at advertising.' But everybody knows, including Andy, that this is a foolish attitude. When Andy cools off a little

[1] *Absentee Ownership.*

he admits that though it was quite a strain working to pay off that furnace, the results are wonderfully worth while. And Andy goes on:

I begin to see that it's advertising that makes America hum. It gives ginks like me a goal. Makes us want something. And the world is so much the better for our heaving a little harder.

Looking at the Advertisements makes me think I've GOT to succeed. Every advertisement is an advertisement for success.

I guess one reason there is so much success in America is because there is so much advertising—of things to want—things to work for.

Another time the little man, whose full nume is Andy Consumer, is emboldened to expound the advertiser's favourite theory of economics:

If you are a manufacturer, don't come round to me with a tape measure and say that you would like to measure me for soup or soap. First go get one million other guys like me and then I'll listen.

My reason for being so inexclusive is this. I figure that if you get one million other customers your soup or soap is bound to be good. You can afford to take pains with it. You can hire a lot of experts to experiment their heads off. You can put in the best soup or soap machinery in the world. Your soup will be SOME soup. Your soap will WASH DIRT.

If I placed my order with you PERSONALLY for one can of soup or cake of soap you might fuss round with it, and it might be good or it might NOT. And if I didn't like it and kicked, you should worry!

But with one million other birds to please you will please or perish. I should worry!

The only way I know for you to get one million other buyers is for you to advertise. I should worry!

Jollied along by Andy Consumer, dazzled by the flow of glittering goods, the American male began to mortgage his future. At the height of the Coolidge prosperity era it was no longer enough for a man to buy a new car every year; he must be taught to buy two cars. He owed it not only to himself and to his family, but to the nation. He must instal, not one bathroom, but two. He must have a radio, not only in his living-room but in every other room. So it went on. Why should a man be allowed to spend the whole day wearing the same pair of spectacles? As early as 1921 the American Association of Wholesale Opticians had begun a campaign to urge people to wear one kind of spectacles for work, another for leisure and another for outdoors. There were limitations to this idea of doubling everything, of course. A woman could hardly be expected to wear two wedding rings; but a singularly successful campaign was run to belittle in woman's eyes a plain gold ring and make her demand a platinum one, preferably encrusted with diamonds. Think how many more craftsmen (sound American craftsmen) she was providing with employment!

Many and importunate were the efforts to widen seasonal trade. The Greeting Card Association of America showed much ingenuity in devising cards for other occasions than Christmas and birthdays—get-well cards, sorry-I-forgot-your-anniversary cards and so on. The country had to be made more and more anniversary conscious, if necessary by creating and fostering new anniversaries. There had to be new pretexts for gallantries. For a long time the florists had been pointing the path—those same florists who at one time had persuaded certain newspapers to ban the regrettable phrase 'No flowers, by request' in death notices. They had now hit on the highly successful slogan 'Say It With Flowers'—a slogan capable of almost infinite elaboration, humorous or sentimental. Between them, the florists, the greeting-card makers, the candy manufacturers and the cable companies fostered one of the most successful sales stimulants in Mother's Day, which was worked up from a sentimental idea to a national racket (Father's Day has never enjoyed the same reverence). In a 'Mom'-dominated land, no son dared *not* to send flowers on Mother's Day, and the florists raised the price of flowers steeply when the Day came. It was almost impossible (in the writer's own experience) to buy a box of chocolates which was not inscribed with a tribute like 'For you, Mother o' Mine.' And the cables were choked with messages (many of them suggested by the companies themselves) like: 'I send a blessing for every thread of silver on my mother's head.' Much of this was achieved by moral pressure on the lines of 'Nothing is too good for your loved ones'—the same tactics which had quadrupled the price of a funeral.

There were other pools into which the American advertiser boldly plunged while Britain—for reasons of nervousness, inhibition or even good taste—teetered on the brink. One of them was the pool of Culture. Sinclair Lewis's *Babbitt* had assured an audience of realtors that culture—in reasonable doses—was manly and American, even though in other countries art and literature were left to 'a lot of shabby bums living in attics and feeding on booze and spaghetti.' Knowledge, Vocabulary, Conversation, Languages, Etiquette, Poise—these were not only worth acquiring, but *must* be acquired. Of particular interest were the reasons now offered why people should learn French. Nearly a hundred years earlier an English publisher had commended his teach-yourself-French book by saying that it enabled a man to learn the language without exposing himself to the corrupting influence of Paris. Now Americans were urged to make themselves worthy of Paris. The risks of social discomfiture were stressed. One advertisement showed a man being mocked by his friends because the waiter had spoken to him in French. Another depicted a dinner-jacketed young man humiliated by his inability to explain the menu to his girl. 'A French phrase deftly turned is a devastating weapon,' cried another advertisement. 'You can gain a quick mastery of smart French repartee.' An accompanying picture showed one female sophisticate being catty to another; the victim vowed, 'Next time I'll get even with that Mrs. B.!'

Other advertisers, instead of needling the reader for being unable to speak French, sought to throw him off his stroke by suggesting that he did not know how to speak English. The boss at his big shiny desk was seen turning down a man for promotion, not because his heels were worn but because he was guilty of saying 'can't hardly.' Whispering women told each other how sorry they were for Mary, married to a man who said 'you was.' How foolish, when nine-tenths of everyday mistakes consisted of a mere twenty-five simple-to-correct errors! Another advertiser said: 'You may be using the right words, but are you sure you are *pronouncing* them properly?' And so it went on. Most to be pitied was the man who had no words at all. His fur-laden wife would nag him on the way home from an evening out, and he would accept it abjectly.

'I was never so embarrassed! Just when I wanted to be proud of you, you sat there all evening without saying a single word!'
'Aren't you a bit harsh?'
'Not in the least. Couldn't you think of *anything* to say?'
'No, I couldn't. How was I to get in on that kind of conversation?

'What did you expect them to talk about—your business?'

'Really Ja——'

'Oh, I'm so ashamed! I wanted to be proud of you, Ted. You are cleverer and more successful than any man at that dinner tonight—but you acted as though you were afraid to open your mouth.'

'I was, dear. What do I know about that philosopher they were talking about—what was his name? Nietzsche. I couldn't even follow their conversation half the time.'

'You should read more. It's pitiful! Why, you didn't even contribute one idea or opinion all evening!'

'I'd like to read more, but you know how much time I have! . . . You made up for both of us, Jane! You were wonderful! How did you ever find out so many things to talk about?'

'I found all that information in Elbert Hubbard's Scrap Book. Now don't tell me you don't know who Elbert Hubbard was! One of America's most versatile men—a writer, craftsman, orator, business man—a many-sided genius. Well, when he was quite young he started reading the greatest thoughts of all the greatest men of all ages. He marked the passages which inspired him most—the *highlights* of literature, the greatest thoughts of the last 2,500 years. He did all your reading for you. . . . It will make you so well-informed—you'll never need to feel embarrassed or uncomfortable in company again.'

Another advertisement showed a man who had swallowed somebody's pocket university holding an audience spellbound with tales of Cleopatra and Diogenes. Such a man, it might be thought, was as likely to be nagged on the way home for hogging the conversation as for failing to enter into it.

Still another short-cut to culture was the *Daily Reading Guide*. A picture showed a harassed young man entering an editor's office and saying:

'I can't read worth-while literature! For the past two weeks I've tried daily to read the works of Carlyle, yet I——'

'Stop,' exclaimed the editor. 'Have you ever tried to eat roast beef three times a day seven days a week? That is what is the matter with your reading. You need variety, *daily variety*! Then you will find the reading of immortal literature one of the most engrossing pursuits of your life. Yes, and the most profitable.'

The *Guide* was designed to give twenty minutes' reading a day. 'It is for busy men and women. One year's reading brings you broad culture.'

'He who runs may read' was adopted as a slogan by the

publishers of the *Golden Book*. They claimed, moreover, that their volume was just the thing to counteract the jazz fever of the day.

Cocktails, dance halls, freak dress, petting parties are simply defence reactions to the present age. To offer the young people something just as daring, just as exciting, just as amusing—but something that leaves a finely stimulated memory is the job of the editor of the *Golden Book*.

The editor of this volume was only one of a great band of advertisers with a touching faith in the power of their products to lure the younger generation from dubious ways. In our own time stay-out-late daughters are shown coming home early, and bringing their boy friends with them, because 'Mum' is using the only permissible sandwich spread.

Though there was no lack of publishers to predigest (or even to rewrite) the classics, there were still determined attempts to market the classics 'neat.' Plato's *Dialogues* were represented as being topical, challenging and smart. A copywriter adopted the Hollywood technique in lauding a new edition of the works of Shakespeare—'every word he ever wrote'—and said: 'Be fascinated by sensuous Cleopatra! Shudder at murderous Macbeth! Chuckle with Falstaff! Thrill with lovesick Romeo!'

Yet there were other things besides culture that the well-rounded citizen must absorb, and the advertiser had them all ready. Babbitt's son had been attracted by the type of advertisement which read.

CAN YOU PLAY A MAN'S PART?
If you are walking with your mother, sister or best girl, and someone passes a slighting remark or uses improper language, won't you be ashamed if you can't take her part? Well, can you?
We teach boxing and self-defence by mail. . . .

Varied and often improbable were the arts and skills which were taught by mail. 'Big profits in Taxidermy,' ran one lure. 'Learn at home *By Mail* to mount Birds and Animals in spare time. Mount trophies for sportsmen. Mount wild game, also common animals, rabbits, frogs, pigeons. Fine side line—quickly learned.' But why stuff rabbits when there was more money to be made out of breeding them? Make $10,000 a year raising Rex rabbits for us. We pay up to $12 each for all you raise. . . .' Another invitation read 'Be a Detective. Make Secret Investigations. Earn big money. Work home or travel. Fascinating work. Experience unnecessary.' For the less adventurous there was another opening. 'Be a Dentician. Learn at home to make plates, bridge work for dentists.' If none of these attracted, there was always the example of the reader who boasted, 'I made $146 my first week with the Red Lion Electric Pants Presser.' (By contrast English newspapers and magazines offered a much less exciting range of home activities, the usual standby being the addressing of envelopes, often at a starvation wage.)

In a more sober field—and it is important to remember that there *was* a sober field—America's leading insurance company was pioneering a form of advertising for which there could be little but praise. Its purpose was to improve the nation's health, confounding those who obstinately believed that insurance companies were interested only in encouraging sudden death. As well as preaching health in the Press, the Metropolitan Life Insurance Company conducted clean-up campaigns in many big cities, organized health exhibitions, distributed millions of pieces of literature. It tried to persuade parents to take their children to the doctor when they were fit and well. This was a revolutionary policy, at a time when many a British insurance firm's notion of advertising was to print the names of the directors and a balance sheet underneath. The Metropolitan claimed that its strategy was richly successful. 'Measured in dollars and cents it meant the payment in 1922 of $11,828,000 less in death claims than would have been paid if the death rate of 1911 had prevailed in 1922.'

At one stage, the Metropolitan, divining that America's besetting ailment was constipation, but deploring the way in which the public was being urged to take daily laxatives, decided to take dignified action. 'One in three suffers from Dyskinesia,' it said, a phrase which no doubt halted readers in their tracks. By the time they found that it meant constipation they were perhaps ready to send for a free booklet explaining how diet and exercise could remove the complaint.

The Metropolitan's concern to save America from its follies went far beyond illness and constipation. Under a bold heading 'The Toll of Water' in the *National Geographic Magazine* of July 1925 the company told how six thousand persons a year were drowned in America, and urged bathers against showing off and taking risks which jeopardized others. Also it urged the public at large to learn the rules of artificial respiration. 'In July 1924,' said the advertisement, 'the number of deaths from drowning among Metropolitan policy-holders was about twice as many as from typhoid fever and diphtheria together.' Three years later the Metropolitan was urging every American to take a sun-bath daily.

Not all insurance companies were concerned with fostering health. It was a tempting field for scare methods like 'What will *they* do if you are knocked down?' or 'Would you want *your* wife to go out and work?' Once again it was implied that no sacrifice was too great for the 'loved ones.' Fire insurance firms sought to shake a man's nerve by showing his house roaring up in flames. Under the heading 'Stick 'Em Up, Santa Claus!' appeared the warning: 'It will be a good plan to apply for insurance . . . the very day you receive your Christmas jewels.' And the Prudential sounded a new alarm, pointing out that the chances of the Stork bringing twins were 'greater than you may think. One in eighty-nine, in fact.'

American bankers also began to burst the fetters of conservatism in which they had been self-confined. They adopted the man-to-man approach. A bank manager was painted as a likeable fellow only too anxious to help a client out. Public utilities, notably telephone companies, began to advertise their services, and better still, to teach politeness on the telephone. The standard of much of this advertising, technically, was very high. Big business tried to appear human, friendly, tolerant, sympathetic. When strikes broke out, a corporation sometimes took advertising space to put its own case; so also, if it could raise the funds, did the opposition. Startling to the English eye was another type of advertisement which sometimes appeared at times of industrial unrest: 'We Break Strikes.' The part played by strong-arm gangs, with their tear gas and vomit gas, in breaking, and for that matter in fomenting, strikes was to cause wide scandal.

The rawest advertising of the 'twenties—the advertising which inspired organized protest—was that of the film companies. It was the time when screen actresses were being built up into *femmes fatales*, whose passion destroyed, whose love was death. Here is the kind of bait which outraged the churches, the women's clubs, the leagues of decency:

HER HUSBAND DREW THE GIRL TO HIM AND —— A long, long kiss, a kiss of love and youth and beauty, all concentrating like rays into one focus, kindled from above; such kisses as belong to early days. Where heart, soul and sense in concert move, and the blood is lava, and the pulse is ablaze.

Hollywood undertook from time to time to restrain its advertising exuberances, but the improvement was not always easy to discern. Even today half-naked lovers are portrayed with lines like 'Emotion swept them like a tidal wave,' and the words 'Shame!' 'Lust!' 'Violence!' 'Vengeance!' stab out as freely as they did in the dawn of moving pictures.

No industry did more to destroy the meaning of words. The follies are too familiar to need labouring here—how the story of a couple of cowboys quarrelling over a girl became an epic, the tale of a small-time 'hoofer' a deathless saga. Colossal, terrific, titanic, stupendous—these words became the small change of film advertising. A reservation was put on a whole series of other adjectives, like throbbing, rending, tingling, pulsating, pounding, sizzling, scorching and searing. When a better-than-ordinary film came along there were no words left to describe it. 'The greatest love story since the world began' meant, in fact, 'the greatest love story since last week.' No film maker dared return to a use of modest words for fear the public should suspect him of lack of confidence in his production. A *Punch* cartoon summed the whole thing up: outside a cinema blazoned with superlatives one citizen was saying to another, 'I wonder if it's worth seeing?'

Cinema managers, on both sides of the Atlantic, were deluged with 'campaign sheets' full of brash and tasteless ideas for engineering local publicity and 'tie-ups.' Any manager who carried out one-tenth of these suggestions was well on the way to becoming the most unpopular man in his community. He was urged to suborn local clergymen, Army commanders and heads of stores to help publicize his attractions; he was told to invite senior pupils from schools to see films about adultery; he was prodded to promote kissing contests and leg competitions, to hire hunchbacks. In a bad week his instructions might begin, 'Get hold of a couple of camels. . . .' If a safety-first drive was in progress he would be expected to put out posters saying 'DRIVE SLOWLY to see "——" '; if a salvage campaign, to say 'DON'T

WASTE a moment: see "———".' He was told in starkest terms how to make the most capital out of an 'Adults Only' film.

In December 1927 came an advertising campaign which roused America to near-hysteria: the proclamation and unveiling of the Model 'A' Ford. For eighteen years the famous Model 'T'—the car which was incapable of improvement—had clattered its way round the world. With deep reluctance, and at fabulous risk, Henry Ford had decided to re-tool his factories in order to produce a new model, which could hold its own with the flashy, multi-coloured Chevrolets and Chryslers which were making the Model 'T' look like a survival from Covered Wagon days. A wildly successful policy of secrecy made the new Ford the nation's main talking-point. Newspaper photographers haunted the roads near Detroit in the hope of catching the new model out on test; they photographed many cars, but not the right one. On December 2, the day of the unveiling, a million people in New York tried to view the Model 'A,' which, by late afternoon, had to be removed from its showroom and installed in Madison Square Garden. In two thousand newspapers, at a cost of $1,300,000, Ford ran a five-day series of full-page advertisements, revealing all that had hitherto been a matter for speculation. The manufacturer who had sneered at fancy colours and styling now admitted that his new model had 'a bit of the European touch in its coachwork.' Henceforth a customer could buy a Ford in any colour so long as it was Arabian Sand, Niagara Blue, Dawn Grey or Gun-Metal Blue.

Ford had triumphed again. And he was active now in another dimension. The copy for his aircraft advertisements of 1928 was rich and visionary:

When forest fires or tornadoes strew the paths of civilisation with wreckage and suffering . . . when levees melt away before uncontrollable floods, and entire countrysides are inundated . . . when blizzards smother city and country under paralysing burdens of snow and sleet, *where does man look first for help from his fellow men*?

Upward! For across the fenceless sky first aid will come!

It was the Ford policy, the announcement said, to plan in advance for great expansion. Already Ford all-metal aircraft had flown over a million miles.

Who has not thrilled with thoughts of the golden pathways that lead across the fenceless sky?

It was a daunting thought that the air might soon be swarming with Model 'T's.'

The depression which began in 1929 gave a swift quietus to hundreds of advertising campaigns. In vain advertising agents quoted precedents to show that a depression was just the time to advertise, and that, in the past, those who had greatly dared had won. Most manufacturers were content to draw in their horns. The Gadarene race was over. Others decided that desperate measures alone could shift the contents of their gorged warehouses; and there were agents ready enough to undertake desperate campaigns, rather than go under.

So, with the depression, began a period of vulgarity in advertising. Most of the offenders were those concerned with products for personal hygiene, a field which left plentiful scope for crudities. 'The comic strip technique was adopted with a vengeance,' writes R. M. Hower, historian of the Ayer Agency. 'The use of testimonials of all kinds increased while premiums were recklessly offered and prize contests swept the country as swiftly as the craze for jigsaw puzzles. The shrieking headlines, gross exaggeration, and even downright deceit which appeared had no parallel except the patent medicine advertising of the nineteenth century, while the use of pseudo-scientific arguments and appeals to emotion and appetite surpassed all previous efforts and violated the previously accepted standards of decency.'

Preoccupation with bodily hygiene and functions had grown steadily during the post-war years. From itching scalp to fungus-ridden toes, no part of the body escaped the accusing arrows and revealing lenses of the advertiser. 'His heart quickened at the soft fragrance of her cheeks, BUT HER SHOES HID A SORRY CASE OF ATHLETE'S FOOT.' A wife obviously near breaking-point appealed to her husband 'Please do something about this!' 'This' was 'white coat collar.' 'Four out of five are pyorrhea's victims,' cried a tooth-paste firm. There were pictures of men purporting to be steel tycoons and movie producers who yet knew so little of the facts of life that they accepted 'pink toothbrush' as inevitable. Every other page would have a close-up of a woman's arm-pit, miraculously cleared of unsightly hair. Here and there was a picture of a man 'burping' in the reader's face (fullness after meals). Intimate details of female hygiene, previously obtainable only by sending to Nurse So-and-So for a discreet booklet, now found their way into bold print. 'Protection' and 'confidence' joined the long list of words debased by the advertiser.

But the greatest obsession of the advertiser was with the human breath. Halitosis (a word unrecognized by the dictionaries of the day) was the spectre which Listerine conjured up, gigantic and menacing, until it shadowed the continent. The slogan 'Even your best friends won't tell you' was sometimes mocked, but it was mocked nervously. Old-time medicine men had been content to call halitosis bad breath, without dilating on its social handicaps; though usually they were too busy 'curing' cancer and tuber-culosis even to mention it. Until halitosis was discovered, an antiseptic had been something for rubbing on a schoolboy's knee.

For sheer fertility in creating situations in which halitosis could spell business ruin and the wreck of romance, Listerine must not be grudged a grain of admiration. There was the straight senti-mental approach, with a colour picture of a lovely woman in distress, exclaiming: 'HER Honeymoon—and It Should Have Been MINE!' More brutal was the picture strip which showed stages in the rise to success of a young fashion artist. His works were approved by the firm's chief client, a fastidious fashion editress. All seemed rosy for the young artist. Then one day the editress rounded on him suddenly and snarled, 'You are a very ill-mannered young man. The sooner you leave the better.' Mystified, he returned to his office, to find that the boss had already received a telephone call demanding that he be discharged.

'I don't entirely blame her,' said the boss. 'Halitosis has no place in business, so take that hint. Use a little Listerine once in a while and come back in two weeks and I will hire you over again.'

This advertisement at least ended on a note of hope. Less cheerful was one which showed a young man eagerly offering his card to a prospective employer. Alas, it contained the words 'formerly with' above the name of his last firm. Any employer seeing those words—'the phrase that wrecks a million men'— could see instantly that here was a fugitive from Listerine on the downward slide.

Another young man whose best friends had failed to tell him was packed off to peddle insurance in the home of a wealthy man who had invited him to a house party. By ill luck the guests were playing 'nose-to-nose, Society's new game,' the rules of which were explained by Jean, the millionaire's pretty daughter. 'You place a piece of tissue paper to your nose and the person next to you must take it from you by breathing through his or her nose. Each one who misses must pay a forfeit. It's barrels of fun and develops your lungs.'

It seemed only fair that the girl who roped in her guests to play this nauseating game should herself be drawn against the young salesman. . . .

Halitosis was such a money-spinner that many other firms, notably makers of dentifrices, 'angled' their copy accordingly. There was another social unpleasantness, hitherto talked about only in the most tactful terms, namely, Body Odour. It was left to Lifebuoy to inflate this rival spectre, which it did with much ingenuity, and with the help of numerous imitators. It has to be admitted that, though these anti-effluvia campaigns were often in dubious taste, the cumulative effect was undoubtedly to make the population look to its pores and its breath, to the benefit of a congested civilization. Because one individual dared not whisper a word to another, it was necessary to shout the word in the ears of millions.

Inevitably, the advertising of perfume also underwent a change. Until the first World War, it was being offered as something which lent the virtuous woman an aura of innocent 'freshness.' In the 'thirties it was beginning to be sold with a wink and a leer; it was now a mantrap, a weapon for stealing the other girl's boy. A shampoo, which had been a means of ridding the scalp of dandruff, was now a weapon by which the typist ensnared her boss. And so it went on. There was hardly a product which could not be sold on raw 'psychological' lines. Razor blades? The Gillette advertising had travelled a long way. 'Keep an eye on your wife!' cried a 1930 advertisement, which contained a picture of a wife looking distrait. The text ran:

Possibly she's not as happy as she seems. Sometimes you may catch her when she's off guard and surprise a little wistful look on her face. Is she worrying about you? After all, most wives are loyal and proud, and rather reluctant to speak up. This may be far from the fact—but there is a chance she's distressed because you aren't as careful about shaving as you were in times past. . . .

For an advertiser to admit that 'this may be far from the fact'

GIVING 'GINKS' A GOAL   225

was unusual. Most copywriters swept the victim swiftly and irresistibly into the snare of their own setting. Their plausible humbugs of doctors in the picture strips diagnosed the complaint before the victim had entered the room. Spectacled and white-overalled, they spouted pseudo-science and bogus statistics, and sent the victim hot-foot round the corner to buy the magic product. Gone were the days when it was necessary to pretend that the secret of an ointment had been whispered to a titled traveller by a dying hermit in a cave at Petra. Now every specific was the result of years of testing in laboratories. Science had found the way 'to destroy millions of germs that swarm into your mouth with every breath and attack teeth and gums.' Science had ascertained that only nine men in a hundred need be bald.

Some time in the 'twenties it was discovered—doubtless in some scientifically conducted poll—that twenty million Americans fell so far short of the ideal of 'gracious living' that they did not buy toilet paper. Here was a challenge to the unfastidious copywriter. How could the shameless twenty million be saved? One advertiser decided to put them all on parade; he set an artist to draw a picture of a shambling, hangdog multitude stretching away into a doomed infinity, each with the mark of infamy on his brow. It was not a very good idea, because to the casual reader there was nothing to distinguish this sorry legion from the twenty (or fifty) million who were needlessly suffering rheumatism through not taking So-and-So's salts.

While the manufacturers strove for the custom of the twenty millions who did not buy toilet paper, they also fought each other vigorously for the custom of the 100,000,000 who did. A full-page advertisement in the *Saturday Evening Post* showed a masked surgeon conducting an unseen, but as the text revealed, an intimate operation. The heading ran: 'And The Trouble Began With Harsh Toilet Tissue.' Another advertiser, taking advantage of the convention that outrageous statements may safely be put into the mouth of a 'cute' child, drew up a full-page advertisement showing a little girl whispering into her mother's ear: 'Mummy, they have a lovely house, *but their bathroom paper hurts!*' Going one better (or worse), Robert Waithman in his *Report on America* tells the story of Joan Foster. In Picture One her job hangs in the balance. She is rebuked (Picture Two) because her department has been slipping lately. She goes to see her

P

doctor (Picture Three) who tells her that harsh toilet paper is making her 'condition' worse. She buys the right kind (Pictures Four and Five). In Joan's next appearance (Picture Six) she is back at her job thinking to herself: 'The work is going smoothly again—thanks to Soft-Weave Waldorf!'

If the inventor of the zip-fastener had guessed how his innocent device was to be exploited in advertisements of men's trousers he might have paused before giving the world the benefit of his genius. One full-page magazine advertisement showed a young man, alert and self-confident, posing in sleekly fitting 'gap-free' trousers, fastened (according to the caption) by a zipper. Beside him, in a negligent attitude, was a young man whose trousers were fastened in the same way that his father's and grandfather's trousers had been fastened. A savage arrow pointed to the offending irregularities, and a black headline cried INEXCUSABLE! Every device was tried to sap the self-confidence of young men walking about in trousers with the old-time closure. They were left to discover for themselves the embarrassment caused by zippers which failed to close.[1]

About this time great emphasis began to be placed on the importance of svelte-fitting undergarments for men, and the reader's eyes were focused increasingly on the male crotch. The men who had conquered the West had done so without the benefit of 'support,' but an effete new generation evidently stood in pathetic need of it. 'Support' had to be achieved without causing the wearer discomfort. Mr. Cecil Beaton is one of many who have come to the conclusion that 'American men must be crotch-bound.'

A few of the more reckless advertisers of the lean years fell foul of the Federal Trade Commission. In January 1930 the *New York Times* was able to report that 'an unnamed cigarette firm' (which most readers could readily identify) had promised to abstain from claiming that 'women retain slender figures' through smoking their cigarettes and to give up using phrases like 'over-weight banished.' The Federal Trade Commission had been invited to take action, not only by envious competitors but by

---

[1] This failing was taken account of in a zipper advertisement published during the Second World War. 'They told me Crown Zippers can't lock open —like this—and I told them about a friend of mine on a recent occasion. Boy, what he would have given for a Crown zipper!'

friends of non-smoking celebrities who were being represented as owing their slender figures to smoking the cigarettes in question. They did so 'for a valuable consideration.' The *New York Times* thought that the Commission's intervention had given national good taste a push forward. Now the cigarette firms would have to fall back upon 'the doubtless, excellent intrinsic merits of the cigarettes as smoking material only.'

The cigarette firms did nothing of the sort. Instead they 'proved' that cigarettes aided digestion, increased alkalinity and saved people from such evidence of jangled nerves as doodling, pencil-chewing and key juggling. 'How are your nerves?' asked one firm, and invited its male readers to try a simple test. This consisted of unbuttoning the waistcoat with one hand, starting at the top, and then rebuttoning it with the same hand, also starting at the top. Bogey for this operation was twelve seconds. If anyone failed it was a sign his nerves were bad and that he needed to start smoking. Or perhaps that his waistcoat buttons were stiff.

A sharp comment on cigarette advertising was expressed in a *New Yorker* cartoon showing a scene in a laboratory. A 'scientist' was saying to his fellow workers: 'It's passed all the tests for coolness, kindness, mildness and freshness. Now if there was only some way we could keep it from tasting lousy!'

The war between the Federal Trade Commission and the American cigarette manufacturers went on year after year and is still in progress. One by one, firms found themselves debarred from saying that their cigarettes contained less nicotine, aided digestion, relieved fatigue, were recommended by nose and throat specialists or were preferred by tobacco experts.

Occasionally, the chewing-gum firms were not far behind the cigarette manufacturers in the fancifulness of their claims. One announcement of this product, headed 'A Tip to Motorists,' said 'Time passes faster—your wits are keener and your nerves are steadier with ——'s help.'

The absurdity and growing effrontery of many advertisements had long been irking an articulate minority, but advertisers were not interested in minorities. An advertising man, H. A. Batten, testified in the *Atlantic Monthly* in July 1932 that 'even a brief excursion through the average newspaper and magazine is, for the advertising man who respects his calling, a disheartening experience.' He noted how some advertisers were reluctantly being forced into sensational advertising because of unscrupulous competition by their rivals, and said, regretfully: 'My own feeling is that there are few of us here on earth with enough moral courage to sacrifice our bread and butter for the sake of an abstract ideal.' The only way to put an end to advertising which was 'a stench in the nostrils of the civilized world' was for individuals to refuse to buy the products thus advertised, and to tell as many as possible why.

There was, perhaps, another way—to deflate advertising by ridicule. In the early 'thirties was published a strangely successful magazine called *Ballyhoo*, which thumbed its nose at the world of publicity. It introduced a character called Elmer Zilch, who propounded such heresies as 'if you can build a lousy mousetrap and spend $10,000,000 advertising it the world will beat a path to your door.' His associate, Harvey K. Poop the Second, was introduced as 'the man who first proved statistically that four out of five have pyorrhea and that nine out of ten believe it.' *Ballyhoo* published a 'Ten Commandments of Advertising,' number three being 'Honour thy Father's Day and thy Mother's Day,' and number ten 'Thou *shalt* covet thy neighbour's car and his radio and his silverware and his refrigerator and everything that is his.' Another time it gave a glossary of advertising terms, which included:

Delicate membrane	any part of the body.
Lubricate the skin texture	put on grease.
Pore-deep cleansing	washing the face.
Harsh irritants	all the ingredients of a competitor's product.
Great scientist	anyone who will sign an endorsement.
Lifetime	until the new model comes out.
Exclusive	expensive.

Readers of *Ballyhoo* were invited to send in samples of folly in advertising and they responded briskly. The magazine carried a small number of genuine advertisements and a large number of bogus ones, also a few indeterminate ones. There was much speculation about a full-page announcement reading:

Be a man and wear a Tarzan chest wig.
Are you bald-chested?

Are you afraid to expose your bare chest? Be a real he-man by wearing a Tarzan chest wig!

Blond chest wig $3.50   Brunette chest wig $3.49.
Tarzan Chest Wig Co.   Chester, Arkansas.

Whether or not there was a chest wig factory at Chester, Arkansas, chest wigs have undoubtedly appeared on the market.

The popularity of *Ballyhoo* inspired many rivals, of varying degrees of wit and irreverence. *Ballyhoo* itself, perhaps under pressure of competition, gradually lapsed from its high purpose and became a journal mainly of leg jokes, interspersed by rather perfunctory tilts at advertising. It was easier perhaps to ring the changes on the oldest joke in the world than on the newest.

The disillusioned view of advertising was intensified by a number of books which 'took the lid off' the business and exposed the chicanery beneath. All this satire and 'muckraking' undoubtedly helped to promote a wariness of outlook in some of the public and eventually to create a climate in which such measures as the Food, Drugs and Cosmetics Act of 1938 could be passed.

To some of the more reputable agents it seemed that the credit of advertising could only be built up again by offering the manufacturer a patently square deal, by confronting him with market research and assuring him that his money would be usefully, intelligently and scientifically spent. As things were, some firms were going back to the oldest methods of advertising. In April 1932 a writer in the *New York Times* noted that since the depression 'barkers' and sandwich-men had come back, many of them in well-cut clothes. 'To be a sandwich-man in these days is to carry the pennon of gentility,' he said.

And while some advertisers were going back to the oldest methods, others were going back to the oldest frauds. The *New York Times* noted how the electric quacks were beginning to make headway again. Not electric belts this time, however:

... they now sell coils of wire which the patient places round his body and plugs into the electric light socket. These objects, which cost perhaps less than ten dollars to produce, are called solenoids and under various fancy names are sold at prices ranging from $40 to $120 each to sick persons who would never think of falling for the old electric belt fraud.

Restoring the credit of advertising was a slow task, but by about 1933 the worst of the depression was over. In that year came the repeal of Prohibition, a godsend to advertising agencies and the Press alike. It was a blow, perhaps, to the soft drink firms, whose advertisements were intoxicating even if their wares were not. A ginger ale company had been running a large advertisement headed:

O MAGIC NIGHTS BENEATH THE MOON
Where Eye Meets Eye Beneath The Southern Cross

There was a great deal more in the same heady strain, revealing finally that the grand catalyst of romance was the 'champagne of ginger ales,' with its 'exhilaration and unusual zest.'

Overnight, drinking of intoxicants ceased to be a hole-in-the-corner hobby, and became a mark of good breeding. In a two-page advertisement addressed 'To The 73 Per Cent Who Said Yes,' in *Life* for January 1934, the Schenley Distillers Corporation touched on a point which must have puzzled many:

After these 14 years of barred distillery doors, of rusting vats and stills, of grapes rotting on neglected vines, and empty warehouses, in which fine old whisky should have been rightly mellowing—after these 14 years of such discouraging inactivity, you must be inclined to wonder how really fine wine and spirits may now be produced or bought. . . .

Some liquor firms, the announcement went on to say, had grown tired of waiting for Repeal and had gone into other business; but 'there were a few who never lost faith in the ultimate decision of America's millions,' firms which went on 'building earnestly, soundly, confidently, through those fourteen years of shadow in preparation for the dawn.'

What all this boiled down to was that Schenleys had spent their time obtaining control of many old-established American liquor firms and more recently had renewed relations with British breweries and French vineyards.

Another firm explained its preparedness by saying that 'even during Prohibition the Company continued to operate under one of the seven medicinal licences granted by the Government.'

Other staples of the advertising pages of the 'thirties were refrigerators, self-changing radiograms, home movies, frosted foods, silk stockings and the new-style brassières ('lift, mould, restrain, hold'). While makers of brushless shaving creams were still crying 'Shaving Brush and Soapy Ear Went Out of Style With Hoops, My Dear' the electric razor came on the market and once more man was nagged to 'revolutionize' his method of shaving. (Astonishingly, after generations of razor advertising, it was discovered in 1950 that only one man in seven in America shaved daily.)

Aircraft lines produced some impressive advertisements, the prize going to the one which advertised *noiseless* typewriters in its flagship. Shipping firms offered more and more sybaritic cruises. One of them ran, year in, year out, a line which seemed to have escaped from a poem: 'Dining-rooms with roll-back domes that open to the sky.'

As the 'thirties progressed, American advertisers tended more and more to write in an invented language of their own. To replace the good English words they had devalued, they devised irritating new ones. The tendency was well summed up in another *New Yorker* cartoon showing a copywriter sitting on the edge of a pool contemplating a swan. He was saying, 'Grace, poise, charm and, ah—floatability.' The motor-car industry, tired of enthusing over windshields on which the rain flowed *upwards*, devised for itself a complete new vocabulary. They offered a levelized ride in a unisteel body, with sound-sorbers, powered by a micropoised engine with an eezedrain sump. There were flashway signals fore 'n aft, the steering was permi-firm or safe-t-flex, and fresh air came in through rear-opening ventipanes, or ventiports.

More excruciating was the line of baby talk developed to accompany the polychromatic pictures showing foods of an unearthly succulence. Breakfast cereals of the 'snap, crackle, pop' variety had long had a nursery nomenclature of their own. Now makers of other foods began to boost their specialities as 'yummy,' 'tangy,' 'zippy,' 'chewy,' 'crispy' (or 'krispy'), 'crunchy' (or 'krunchy'), all just the thing for 'oomph 'n' energy.' The exasperating device 'n' had been popularized, no doubt, by 'Amos 'n' Andy'; it became the scourge of magazine copy. So did the process of hyphening up, as in jiffy-quick, sun-sweet and oven-hot. Stretch became s-t-r-e-t-c-h, cool became c-o-o-l. Coy apostrophes crept in everywhere—'specially for you. Bafflingly, the word 'eating' became an adjective—'a wonderful "eating" cheese'; then followed 'eatingest'—the 'eatingest corn that ever tossed a golden tassel.' This 'word magic' was carried sometimes to distracting lengths. The phrase about 'the eatingest' corn came from a Bird's Eye frosted food advertisement which also contained the phrase 'picked when the tender kernels are welling with milkiness.' Ordinary natural processes were described in the language of the Song of Solomon. Perhaps 'welling with milkiness' is as good a description of this style of copy as any.

'Word magic' was frowned on by the inventor of a much-discussed system for assessing 'readability': Dr. Rudolph Flesch.[1] This pundit out of Austria held that most advertising copy of the late 'thirties was being written to please the seller rather than the buyer; indeed, he might have said that it was being written to impress fellow copywriters. It fell to Dr. Flesch to make the discovery that sentences of up to eight words were very easy to read; up to 11 words, easy; up to 17, standard; up to 23, difficult; up to 29 and over, very difficult. There was a little more to it than that, however. Dr. Flesch counted the number of affixes in any given 100 words; 54 or more put the writing into the 'very difficult' class. Counting affixes, incidentally, was skilled labour, for it was necessary to count the am- in ambiguous, the apo- in apostasy, the dys- in dysentery, the -ade in lemonade. The doctor also took into account the number of personal references per 100 words—words like you, me, I, wife, husband, dame, pal, and so on. Nineteen or more of these put the writing into the very easy class, fewer than two into the very difficult class.

This is a suitable point at which to review some of the other copy-testing devices which were tried out in America in the anxious years after the depression. Names like 'consumer jury' and 'unaided recall' were used to dignify methods which often were on the same level of 'science' as the much-boosted tests of deodorants and depilatories. One method involved submitting differently 'angled' versions of the same advertisement to a large number of women, and inviting them to pick out the presentations most likely, and least likely, to spur them to go out and buy the product. Sometimes the jury agreed that a certain presentation was outstandingly good; at other times they disagreed hopelessly. It was not long before someone hit on the happy idea of submitting to consumer juries advertisements which had already proved their

[1] *The Art of Plain Talk.*

worth (as judged by the number of keyed replies received). The
juries frequently picked out for praise the least effective advertisements. The same test was then applied to highly paid advertising
executives, many of whom also confidently chose the worst-
pulling advertisements. The most that could honestly be said for
the 'consumer jury' system was that it might, in certain circumstances, be better than nothing. It was important, pleaded the
defence, that those questioned should be people with a 'consumer
interest.' That is, it was no use asking non-smokers to criticize
tobacco advertisements, or low-paid workers to consider exhortations to visit Italy. Again, it was essential that a member of the
jury should be intelligent, equable, normal and above any
temptation to flatter the advertiser. Where was this prodigy to
be found?

Another method was for the tester to sit down cosily with an
'average' housewife and go, page by page, through a magazine
which she admitted having read, and noting which advertisements
had impressed her eye and her memory, which ones seemed
credible, and how far she had read them before turning over.
Many readers, it was suspected, read the eye-stopping headlines
and little more. In an attempt to discover how far down certain
advertisements were read, the 'hidden offer' idea was tried out.
In modest type, near the end of the advertisement, a free gift
would be offered; there would be no prominent headline crying
'Sensational Free Offer!' Then the number of applications
received would be carefully analysed. The system known as
'unaided recall' involved asking readers questions like 'Which
razor blade manufacturer urges "Banish five o'clock shadow"?'
Or perhaps the guinea-pig would be asked to lie down on the
equivalent of the psycho-analyst's confessional couch, and would
there be subjected to a list of words like 'toothpaste' and 'beer,'
to which he would respond with those proprietary names which
first sprang to mind.

But more remarkable methods of pre-testing were being
developed. From time to time newspapers had carried intriguing
reports of 'intimate' devices used to measure the emotional effect
of films on susceptible audiences of young men and women.
Variations of this device were used to measure the amount of
interest aroused, if any, by given advertisements on selected
members of the public. Relaxed and incorruptible, the guinea-pig

234 · THE SHOCKING HISTORY OF ADVERTISING!

was seated in a comfortable chair, with no distractions other than electrodes attached to his arms. When he felt at peace with the world, he began to study advertisements set before him and as he did so instruments in an adjoining room charted his interest or apathy as the case might be. The dubious theory behind this device was that a person whose emotions were aroused was likely to go out and buy the product; no allowance would appear to have been made for the individual whose actions were not entirely governed by his emotions. Another difficulty was that pleasure and dislike both agitated the needle equally. Other devices involved the guinea-pigs pressing buttons inscribed 'like' or 'dislike' (this method was often used in testing radio programmes —*see* Chapter Twelve).

One additional test of copy would seem to be to have the copywriter recite it when coupled up to a lie-detector; though for all the writer knows this may already have been done.

1939–1952

SOBERING DOWN

MOST readers will not need to be reminded at length of the advertisements of the Second World War. It was the inevitable pattern. Boot polish firms brought out the comic sergeant-major to commend their wares; girls balanced military hats, not always at military angles, on their shampooed locks. Soon the cry was 'Go easy with ——,' 'Please use —— sparingly.' Firms boasted how they had given up making saucepans to make steel helmets. Economy was an easy wagon on which to ride; by using such-and-such razor blades, which lasted longer, a man could help conserve the nation's supplies of steel. Proprietary medicine firms had magnificent new opportunities ('Worry floods the stomach with acid'). There were 'blackout nerves' to be conquered. Tonic wines were more than ever necessary for 'heroines of the home.' Trying to strike a bright, convivial note, one firm advertised 'the cider for the shelter.' And on top of it all the Government nagged everyone to be brave and cheerful.

Much advertising space was 'presented to the nation' by private firms; only the churlish reader reflected that this was as good a way of spending taxable money as any. By the war's end some of the public had grown exasperated at the constant reminders of goods which were not in the shops. They grew still more exasperated when, in the years of peace, they found that these elusive goods were being shipped overseas. 'Yes, you want a —— sweater. So do thousands of American women. Only about 20 per cent of American women who want —— get ——.' The British housewife found it difficult to shed tears over the deprivations of the American housewife.

In the expanding of overseas markets advertising men had their chance to do their country a powerful service. Many of them rose admirably to the challenge. To help agencies, an information service was formed under the initials B.E.T.R.O. (British Export Trade Research Organization), and technical knowledge was shared out by B.E.T.A.C. (British Export Trade Advertising Corporation).

The shortage of newsprint, which had strait-jacketed the Press during the war, continued to do so afterwards. Some of what the Press lost the hoardings gained. By the 'fifties the fast-rising costs of newsprint forced the newspapers to raise their advertising rates, and the queue of firms seeking space thinned out.

Widening of the health services and the improvement in the nation's physical standards were widely thought to have lessened the national addiction to self-medication. But the chairman of the Beecham Group, Sir J. Stanley Holmes, told his shareholders in 1951: 'The introduction of the National Health Service has had little effect on the sales of proprietary medicines. . . . In the main [these] provide standardized home remedies for use against minor ailments when it would be a waste of both doctor's and patient's time to make use of the Health Service.'

The advertising of many popular specifics was now a good deal more restrained. For the worst type of curemonger there were few opportunities left. In 1939 the Cancer Act had banned the advertising of cures for cancer, and the Pharmacy and Medicines Act of 1941 at last made illegal the advertising of cures for Bright's disease, cataract, diabetes, epilepsy, fits, glaucoma, locomotor ataxy, paralysis and tuberculosis. With 1950 came a new British Code of Standards on medicines and treatments, consolidating and extending earlier codes. It was approved by the Advertising Association, the Newspaper Proprietors Association, the Newspaper Society, the Periodical Proprietors Association, the Institute of Incorporated Practitioners in Advertising, The Incorporated Society of British Advertisers and other bodies; and it was drawn up in conjunction with the Proprietary Association of Great Britain. The Code is worth summarizing. It forbids any claim to cure any ailment or symptom of ill-health, any misleading or exaggerated claim 'as to composition, character or action of the medicine or treatment'; the disparaging of other products or of the medical profession; the use of words like clinic, college and laboratory unless such establishments exist; the use of the terms 'Doctor' or 'Dr.' in the name of a product, unless it was on the market before January 1, 1944; the use, in advertisements of medicines or treatments for women, of any phrases implying that the product can be effective in inducing miscarriage—for instance, 'Female Pills,' 'Not to be used in cases of pregnancy,' and 'Never known to fail'; the use of words like magical and miraculous; the inclusion of references suggesting that the product or treatment has some special property 'which is in fact unknown or unrecognized'; and the use of phrases suggesting that a product will promote sexual virility.

A long list of diseases, illnesses and conditions for which medical treatments, products or appliances may not be advertised includes: anaemia (pernicious), arthritis, baldness, blood pressure, heart troubles, gallstones, indigestion (chronic or persistent), insomnia (chronic or persistent), leg troubles, pyorrhoea, rheumatism (chronic or persistent), and varicose veins.

Asthma may be mentioned only if it is made clear that the product is merely for the alleviation of an attack, and if the advertisement recommends sufferers to seek medical advice.

As for slimming, 'no reference may be made in any advertisement to weight reduction or limitation, slimming or figure control,' though this does not apply to offers of exercise courses or articles used for physical exercise.

The Code is not without its loopholes. It does not wholly frustrate anyone determined to invent a new 'disease.' There are many useful and hard-worked near-synonyms for 'cure.' Some critics would like to see the spirit of the Code extended to cover the advertising of certain foods and drinks, and other commodities to which powerful virtues are ascribed. But in the field of medicines the Code does mark a big—and a voluntary—step forward.

Besides critically examining claims made on behalf of new medicines and treatments, the Advertising Association during the post-war years continued to tackle abuses in other spheres—bogus home-work schemes, the offering of worthless diplomas, and so on. It was instrumental in prosecuting offenders or running them out of business. The Retail Trading-Standards Association also harried advertisers who too lightly employed words like 'wool' and 'linen.'

Those who had looked for a brave new world in which advertising would be found serving the fundamental needs of the community, as distinct from the profit-makers in that community, were still not satisfied. A Labour Party discussion pamphlet issued on the eve of the General Election of 1951 attacked advertising for its continued part in sustaining monopolies:

Vast sums of money are spent in attempts to convince the consumer that the particular advertised goods are unique—even when they differ from their rivals only in the colour of the label or the shape of the bottle. A monopoly is created in so far as advertising convinces the customer that no substitute exists.

The Times thought that much of the sting had gone out of the old accusation that advertising encouraged wasteful competition. In a leader on July 9, 1951, it said:

The danger for consumers lies, today, not in too much competition, taking expensive forms, but in too little, not in too much duplication of efforts to satisfy consumers' wants but in too many limitations that may require them to take what they can get and embolden their suppliers to adopt a 'take it or leave it' attitude.

Under suitable safeguards, advertisement could provide a healthy restraint on this growing tendency, said *The Times*.

It would have been interesting to hear the view of *The Times* on a scheme, in 1951, to promote 'Father's Day' in Britain. The *Sunday Pictorial* strongly urged its readers to let this occasion slip by unobserved, regretting the cynical enthusiasm with which salesmen sought to 'cash in' on special occasions. Christmas and Easter had already been converted from 'religious festivals which drew the family closer together' to 'commercialised spending sprees,' and Mothering Sunday, 'a centuries old British feast, had been ballyhooed into Mother's Day.'

The most spectacular competition in the post-war period was between the makers of soap powders and soapless detergents. In 1950 Oxydol spent on Press advertising just short of £300,000, and Rinso, Dreft, Wisk and Persil more than £200,000 each. These budgets were double those of the leading proprietary medicines. In 1951 Sir Geoffrey Heyworth, chairman of Lever Brothers and Unilever, said that the advertising expenditure on Persil was 6·2 per cent of the consumer price in Britain, 5·6 per cent in France. 'These advertising expenditures sustain the necessary demand to bring about savings in production costs which, although they cannot be exactly calculated, are probably greater in amount.' (Thomas J. Barratt had been more positive than that!) Advertising, Sir Geoffrey Heyworth pointed out, also decreased the costs of retailing by speeding up stock turnover.

No revolutionary new techniques in Press advertising were to be detected. The picture-strip was still popular. There was a short-lived campaign on these lines in the summer of 1951 which deserves especial mention. At first sight it looked like just another in the series showing how foreign correspondents and continuity girls on the edge of failure were saved by drinking the right night-cap and thus ensuring a night's sleep which would reach down into their subconscious. The first picture, entitled, 'Jim took his chance,' portrayed a distressed young husband being consoled by his pretty wife. 'Don't carry on so, Jim,' she said, with tears in her eyes. 'I believe in you. I will stand by you if you want to take a chance and have a go at another job.' Reflecting, 'Well, it's a free country,' Jim gave his firm 'the push.' Two months later he was shown receiving promotion at another factory. And that night he told his wife: 'Betty, darling, I've got a better job and more money already and it was you who gave me the confidence to take a chance.'

Underneath, to clinch the whole thing, ran the slogan:

FREE ENTERPRISE GIVES EVERYONE A CHANCE

The fall of the Socialist Government was given as the reason for discontinuing this campaign. It is conceivable that not all employers relished the idea of encouraging ambitious young men to give their firms 'the push.'

At the time this campaign was running a suggestion was made that a national advertising scheme should be launched to promote chastity in Britain, to make young people 'feel that illicit relations are unworthy of them.'[1] It is interesting to speculate how this subject might have been tackled on the lines of the 'private enterprise' campaign.

'Word magic' was not entirely a forgotten art. There was a notable outbreak in *The Sphere* of October 27, 1951.

the luxury topcoat of the world
that has *devastated society* like a theme song
cleverchange worn with hood or without—half belt or unbelted
originated (and patented thank you) by wetherall
for our uncertain climate *blissfully warm ethereally light and watertight*
cut with the sweep of inspired shears
from the most benevolent *blu blooded cashmeredlama lambs*
in camel budgeblu snuff huntin' pink (woven to our own design).

[1] In the book *English Life and Leisure* by B. Seebohm Rowntree and Commander G. R. Lavers.

There was another form of 'word magic,' which could be described, a shade unkindly perhaps, as 'brewers' patriotic.' It involved using words like 'doth' and 'wherefore.' A sample:

LIKE SOME BELOVED and familiar face that we do hardly note till fear or danger bring it sharp before our eyes, so does This England bloom again in every heart. (Ill indeed is the wind that bloweth no man good.) For we are not aggressive patriots, with insistent symbols and official cries; there is no need. We love England for itself, not for the name; an England whose history is alive in beauty. . . .

Beer, this copywriter asserted, was an integral part of England's courageous, lusty past. He did not say that beer had given England her courage; but another brewer was heading his advertisement 'If you want to feel brave ——' and following up with 'After a —— you feel a bit more able to deal with difficult situations.'

In the summer of 1951 an international advertising conference was held in London. As is customary on these occasions, a great many words were uttered without a great deal being said. There were some illuminating statements, however, on the status of advertising. Mr. J. B. Nicholas, an advertising agent, said that 'in comparison with other professions—the Church, Education, the Law, the higher levels of journalism, and the B.B.C.—I am afraid it must be admitted that advertising sits rather below the salt. A Chair of Advertising should be established without delay in our leading universities, not to deal with technical aspects . . . but to study and examine particularly its social implications and its service to human relations.'

To Mr. Cyrus Ducker, director of the London Press Exchange, the trouble with advertising was the Fifth Column of cynics within its gates. He thought that when the new population census was issued very few would be found to have given their occupation as 'advertising.' The advertising man had been portrayed on film, stage and on the radio as a cold-eyed, hard-faced, back-stabbing desperado who would cheerfully sell his best friend down the river and cheat his own mother for the sake of a good laugh. But the advertising man of today, at the top level, was

. . . generally a kindly and respectable-looking man of rather more than middle age, who lives in the best suburb, belongs to the best clubs in Town, avoids publicity like the plague, seldom goes to the pictures, always reads *The Times* and never goes to the dogs.

To make the picture complete, Mr. Ducker might have added that this dweller in the 'best suburb' could be relied on to fight to the death any proposal to put up hoardings near his house and to write angry letters to *The Times* complaining of low-flying aircraft towing advertising banners.

America: Back in the Groove

It was in 1943 that Mr. Herbert Agar, in his book *A Time for Greatness*, protested against 'the repeated suggestion of a million [advertising] displays . . . that there must always be an answer to every problem and that answer is something money can buy.'

Morale was now a commodity to be purchased over the counter. Asked one advertiser: 'In bewildered times, where shall a man turn to replenish the wells of his courage, to repair the walls of his faith?' The answer was: beer. Another cried: 'We must guard the growing generation which will make our post-war dreams come true. It must be given the spirit and the strength. . . .' The answer this time was: meat. ('You must learn how to prepare less familiar cuts appetizingly.')

Women, superfluous to add, fortified their faith out of jars and pretty phials. But one day, unexpectedly, into the fog of humbug blew a gust, a perfumed gust, of common sense:

We wish it were otherwise. But, frankly, we don't think that Germaine Monteil's Face Powder and Beauty Balm will build morale or help preserve our way of life. *Their* job is to make you look prettier, which they perform brilliantly.

The gust quickly died, and the humbug closed in again. There was a full-page advertisement showing a woman with her chin defiantly tilted:

A wonderful surge of courage brings your head up fiercely in the face of threats. A flash of your eyes measures the enemy.

Sacrifice? Your answer is a short laugh. Sacrifice is a pleasure. It's something to *do*. It's a way to help. And you—magnificent lady—*you*'ll help. You'll toil. You'll fight like a tigress. We know. We've seen it in the lift of your chin.

There was a good deal more of it, finally leading to a disclosure of the sacrifice which the magnificent lady was making: she was doing without a brand of bed sheets, which were needed by the Services.

Q

To women in lands where sacrifice could not always be dismissed with a 'short laugh,' advertisements like this were painful reading. It is possible that they were painful reading in America too. 'Buy furs wisely . . . and you can save to buy War Bonds' was one advertiser's idea of retrenchment.

The theme of countless advertisements was 'Be lovely to come home to'; but the scent-makers seemed anxious to turn the waiting American housewife into the priestess of an unholy altar. Names of perfumes included My Sin, Menace, Intoxication, Frenzy, Shanghai, Lotus, Surrender, Tigress, Wild Harvest, Voodoo and Tabu. Jean Patou continued to market Joy, with its inspired slogan 'the costliest perfume in the world.'

Another way to be worthy of a man was by taking the right vitamin pills daily, thus keeping both lovely and lively. It was to vitamins that the actress Mary Martin owed her euphoria—a libellous-looking word which, the copywriter explained, was a medical term meaning *good* good health.

Of all the war-time adjurations to American women, one of the oddest was that by the firm of Goodrich. After the war 'when your husband goes out to buy tires for the family plane, exert your important family influence in favour of smoother, safer-landing B. F. Goodrich Silvertowns. . . . Of course, you'll want brakes that stop your plane safely and smoothly with only a slight pressure of your toe. So—remind him that B. F. Goodrich Expander Tube Brakes do just that (even on a 30-ton Flying Fortress).'

When the war was over the advertisers were forced back on the old familiar angles. AN HOUR UNDER THE MISTLETOE AND NOTHING HAPPENS. . . . HOW DO YOU GET TO BE AN OLD MAID, AUNTIE? . . . A MAN CAN CHANGE, JUST LIKE THAT. . . . 'ME, JOHN? ME? UNRESPONSIVE—COLD?' To many it seemed, however, that some of the last reticences were being abandoned. The 'Me, John? me?' headline, from *Look* in 1949, was accompanied by a picture of a pretty woman registering apprehension as the icy fingers of inhibition gripped her shoulder. The text below gave so intimate a talk on feminine hygiene—naming parts hitherto not named in the public prints—that it was hard to see what extra information could have been gleaned by sending a coupon for an explanatory booklet.

It was the old pre-war world again, plus television, plus a few new wonder drugs (one antihistamine was sold under the slogan 'One person in every two suffers an allergy'). It was the old frenzied world of ear stopples and blinkers (without which no one could be expected to sleep); though now there was a clock-radio which could combine the feats of lulling and rousing. 'It soothes you to sleep, *turns itself off* . . . and next morning it *wakes* you to music, automatically!'

The goal was still 'gracious living.' In what new ways could this happy state be realized? Once again the answer was contained in one familiar word: beer. The American brewers' advertisements at this stage might have been written by the same hand as the British ones; they were full of high-falutin' talk about freedom and patriotism.

Plumbers were out to promote gracious living, too. In a full-page advertisement in the *Saturday Evening Post* of October 2, 1948, a salesman and a housewife gazed with a mixture of reverence and ecstasy at a glittering object, fashioned from newest plastic, and available in golden peach, sea-green, powder blue, rose orchid and sparkling white. It was manufactured by the Federal Seat Corporation of Long Island.

An advertisement in the *New Yorker* of January 27, 1951, was headed 'Introduction to Social Poise.' The text began: 'Give your children the right roots to grow on. Let them absorb the grace of tasteful, relaxed living from their earliest experiences and memories.' The product advertised would 'help to give growing children social poise . . . free them from self-consciousness, awkwardness and unnatural restraint.' Prolonged guessing on the reader's part would probably fail to identify the product: a brand of dinner-table candle.

The highest levels of gracious living were being achieved in the air. In double-deck Strato clippers young women of splendid poise were pictured descending staircases into spacious cocktail lounges, where more young women of splendid poise sat in foam-soft seats with their long legs crossed. 'Magnificent seven-course dinners,' cried Pan-American, 'champagnes and liqueurs, music, bed-length sleeperettes, five extra cabin attendants, and— for the ladies—Lanvin's *Arpège* perfume and orchids. Small surcharge.' Then, as an after-thought, 'a blue carpet is rolled out for your departure.' And all this, apparently, in all five continents.

The zeal for gracious living may also have accounted for a new device which appeared on the market in 1951: a combined tooth-brush and tongue-scraper. 'Made of curved smooth plastic [the tongue-scraper] has a patented vacuum-action groove that gently sucks out the harmful bacteria. Now the tongue can be cleaned off, simply and quickly, leaving the mouth clean and your breath sweet.'

This remarkable 'gimmick,' it was explained, ended man's long and restless quest for a means of cleaning his tongue. In the past, people had been obliged to improvise, sometimes using the bristles of the toothbrush, the back of a nail file, a piece of gauze, a spoon, and 'even the upper teeth.'

The tongue-scraper seems to have been less successful than some other post-war novelties. For example, the ball-point pen. 'It writes under water' was the slogan with which this novelty was launched, a Barnumesque touch intended to make persons exclaim to each other about the folly of such a claim, and in so doing to spread the news of the pen. Less widely quoted was the tribute of a nib-pen manufacturer: 'The only pen that will make eight carbons and no original.' Five thousand people waited outside a New York store on an October morning in 1945 to buy the first pens—at $12.50 cents each.

The ball pen, which swept the world at a fast-falling price, was the first big promotion of the atomic era. At one stage it was hailed as an 'atomic age marvel,' as indeed were many other products. But in due time the word 'atomic' was used less reck-lessly. As the world situation worsened, 'atomic shelters' began to be offered in California and elsewhere, and business men were being urged to store their records and valuables in the atom-proof Lincoln Mountain Vaults. Another advertiser said: 'Afraid of A-Bomb Contamination? In the event of an A-Bomb attack wash contamination away with Flobar . . . it can be carried about for instant use.' Just like something for chapped hands.

The sting was still being taken out of death, and the incon-veniences of mourners were being solicitously studied. A burial-ground advertisement took the form of a telephone dialogue between two women, one of whom was recommending the estab-lishment on the grounds that the parking-place was centrally located, and husbands were less likely to grumble about the nuisance of having to park a long way from the grave-side.

*   *   *

'Word magic' burgeoned in new, sometimes emetic, forms. The most wanton havoc to the English language was achieved by the copywriters (male or female?) engaged in boosting female underwear. One advertisement began:

Darling, we'd like to put our charms around you!
How Warner's 3-Way-Sizes can curve a beautiful comfy you.

It went on, 'And while you're being "pick-ticular" you'll honestly go swoony over the skillions of styles. . . . Even with a daily "bra-th" the cups dry into the same smooth-fitting loveliness.' There were 'styles that lift-a-little and styles that lift-a-lot,' though neither of these was quite right for an 'in-betweenie.' The firm also undertook to conquer 'tummy roll,' claiming on behalf of its 'you-shaped bones' that 'not even an admiring glance could follow your curves so closely.'

Yet some may prefer the archly drooling style of Warner's to the Smart Aleck manner of Springmaid, as exemplified in various magazine advertisements in 1948. The copywriter told how, during the Second World War, the Springs Cotton Mills developed a special material for jungle camouflage, impregnated 'with a permanent odor of hibiscus, hydrangea and old rubber boots.' Obviously a discovery of this kind was adaptable to the ways of peace:

This process has been patented, and the fabric is now available to the hip harness and bosom bolster business as SPRINGMAID PERKER, made of combed yarns . . . the white with gardenia, the pink with camellia, the blush with jasmine and the nude dusty.
If you want to achieve that careless look and avoid skater's steam, kill two birds with one stone by getting a camouflaged callipygian camisole with the SPRINGMAID label. . . .

Another variation of this advertisement began 'Defy Diaphoresis!' A footnote explained that diaphoresis was 'commonly known as Rhumba aroma.'

Once again, here was an advertisement which contained the phrase to describe its own literary style—'impregnated with a permanent odor of hibiscus, hydrangea and old rubber boots.'

American advertising was still being mocked by 'sophisticated urban elements.' When the British magazine *Horizon* published an American issue in October 1947, Herbert Marshall McLuhon contributed an article on the state of advertising in that continent. 'The American is in a much happier position than the Englishman, whose advertisements are such half-hearted efforts to externalize his hopes and fears and appetites. American advertising is Cartesian. The English is Baconian,' said Mr. McLuhon. He then unbent sufficiently to quote some recent advertisements, one of which alone was worth the price of a year's subscription to *Horizon*.

This was the picture story of Tommy, who had come home from school with a black eye. Questioned by his lovely young mother, he said that the boys had been taunting him because his father had begun to go out with other women. Tommy had lashed out in defence of his mother's sex appeal, but had been unlucky enough to receive a black eye. Mortified, the young mother ran out to buy the only talisman which could bring back her husband's love—and began to rub it on her teeth. Next morning, radiant in panties and brassière, she whispered to Tommy, in the bathroom, 'It works.' A later picture showed the children looking round the corner into the living-room where dad was waltzing mom to radio music. 'Gee, looks like he's going to haul her off and kiss her,' said one of them. 'Yep,' replied Tommy, 'you can't say my Dad hangs around with other girls now.'

All that need be said about Tommy is that he is right up in the same class as Jane Porter and her Soft-Weave Waldorf.

* * *

American advertisers did not have it all their own way in these post-war years. In 1951 the Federal Trade Commission directed a tobacco firm to refrain from claiming that its cigarettes, by virtue of containing a certain moistening agent, produced 'less irritation.' Obstinately the Commission took the old-fashioned view that the chief irritant in tobacco was tobacco, irrespective of any chemical additions. Before the ruling was finally imposed an astonishing series of 'scientific' tests was conducted. The firm bubbled smoke from various cigarettes through water and dripped the solutions on to the eyes of rabbits; only the solutions of rival brands, it claimed, caused irritation. Embattled (and embittered) rivals devised their own smoking machines to blow smoke against rabbits' eyelids. All smokes, they reported, had an identical effect. Another test (subsequently disallowed by the Federal authorities) involved cutting off the rabbits' upper eyelids, weighing the membraneous linings, drying them in an oven and weighing them again. The firm under attack then cut holes in the air passages of the rabbits and pumped smoke into their lungs (presumably because the rabbits were reluctant to inhale). Five of the animals died, but (argued the experimenters) they were all smoking rival brands.

It was a haunting glimpse into the mad laboratories of advertising, but the public laughed and passed on. It was still prepared to overlook all manner of wayward practices in the name of advertising, right down to the attaching of advertisements to girls' legs (the theory was that this was where everybody looked). Yet on one issue the public rebelled, or was induced to rebel. That was when it found itself being bombarded by loud-speaker advertisements in New York's Grand Central station. The campaign of protest was led by the late Harold Ross, editor of the *New Yorker*. As a result, the nuisance was stopped. Ross then turned his attention to the loud-speaker advertising which had been started in public service vehicles in Washington. The *New Yorker* said:

> The role of the advertising man in this modern drama is unique, for he not only dreamed up the technique of catching the consumer when he was helpless but made the fatal blunder of calling his victims by their exact name, 'captive audience.' This phrase, coined in a moment of triumph, turned and bit the advertising man, and it will live to bite him again. There is just something in the American temperament that doesn't like captivity—even the mild captivity of a street-car ride with a radio that cannot be turned off.

On another occasion the *New Yorker* said:

> The issue of the captive audience is simply the issue of the life contemplative; whether or not there is any obligation to preserve the individual's mental quietude, whether a citizen has a right to twirl his thoughts round as he pleases, or whether his thoughts may be twirled round at the pleasure (and profit) of a transit company. . . . Free government cannot thrive without Contemplative Man.

And a spokesman of the American Civil Liberties Union was quoted as saying 'The Bill of Rights can keep up with anything that an advertising man can think of'—a heartening assurance.

1900–1952

HOARDINGS IN RETREAT

W HEN the twentieth century came in, many a hoarding in
Britain was still a sorry hodge-podge. Big posters and small
were pasted side by side, above and below each other according to
the whim of the man with the brush. A hoarding of this type
might run housetop-high for the length of a street. There was some
excuse for artists of repute refusing to design posters when they
knew their works would inevitably be jostled by highly coloured
crudities. Some improvement was to be seen, however, in 1904,
when one contractor began to erect 'solus' sites, that is, sites
exclusive to one advertiser.

In 1905 Parliament was invited to pass an Advertisement
Regulation Bill which would consolidate some of the ideas contained in the protective Acts secured by Dover and Edinburgh.
The sponsors of this measure recognized that it was no use
appealing any further to the good sense and good taste of the
outdoor advertiser: competition was far too intense. The Bill
reached the Statute Book in 1907. It empowered local authorities
to 'regulate and control' hoardings over twelve feet in height and
to 'regulate, restrict or prevent' advertisements overlooking
pleasure parks and promenades, or disfiguring 'the natural beauty
of the landscape.' This Act inspired many edifying, but incon-
clusive, arguments in court on such questions as 'What is natural
beauty?' and (better still) 'What is a landscape?' For instance,
was the bare sweep of the Sussex Downs a landscape within the
meaning of the Act? There was nothing there, as Kipling had
testified, except

our close-bit thyme that smells
Like dawn in Paradise.

Surely (it was argued) a landscape needed trees, a river, a church spire or a stately home? How could beauty dwell in emptiness?

In spite of these uncertainties, a number of local authorities did pass protective by-laws and the bill-posting interests were soon complaining loudly of the conflicting rules which confronted them up and down the country. Sensing the drift of public opinion, a few firms, notably Michelin, began to take down their rail-side signs.

In towns, a flagrant new eyesore was the cinema poster, as unforgivably crude, as unregenerate as it often is to-day. Harry Furniss had this to say about cinema advertising in *Our Lady Cinema* (1914):

Any ordinary theatrical venture would be ruined instanter by the exhibition of posters such as these. They are fifty per cent worse than the most atrocious poster advertising the most plebeian play in the vilest and most poverty-stricken purlieus frequented by the veriest riff-raff of the amusement-going public. Decent people are instantly shocked and repelled by their flaunting hideousness, and that the less educated section of the community is in any way attracted to them is open to considerable doubt.

John Hassall's view of cinema posters was shorter but just as crushing: 'Artistically too bad for words.'

When the National Council of Public Morals issued the report of its inquiry into the cinema in 1917, it said that censorship of posters was 'in some respects even more necessary than of films.' Although the billposting trade had power to exclude objectionable posters from the hoardings, it could not touch the posters on the cinemas themselves.

The First World War gave a violent impetus to the poster industry. It has been computed that two-and-a-half million posters, by more than a hundred artists, had been pasted up before conscription came in. Alfred Leete's Kitchener poster— 'Your Country needs YOU!'—was the most famous and inescapable. 'Women of Britain say "Go!" ' was the title to a picture of a woman looking down, brave but fearful, from an open window. John Bull, wearing a Union Jack for waistcoat, joined in the finger-stabbing, crying, 'Who's Absent? Is it you?' A spirited picture of the *Lusitania* sinking was headed 'IRISHMEN! Avenge the *Lusitania*! Join an Irish Regiment to-day!' Not all these rousing pictures were sponsored by the Government. One, entitled 'The Vow of Vengeance,' showed a soldier looking up from a woman's corpse to shake his fist at a German airship. Underneath was the heartening reminder: '*Daily Chronicle* readers are covered against the risks of bombardment by Zeppelin or aeroplane.'

Some of these wartime posters were crude in execution. A few were magnificent. The most illustrious artists now recognized that painting posters was their patriotic duty; there could be no question of the hoardings being beneath them. Yet in 1917, when Whistler's 'Mother' was set to work on behalf of War Bonds, there were still many who protested that art was being wantonly degraded.

When the war ended, the public were in danger of being poster-weary. London was seedy-looking under the remains of the recruiting posters, partly over-pasted by the pill-men. The bill-posting industry began to clean up its heritage, and to design new standard hoardings on the American pattern, with frames protecting the sheets from wind and rain.

Hundreds of rail-side hoardings were now falling to pieces; hundreds more had been voluntarily removed. Most of the Bovril boards had gone, and Ingersoll began to dispose of their field sites. A pill company is said to have defended its field signs on the grounds that they were made of tastefully enamelled iron and were therefore unexceptionable. Such concessions as were made were more than offset by the rush to build hoardings along the highways. Motoring was at last becoming a popular pastime (the Austin Seven emerged in 1922) and there was a real danger that thousands of people might remove themselves beyond the reach of the advertiser every week-end. Along every highway the boards began to multiply. Though a motorist was expected to be able to see a pedestrian at fifty yards in pitch blackness, he was assumed to be incapable of spotting a petrol pump by day unless it was prefaced by a series of overbearing announcements. In some places green English hedgerows which had stood for generations were pulled up and replaced by hoardings. If a tree hampered the traveller's view of a giant sauce bottle, it was cut down. Metal railway bridges, often eyesores in themselves, were made quadruply more offensive by the posting of announcements on the sides, underneath the arch and along the adjacent embankments.

Almost every year from 1920 onwards, Bills were brought forward in an effort to check these excesses. Some of them wilted under the sneers of Lord Birkenhead, the Lord Chancellor, in whom outdoor advertising inspired a curiously warm-hearted tolerance. On railway journeys, said the Lord Chancellor in 1921, it was common to see a large bottle appearing at frequent intervals by the rail side:

I will confess that I am so unaesthetic and so unexacting in this matter that if the bottle gives me the information how many miles we have passed since London was left, how many miles remain before London is reached, I withdraw all my aesthetic objections, because I consider that the bottle has played its part. The bottle very soon disappears. . . .

Lord Birkenhead seems to have based some of his opposition on the ground that 'many of the men who have undoubtedly developed British trade in foreign countries have been among the largest of our advertisers.'

Sponsoring an unsuccessful Bill in 1922, Lord Newton said that if the Lord Chancellor had to live permanently in the neighbourhood of a bottle or a sausage he would probably regard such sights with different feelings.

Vested interests were not necessarily hostile to Lord Newton's Bill. Lord Riddell had let it be known that he wanted to see outdoor advertising suppressed, an avowal which (said Lord Newton) must have caused him 'many pangs,' in view of the open-handed way in which his newspaper was advertised. The 1922 Bill was described by Lord Birkenhead as 'futile and unnecessary.' Local authorities, he said, did not want it, and would not even use the powers they already had.

Readers of *The Times* held much debate about the extravagances of outdoor advertising in the early 'twenties, and the newspaper itself sought the views of many authorities. A Mr. W. H. Atkinson, of Ealing, voiced the view of 'those with the misfortune to live in a street where their view is limited to the distance from their windows to the hoarding on the opposite side of the street.' He said:

Many of the manufacturers of goods so publicly eulogised are titled gentlemen and perhaps collect works of art. I wonder what they would think if they looked out of their windows one morning to find their beautiful trees and Japanese gardens hidden by a hoarding displaying pictures of oil engines and coal scuttles.

It was fair comment then and it remains fair comment now. A generation before, Thomas Holloway had retired to a spot where he was unlikely to be vexed by the sight of his own name. The merchant princes of the twentieth century lived in districts which jealously defended their amenities. Only advertising could bring worldly success, and only worldly success could bring relief from advertising. Some merchant princes even built, for their work-people, model towns like Port Sunlight and Bournville, where the gable-ends were left unpapered. Yet a few miles away less privileged communities would be plastered with posters for 'Sunlight Soap' and 'Cadbury's Pure Milk.'

The Times noted that there was a general agreement on electric signs, which were 'all for the increasing of public happiness. They are an unfailing source of wonder to visitors from the country; they reassure the crumbling belief in magic of the youngest revellers and they provide a field of considerable dimensions for the exercise of ingenuity.'

The poster firms were by now inured to unfriendly criticism, yet sometimes praise fell from unexpected quarters. At the Royal Academy banquet of 1923 the Prince of Wales (now Duke of Windsor) described hoardings as 'the art galleries of the great public . . . their refinement has advanced by leaps and bounds.' But only two days after it reported this speech, *The Times* lost its temper with outdoor advertisers: 'The motorist and the bicyclist, the pedestrian, the excursionist and the native are alike disgusted at the insolent vulgarities which so constantly thrust themselves upon the eyes of every user of the roads.' There was a 'system of anarchical assault on the eyes' by 'ugly and lying puffs,' and bye-laws were frequently defied. The occasion for this tirade was the introduction of still another Advertisements Regulation Bill. The Government had failed to support any of the previous measures, complained *The Times*. Lord Newton's new Bill was intended to protect historic buildings—'it will no longer be legally possible to prevent anyone from seeing Tintern Abbey, Magdalen Tower, or Kenilworth Castle without also seeing an advertisement of somebody's boots or soap.'

That same year the Minister of Transport noted with displeasure the way in which hoardings were being erected along London's new arterial roads even before they were opened. He issued a circular to road authorities reminding them of their powers and urging them to take action. But the most encouraging development of the year was the lead given by the big petrol companies in removing, at heavy expense to themselves, the most obtrusive of their rural signs. The great retreat began when the Isle of Wight Chamber of Commerce suggested to the Shell-Mex, British Petroleum, and Anglo-American companies that they should remove their boards from the island. They did; and Anglo-American offered to withdraw its field sites throughout the rest of the country if the others would follow suit. Shell-Mex, not to be outdone in public spirit, started pulling up its signs without more ado. Soon the three companies were joined by National Benzole, United Petroleum Products, Dunlop, and others. It was 'a triumph on the heroic scale,' said Richardson Evans, of S.C.A.P.A., and nobody grudged the oil companies the virtue in which they basked. On town sites, and filling stations, the same firms still retained their advertisements.

Ironically it was the railways, drawing an impressive revenue from the eyesores on their bridges and embankments, which conspicuously improved the level of poster art after the First World War. The movement had begun just before the war, when Frank Pick began to commission distinguished artists to paint posters for the London Underground. Pick has been described as the nearest approach to Lorenzo the Magnificent that a modern democracy could achieve. After the war the big railway companies also began to give a free hand to leading Academicians. Some of the railway directors were unhappy about the pictures that were painted; so, for that matter, were some of the public. What (the directors may well have thought) would King George V say when he saw Clive Gardiner's poster of Windsor Castle, unrecognizable as such? The artist Oleg Zinger, after viewing (presumably) all the glories of Hampton Court, had elected to paint a single water lily. It was a very good water lily, but it was still only a water lily. There were some who preferred the more intelligible John Hassall Underground poster showing an old lady at the entrance to a Tube station—'No need to ask a p'liceman,' or Alfred Leete's night watchman, with the comment: 'The roads are never up on the Underground.'

Some Royal Academicians were not over-successful at executing posters. There was no comfort for them in the view expressed by E. McKnight Kauffer that bad painters designed bad posters and that good painters always designed good posters. McKnight Kauffer, who himself excelled at expressing the bold essence of an idea in arresting colours, published his poster 'Bible' in 1924: *The Art of the Poster*. The reproductions consisted mainly of travel posters. There was one solitary film poster—by Will Dyson, advertising *Moriarty*, a Goldwyn picture. And there was one of a lavatory cleaner. 'The appearance of a really good poster for an everyday commodity is still something of an event,' said Kauffer.

The new poster names were now those of Norman Wilkinson, Laura Knight, Edmund Dulac, G. Spencer Pryse, Maurice Greiffenhagen, C. R. W. Nevinson, E. J. Sullivan, Graham Sutherland and C. Lovat Fraser. These artists had the advantage that they were able to draw on the wealth of Britain's scenery and historic places for their subjects. In due course they, and others, were called upon by the Empire Marketing Board, which in its heyday had twenty thousand hoardings of its own design. Seaside towns and inland spas were also crying for scenic posters (the Health Resorts and Watering Places Act of 1921 had empowered them to advertise out of the rates). Many of the resorts ordered pictures of bathing belles, which did not please the more conservative ratepayers. One of the best-remembered seaside posters was John Hassall's ebullient fisherman, who spread the fame of Skegness.

The improved Advertisement Regulation Act for which *The Times* had been calling was eventually passed in 1925. It gave local authorities power to restrain advertisements which would spoil a view of rural scenery from highway or railway or from any public place or water, or destroy the amenities of a village or historic place or monument, or of any place frequented by the public because of its beauty or historic interest. Model bye-laws were prepared by the Home Office. The problem now was to induce local authorities to use their powers, and to see that they were not openly defied.

A *cause célèbre* of 1925 followed an act of defilement on the much-abused South Downs. Hove County Council prosecuted several defendants for erecting unsightly and intrusive hoardings, one of them 170 feet long, near Patcham. The owner of the land had himself put up a large poster which read.

> Watch and pray.
> The time is short and man brings about his own destruction.
> The air battle will be the end of the world.

As the new Act was not yet on the Statute Book, it was necessary to prove that the scenery affected was a landscape. A representative of the Brighton Arts Club testified that, in his opinion, it was, and that the hoardings ruined it even when the viewer was a mile away. For the defence, it was argued that the adjurement to 'Watch and pray' was not an advertisement. Surely the Court would not rule that a man of strong religious convictions was barred from putting up a text on his own ground? The Court decided that texts ought not to be propagated in such a way as to exasperate the public.[1]

Though the Act of 1925 was a step forward, it still allowed the flouting of urban and near-urban amenities. To take one example at random, a contractor set up in Southborough, Kent, a hoarding 12 feet high by 120 feet long. More than seven hundred signatures were collected in protest, but no action could be taken because Southborough was not a village and the hoarding did not obstruct the view of rural scenery. Industrial towns suffered renewed indignities. Here the bill-posters' argument was the old, familiar one that there were no amenities to destroy. The streets were so drab, they said, that the plastering of bridges and gable-ends could only serve to brighten them. To some observers it seemed that these mean streets might recover a little of their lost dignity if they were stripped of the advertisers' motley. It was a strange arrogance on the part of a soap-maker or a pill-seller that he should presume to decide which streets stood in need of 'brightening.'

In 1930 a Countryside Conference and Exhibition was held at Leicester. It had the effect of inducing more roadside advertisers to withdraw their placards, as the petrol companies had done. There was now quite a long list of firms which had voluntarily abstained from highway placarding, and there was little doubt that many other firms were advertising only because their rivals

---

[1] Some of the most obtrusive 'advertisements' in rural areas have always been religious texts and exhortations, notably 'Prepare To Meet Thy God.'

had forced them into it. Certain counties, notably Kent and Surrey, were more active in invoking their powers than others. Many hoardings were removed after amicable negotiations. Old quarry faces continued to exercise an inextinguishable fascination for some advertisers. In 1930 there were several outbreaks of advertising by turf cutting; on Cissbury Down, near Worthing, an advertisement 200 yards long, visible for miles, was hacked in the chalk slopes to advertise a building estate. Each letter was 45 feet long.

The vulgarization of the highways could not be blamed exclusively on the poster firms. Crude signs erected by café owners, painted walls, whitewashed slogans on corrugated iron roofs, fly-posted bills on backs of farm buildings, enamelled plaques on village shops, bills in house windows—these often were more repellent than the hoardings themselves. There was always someone ready to ruin a neighbour's view for the sake of an occasional pair of theatre tickets or a subscription to a magazine.

There had been a time when the cloak of night had concealed the worst of these excrescences. Now, however, reflecting signs sprang into dazzling life at every bend in the road, and neon signs were spreading out from the cities to the smallest villages. Few novelties created more controversy in the 'thirties than the 'red rash' of neon. It imposed its fiery outline on the bulls and griffins of inn signs; it glimmered under the thatch of tea shoppes. In his *Second Essays on Advertising* Mr. J. Murray Allison said:

Some electric light signs are very beautiful—the neon light, for instance. In my opinion it beautifies every position it occupies. The *Daily Mail* in neon on the south side of the Thames near Blackfriars Bridge is a most glorious thing and the light it sheds upon that portion of the river is just as beautiful, I believe, as the light that Whistler saw at Battersea.

So convinced were some advertisers of the glory of neon that they introduced the neon boat at seaside resorts. Hardly had the sunset died before a garish craft would be towed across the bay, covered with brilliant illuminated signs.

One objection levelled against extravagances like these was: 'How should we celebrate a great victory, a royal jubilee, when we make every night a carnival night?' A more weighty objection, perhaps, was that the multiplicity of signs was a danger to life.

Often a motorist entering a strange town at night had great difficulty in distinguishing the modest red-and-green of traffic lights against the effulgence of light on almost every gable-end and façade. Advocates of safety first on the highways did not fail to seize on this eye-distracting aspect of outdoor advertisements.

Between the world wars, the efforts of S.C.A.P.A. had been heavily reinforced by the Council for the Preservation of Rural England, which carried out some illuminating surveys of the number of advertisements per mile on popular highways. Some progress was being made towards further legislation when the Second World War broke out and once again the hoardings of Britain were monopolised by Government exhortations—Dig for Victory, Careless Talk Costs Lives, Arm Him, Help Them Finish The Job, 'Let Us Go Forward Together,' Bravo British Shipyards, and a hundred others. After the war the Government retained its grip on the hoardings, even while the Minister of Town and Country Planning was seeking to prevent amenities being ruined by posters—including Government posters.

In 1946 the Council for the Preservation of Rural England conducted a survey of the London–Hastings road. It listed 1,075 separate advertisements, of which more than 400 were on gable-ends of buildings. Of the grand total no fewer than 744 were encountered on the ten miles between London Bridge and Bromley. In some stretches of Sussex there were only one or two advertisements to the mile. Clearly it was now the urban areas which stood in need of protection from the advertiser.

Mr. (now Baron) Silkin's Town and Country Planning Bill 1947, which came into force on August 1, 1948, laid down a code for the complete control of outdoor advertisements in England and Wales. Local authorities were now empowered (though not compelled) to nominate rural districts as 'areas of special control' and to limit advertisements therein as stringently as they wished. Control of posters in general was to be considered from the dual points of view of amenity and public safety. When reviewing an advertisement, a planning authority could consider the general characteristics of a neighbourhood, without reference to any existing posters. As from August 1, 1948, no new advertisements were to be set up without consent of the planning authority; and as from August 1, 1951, existing advertisements could be challenged by the planning authority, if it felt impelled to take action.

R

The poster firms showed a certain nervousness as August 1, 1951, approached, but there was no immediate rush of challenges. This was partly because the Minister had urged local authorities to settle disputes amicably, partly because local councils were overworked, and partly because the ordinary citizen was not yet aware of his new privileges. It seemed probable, however, that one of the first battle-grounds would be Trafalgar Square, where advertisers had been encroaching for many years.

From time to time the *Advertiser's Weekly* reproduced photographs of advertisement sites banned by the Minister after contractors had appealed. The Minister did not take the trade view that the existence of a number of posters was sufficient excuse for adding another. He apparently disliked gable-end signs. And he disapproved of many advertisements on the sides of railway arches; these, he ruled, were likely to distract drivers at critical moments.

Some poster firms accepted that they would be expected to give better value than hitherto. Any new site would have to incorporate a garden or ornamental plot, perhaps a shelter or a rustic seat. Many of these embellished sites now began to appear. Sometimes the posters behind them were a happy choice; as often as not they showed soap packets and sauce bottles. Sir Hugh Casson, the architect, was unkind enough to stigmatize garden sites as 'the ultimate hypocrisy.'

The craving for gable-ends persisted. In a supplement to *World's Press News* of November 10, 1951, appeared an advertiser's announcement depicting a 'before and after' view of a gable-end in an unpretentious city street. The 'before' picture showed the wall covered with tatters of paper, the remains of haphazardly posted bills: an undisputed eyesore. The 'after' picture showed the wall cleaned and painted white, and bearing a single large advertisement, not less than fifteen feet in height, reading 'Nestlé's Milk—Richest in Cream.' The legend said: 'This photograph of a —— Solus Site shows how a derelict wall can be cleaned up and re-modelled to become an attractive, strong-selling poster position—and, at the same time, greatly improve the local amenities.' The average man of goodwill will probably find the greatest difficulty in understanding how a sign of these dimensions—bearing a bold boast, and nothing else—can 'greatly improve the local amenities.' At that point he recognizes that he and the professional advertiser inhabit different worlds.

If, as some said, the hoardings were now lamentably respectable, the cinema industry—still a law to itself—could be safely excluded from the charge. After the war films were publicized more and more on the appeal of sex and violence. The most notorious poster was the one which advertised 'The Outlaw.' It showed a skimpily clad Jane Russell, her physical charms heavily emphasized, reclining with a long whip, and trying her best to look 'Mean, Moody, Magnificent.' Film after film was sold on the female bosom, or on pictures of men leering after girls' legs. Many a hint was dropped that the film industry should introduce voluntary censorship, if only to prevent a general compulsory censorship; but all were disregarded.

To the man in the street, the most conspicuous development in outdoor advertising since the Second World War was the craze for luminous inks, an idea developed from a war-time invention. When the first two or three advertisers used these brilliant colours, they outshone all other posters in the vicinity. The result was a general rush to use the new inks, and because everybody strove to catch the public's eye, only the biggest and most blatant users succeeded in doing so. It was the tale of neon all over again (and, incidentally, neon was now available in more than fifty shades).

America: Billboard Blues

In America, the passion for daubing slogans on rock faces had begun to abate by the time the twentieth century dawned. The tendency now was to erect hoardings in front of the beauty-spots. 'The distinction is a fine one, but it means some gain,' wrote Charles Milford Robinson, a leader in the struggle against disfigurement, in the *Atlantic Monthly* of March 1904. As in Britain, field signs had sprung up in thousands beside railway lines, a practice which, to their credit, many of the railways actively resented. One company planted quick-growing trees to conceal the signs; another put pressure on landowners to reject poster advertisements. There was an attempt to foster the idea that a farmer who filled his fields with signs was thereby proclaiming his own poverty and ill-success.

Urban hoardings followed the British pattern, and the sky

sign had now come to stay. 'The glory of the sunset silhouettes against the sky the title of a breakfast food; and the windows of the defenceless home look out on circus girls, corsets, and malt whiskey,' complained Charles Milford Robinson. A widespread infliction was the setting up of large hoardings overlooking parks. Chicago and many other cities took special measures to frustrate such enterprise. Two of the New England States passed laws to prohibit advertising on trees. All over the continent there were moves to limit the size of posters. Of their own accord, contractors began to standardize hoardings and to keep them in better repair. The 'solus' hoarding was devised earlier than in England, and some advertisers found it worth while to lease, but not to use, adjacent advertising rights in order to ensure better display. In 1914 the Poster Advertising Association drew up a uniform specification for poster sites, and began voluntary censorship.

Between the wars, the advertiser flagged and flogged the motorist to an extent unmatched anywhere in the world. The present writer, who drove some thousands of miles over American highways in 1936, remembers chiefly the inescapable word 'Eat,' used as an imperative and as a noun with equal impartiality: 'Eat Here,' 'Joe's Eat,' 'Billy's Eat,' 'Good Eats,' and just plain 'Eat.' The other ubiquitous three-letter word was 'Gas.' Crude and often home-made signs reading 'Orange Drink,' 'Auto Camp,' and 'Comfort Station' did probably more to vulgarize the highways than giant hoardings. Aggressive, too, were the thousands of bright red Coca-Cola signs—the same red signs that to-day spread like a measles rash over scores of countries, notably in the Middle East.

One coast-to-coast advertiser had hit on the idea of running four-line verses, one line to a board, with the boards mounted in series, so that the message could be assimilated at speed. Thus the first board would read 'TO GET AWAY'; the next a few yards further on, 'FROM HAIRY APES'; the third 'LADIES JUMP' and the fourth 'FROM FIRE ESCAPES,' with the name of the advertiser bringing up the rear, 'Burma Shave.' If a verse could be serialized in this fashion, why not (said the wags) a short story—or even 'Gone With The Wind' for transcontinental reading?

Harsher critics said serial signs were dangerous; but some advertisers argued that there was so little to occupy the motorist's mind on these endless, fast highways that their messages were doing a public service in keeping him awake and entertained. Over a dull route in Indiana, the writer encountered a series of recreational signs, bearing no sponsor's name, which carried the kind of statements once popular as 'fillers' in magazines: 'The vocabulary of the average man is 3,500 words,' 'The voyage of Columbus cost only 7,000 dollars,' and so on. After a while the anonymous advertiser began to conduct a quiz. 'Who said, "Don't shoot till you see the whites of their eyes?"' and 'What three coins make 76 cents?' The answer would be given after a suitable interval. When this palled, there came a series of French lessons, then algebra problems and other brain-teasers. No clue was given as to the purpose of the signs; no doubt it was some contractor's idea of creating goodwill, or drawing attention to his business. He desisted only when the approach of a big town offered the motorist a more generous ration of reading matter: 'Big Hop To-Nite,' 'Burlesk,' 'We Buy Pawn Tickets,' and all the rest of it.

At any time between the wars, a battle was going on in half a dozen States in America between 'billboard' interests and local ratepayers' associations, women's clubs, chambers of commerce, safety-first associations and architects' institutes. Legislation was piecemeal and varied from State to State. Advertisers were persistent and ingenious; sometimes an exasperated local authority would set up screens in front of offensive hoardings. In one instance in Ohio, poison ivy was grown on a long embankment to deter advertisers.

Outdoor advertising, like all other forms of publicity, had been put on as 'scientific' a basis as possible. Statisticians in the Traffic Audit Bureau could quote, or at least estimate, the 'circulation' of any advertisement, that is, the number of persons likely to pass the point of exhibition daily. (A big sign in Times Square, New York, was said to attract more than a million pairs of eyes in the twenty-four hours.) Cities were meticulously mapped to show all the available advertising sites and the numbers of persons whose attention could be challenged over a given period.

In the field of 'electric spectaculars' the big American cities—though they got away to a slow start—had little serious competition. There were many claims to have erected the 'biggest sign in the world'—but how was bigness to be measured? By area covered (there have been signs two hundred feet long)? By number of bulbs (there have been signs with 30,000 bulbs)? Or by the distance at which the sign was legible? Then there was the competition for the most costly sign, or the sign with the 'longest run.' An historic electric sign erected about 1910 over Herald Square, New York, showing a Roman chariot race, ran for four years and lured uncounted thousands of sightseers to New York. A Wrigley's sign of vast brilliance and complexity, installed during the First World War, ran for eight years. Millions who have never visited New York know, through the cinema or through illustrated magazines, that Times Square is dominated by Wrigley and Chevrolet signs; an unseen audience which no Traffic Audit Bureau can count.

'Electric spectaculars' on the major scale are launched with something of the ceremony associated with a first night, or with the naming of a ship. Dinners are held and toasts are drunk.

Though Times Square, New York, may well be the most ruthlessly exploited area in the world it is impossible not to be awed by the wild exuberance of light, by the blinding multi-coloured cliffs soaring skywards, dripping with fire. 'Magnificent— if only one could not read!' is said to have been G. K. Chesterton's comment. It is a sad thought that a savage's dream of beauty should resolve itself, in the mind of literate man, into a boast by the Supreme Pants Company.

If the electric sign advertisers ever decided to call off this free entertainment, it would probably pay the city of New York to run the signs on its own account. The situation seems unlikely to arise. Both the advertisers and the city authorities are proud that, on a clear night, the red glow in the sky above Broadway is visible some fifty miles out to sea.

THE SKY'S THE LIMIT

THE idea of advertising on the sky had been a popular joke for generations. Between the world wars, like many popular jokes, it became a reality.

In 1886 *Punch* had published a cartoon showing a plain blunt business man and his wife gazing at the night sky. The wife was rhapsodizing over the beauty of the full moon, but the husband was sighing for lost opportunities. If only the moon had 'Blokey's Pickles' printed across it . . .

Also in the 'eighties, Villiers de L'Isle Adam wrote an extravaganza entitled 'L'Affichage Céleste' in his *Contes Cruels*. In this story the night sky became a hoarding, on which the Great Bear was embarrassed to find between her paws the legend, 'Faut-il des corsets, oui ou non?' and on the cluster of Virgo an angel appeared holding a flask and saying, 'Dieu, que c'est bon!' On seeing these mirific visions in the sky, the brawling citizens of Lyons and Bordeaux were so impressed that they forgot even the bitterest family feuds and sat down amiably together to study the new wonders of the firmament.

Villiers de L'Isle Adam may well have been inspired to this fantasy by a news item of the day, for inventors were already busy with monstrous lanterns. In 1893 a cloud projector was set up on the roof of the Manufactures Building at the Chicago Exhibition; it was used to announce how many people had visited the Fair during the day. At the close of the Exhibition it was installed on the roof of the Pulitzer building in New York. When there were no clouds it was necessary to make them—with the aid of high-exploding rockets.

Inventors continued to experiment along these lines, but little more was heard of sky advertising until the period between the world wars. Then four main types of sky publicity were to be distinguished: smoke-writing, cloud projection, sky-shouting, and banner-towing. Much of this enterprise outraged the sensitive, but among the bulk of the population each new assault on the firmament provoked little more than an ingenuous admiration for man's ingenuity.

A glimpse of what was to come was apparent as soon as the First World War ended. In Britain were hundreds of unwanted military aircraft, thousands of unwanted pilots. It was not long before units of this disintegrated air force began to fly on less heroic missions. As early as 1919 the Air Ministry was appealing to the public to report all instances of pilots dropping leaflets and other advertising matter. The Ministry also sought to prevent pilots from covering their registration marks with advertisements pasted or painted over wings and fuselage. Some pilots did not even pause to remove the military markings from their machines before taking wing in the service of commerce. But painting slogans on aircraft was too primitive a method of advertising; moreover, aircraft had to be flown dangerously low for the messages to be read. And the public gradually tired of the novelty of scrambling for coloured leaflets fluttering from the skies.

Smoke writing was the first effective form of aerial advertising. In Britain it was taken up with eagerness and much self-congratulation by the *Daily Mail*, and was used with startling effect above the heads of the Derby crowds in 1922. Delightedly, the *Daily Mail* next day devoted its leading columns to a description of its own enterprise. Readers were told that the invention, full details of which could not be divulged, was that of Major J. C. Savage, late Royal Flying Corps, who had been experimenting since 1913. He and his pilot, Captain Cyril Turner, had spent more than three months 'learning to write and think backwards,' for the technique was not the same as for ordinary writing. The machine used was a Sweep racing aircraft, and the total length of the letters traced was ten miles. Writing the words took two minutes and the effect lasted for five. As soon as the multitude saw the letters 'Dail——,' according to the report, they burst into a chorus of 'Daily Mail!' From no other daily newspaper was such enterprise to be expected. The spectacle was said to have caused wide satisfaction over eighty square miles.

Next day the feat was repeated over London, the trace being seen by 3,000,000 people over an area of a hundred square miles (how this was calculated was not made clear). A number of children

in a north London school wrote to the *Daily Mail* expressing gratitude for this handsome entertainment, and a schoolmaster quoted one of his younger pupils as saying, 'Is it an angel writing in the sky?' The public were eagerly debating how the trick was performed. In answer to inquiries, the *Daily Mail* explained that the pilot did not loop the loop. The writing was all done on a horizontal plane, except for an occasional deviation to avoid smudging part of a letter already written. Captain Turner disclosed that writing a large 'D' was child's play; the really difficult letter was the small 'y.' *Daily Mail* cartoonists quickly made capital out of the new invention. One drawing showed holidaymakers idling at the seaside, while an aircraft labelled 'hostile' traced the word 'Danger' overhead. Only a few months after the words 'Daily Mail' had been triumphantly scrawled across the firmament, the creator of that newspaper died.

Although the skies of Britain rarely offer a suitable background for skywriting, the *Daily Mail* and Major Savage persevered. In the summer of 1924 the familiar advertisement was being written over nearly a score of seaside towns. That same year readers of the newspaper were invited to admire a photograph of St. Paul's with 'Daily Mail' proudly scrawled above the dome. The *Daily Mail* also published a large photograph taken in the grounds of the Danish Embassy in London, showing the King of Denmark excitedly pointing out the smoke-writing aircraft to his guests. The inscription which so captured the royal interest was executed in 'huge, flame-coloured letters.'

Little public controversy seems to have been roused at this stage by smoke-writing, which indeed inspired in most people only an ungrudged admiration for the skill of the pilot. The eyesore, if eyesore it was, was quickly dissipated on the breeze. In support of the practice it could be—and was—argued that skilled pilots were kept in training at no cost to the State. It was also hinted that the Air Ministry was keenly interested in the signalling and smoke-laying possibilities of the invention.

A less friendly reception—in some quarters, at least—was accorded to the practice of cloud projection, in which notable technical advances were made soon after 1930. One method involved inserting a stencil into a beam of light, another employed an elaborate system of mirrors.

Early in 1931 there were reports that Alfred Ganthier, of New

York, was working out the final details of a 91,000,000 candle power projector capable of projecting an advertisement fifty miles. Clouds were unnecessary; the message appeared as if fixed in the beam, at a predetermined range. One experimental message was projected over Brooklyn Bridge and a larger one over New Jersey. A rumour gained currency among the watching crowds that bootleggers had discovered a new method of signalling to ships at sea.

That same year strange signs began to appear in the night sky of England; and once again it turned out that Major J. C. Savage was the brains behind the venture. On the first day of 1932 *The Times* printed an enthusiastic article by its aviation correspondent describing Major Savage's methods. Messages flung on the clouds were clearly legible six or seven miles away, 'and in one case where the operator followed the last retreating cloud towards the eastern horizon the legend cast upon it was read fifteen miles away.' The aviation correspondent thought that there could be little criticism on the grounds of amenities, for the curious reason that the message 'occupies comparatively little space.' He pointed out, almost in the same breath, that there was nothing to stop projectors being mounted in tandem. 'The best conditions,' he said, 'are given by high solid clouds with a clean regular base.'

This New Year message of cheer was sourly received by readers of *The Times*. Indeed, one of the first to condemn such enterprise was *The Times*' own leader writer. The best he could say for the invention was that it might be of some use in time of war, by throwing a grid of light over a raiding aircraft, to help anti-aircraft gunners. Otherwise, the idea was intolerable. 'If it is sentimental to object to the use of the sky as a billposting station, let us be sentimental and proud of it. . . . Best of all would be a Government declaration that this was an indecent form of advertisement to which no civilized nation ought to be subjected and that it was therefore unconditionally forbidden.' Mr. Lionel Curtis wrote protesting against 'the most comprehensive vulgarization of Nature that the wit of man can devise.' Professor G. M. Trevelyan thought that a project of this kind would 'brutalize life,' and urged a Government inquiry. Then the legal issue was raised. Miss A. Mure Mackenzie wrote: 'The law forbids anyone to hang up in my garden an advertisement of, say, pills. Will it permit anyone to hang it above my head on a surface which belongs to me in common with the rest of the nation?' The answer from Lord Dunedin was not encouraging: 'He who owns a plot of the soil owns all that is above and below it; a tapering wedge towards the centre of the earth, an expanding wedge towards the heavens.' Unfortunately, he said, it was not possible to plot accurately the individual's portion of sky infringed by an advertiser.

Not all those who joined in the correspondence were hostile to the new invention. Sir A. Verdon-Roe said that 'if the unimaginative are to have their way and crush the activities of the progressive, we are finished as a nation. England owes her present position to the enterprise of men like Major Savage. This hysterical outburst reminds me of the outcry raised against railways when they were first suggested.'

Major Savage was soon to have an opportunity to defend his brainchild, for the agitation in *The Times* resulted in the appointment that year of a Select Committee on Skywriting. His arguments appear to have greatly impressed the committee. What was the difference in principle, he asked, between smoke-writing and cloud writing, that one should incur such odium? 'The younger generation regard the sky as a thing of utility.'

Major Savage then told how men had striven to make cloud projection a reality in the previous century, when the first patents were taken out. There had been much experimenting in Europe by the firms of Zeiss, Leitz, Goerz, and Galileo, and also by firms in America. During the past ten years he and his associated companies had sent up sky-writing aircraft into the skies of America, France, Belgium, Canada, Cuba, Holland, Norway, Germany, Austria, Hungary, Poland, Italy, and Australia. 'We were the first ex-enemy airmen to fly in Germany after the war. . . . There was a magnificent chance for someone to complain terrifically, but we received no complaint at all.' Instead, the Germans had shown enormous enthusiasm for this novelty, and displays had been given over every German town of more than 5,000 population.

Major Savage said that he had inserted advertisements in English newspapers inviting the public to say what they thought of his advertisements projected on the clouds. With one exception, the replies were all favourable. He produced a box containing 1,600 letters, of which specimen tributes were 'I saw the most wonderful writing in the sky,' and 'I have never seen such a beautiful advertisement.' When asked whether he really thought that a very large number of the population would welcome a message on the clouds 'Buy Baxter's Pills and Cure Constipation,' the inventor said, 'I often wonder why it is that when approaching this question my opponents always think of the most beastly kind of slogan.'

The committee went to some pains to elicit from Major Savage exactly what type of image he could throw on to the sky. 'A beautiful glass of beer, for example?' suggested one member. The Major replied that he could project only a very simple silhouette. But another witness, Major C. F. Davey, M.C., of Sky Publicity Ltd., said he could transmit coloured images; and, as an illustration of his firm's virtuosity, he added: 'We can put a clock in the sky with the hands keeping time.' From this, the least imaginative could begin to visualize moving pictures in the sky.

One of the witnesses who unreservedly opposed sky projection was the Dean of Westminster. Asked whether he would object to the clouds on a dull day being 'fretted with golden fire,' he said he would not mind so long as the fire was Nature's own— 'the clouds are no less beautiful than the rest of the sky.' A suggestion was made that prayers or texts might be projected in the sky. To this the Dean's comment was that such a development would be the one thing needed to give Christianity its quietus in Britain. As for the charge that he was condemning something he had never seen, the Dean answered that he did not need to see a drunk man to know that he ought not to be drunk.

Another witness, Sir Leslie Scott, K.C., was asked whether he would object to the sight of a rainbow in the sky. He countered with the story of the small boy who, on seeing a rainbow for the first time, asked his mother what kind of pills were being advertised.

Stung by the Dean of Westminster's evidence, Major Savage reappeared before the committee to point out that the Dean seemed to forget the enormous service once rendered to Christianity by a sign in the heavens. In A.D. 300 had not Constantine seen a flaming cross in the sky inscribed 'In This Sign Conquer,' and thereafter become a convert to Christianity? Then Major Savage played his trump card; he himself had been invited in his professional capacity to project texts in the night sky over

Dublin, for the benefit of the Eucharistic Congress, and though a Nonconformist he was prepared to accept the contract. It was a dark hour for the Dean of Westminster.

The committee, announcing their findings, declared that they were 'not much impressed by the evidence of persons as to the hideousness of a sight which they had never witnessed.' Their view was that sky projection—

. . . forms a relief to the squalor of the poorest streets and to the dull monotony of many others. It is open to question whether the leaden gloom of heavy clouds will be seriously desecrated by the loom of an unseen light. It is not necessary, unless one wishes to do so, to follow the beam to its termination. In fact this form of advertising may be less obtrusive and therefore less offensive than brilliantly lit signs or buildings at such a level that the eye cannot avoid seeing them without being lowered to the ground.

The only restrictions proposed by the committee were that advertisements should not be projected on the sky in rural areas, or in the vicinity of famous buildings, or on Sundays. All in all it was a victory for the 'progressive' over the 'unimaginative.' Cloud projection continued on a modest scale and created no more furores.

The committee's terms of reference had included an inquiry into sky-shouting, an art which had been practised in America, Sweden, and Italy, but not as yet in Britain. After some difficulty, a witness was found who had experienced this form of attack from the receiving end. 'Suddenly you will hear a voice from heaven shouting "Smoke Old Gold," and then you will hear a bit of music. It is very discouraging to any mental application,' the witness said. This time the committee were ready to condemn what they had not experienced. Sky-shouting, they said, would be 'an unnecessary and intolerable imposition,' and they were pleased to note that it appeared to have met with little commercial success.

Sky-shouting, it is worth noting, did not always meet with 'consumer resistance.' When readers of the *New York Times*, in the summer of 1933, were debating whether the practice should be tolerated, a Brooklyn resident told how he and his wife had been so impressed by a sales talk from a low-flying aircraft that his wife had gone out and bought the article advertised. 'I would rather listen for a moment to such a message and have it over with, instead of tuning in on my radio and being compelled to listen to many minutes of blah about Ajax Dog Blubber in order to hear a good dance orchestra.'[1]

Meanwhile, a new method of sky advertising was being pioneered—banner-towing. One of the first demonstrations, perhaps the first, was held at Hanworth Air Park in July 1930 (in the same month that a dirigible inscribed 'Advertise by airship' flew over London). Royal Air Force aircraft had been towing gunnery sleeves for some years; now, with the devising of a paravane, it had been found possible to tow a long advertising banner, steadily and safely. Flown at 3,000 feet, the banner could be read (or so it was optimistically claimed) eight miles away. The cost was £100 an hour; minimum charter, five hours. Banner-towing aircraft were not widely used, however, until four or five years later. At first the public response was the usual one of admiration for man's ingenuity, rather than regret at his talent for importunity. Then, as the novelty began to wear off, there were many complaints that pilots flew too low over cities and too intrusively over public gatherings. It was even suggested that the aircraft companies deliberately put old and noisy aircraft on to this service, in order to be sure of competing successfully with urban noises. Derby Day seems to have encouraged pilots to audacities. They were cautioned against flying low over the London Zoo, lest they should stampede animals carrying children. One pilot was carpeted for flying in the vicinity of a Buckingham Palace garden party; he was dismissed with a caution. Not so lucky was the pilot who towed a banner over the City of Manchester during the Two Minutes Silence on November 11, 1937; he was fined £3.

One man who clamoured for action against low-flying advertising aircraft was Mr. (now Sir) Alan Herbert. *Hansard* for July 11, 1938, contains this *cri de cœur*:

Mr. A. P. Herbert: I was unable to hear your last ruling but five,

---

[1] Sky shouting has since been employed in various ways for non-commercial ends. During the Second World War General Mark Clark, United States Army, when hovering over his North African headquarters, used to shout down for his car to be sent to the airport. In Korea in 1951 Easter messages were shouted from aircraft by U.S. chaplains to front-line troops. The device has also been used over Australian bathing beaches to give warnings of sharks.

Mr. Speaker, owing to an advertising aeroplane passing across the
sky. Can you give orders that our proceedings shall not be disturbed
in this manner?

No reply was given. That year Mr. Herbert introduced a
private Bill to abolish aerial advertising, but it was lost in the
press of Parliamentary business.

Finally the practice of banner-towing came up for review by
an Air Ministry committee set up late in 1938 under Lord Gorell
to consider the control of flying. According to the committee,
the reports of disturbance by banner-towing aircraft were somewhat exaggerated, but the members agreed that there were many
people who thought this form of advertisement added 'an unnecessary quota to the burden of noises that have to be endured.' Some
witnesses had called it an indecency to use the sky for the benefit
of the few. The committee recommended that no more aircraft
should be licensed for banner-towing, and that the licences of
aircraft so employed should not be renewed after October 1, 1941.
By that date there were more urgent problems than the control
of aerial advertising.

After the war no petrol was available for aerial publicity
until the spring of 1950. Then banner-towing aircraft began to
reappear over British towns. On April 19, 1951, the *Advertiser's
Weekly* noted the formation of a new company boasting 'the
longest banner ever towed with a different message on each side,
giving up to two miles of readability on either side of the line of
flight.'

In post-war America aerial advertisers were able to resume
their activities more quickly. Over New York by night cruised
neon-lighted blimps advertising films, and by day sky-writers
tried out new rainbow smokes. According to Mr. Don Iddon, at
one stage the competition was such that when a pilot wrote his
appeal to 'Buy so-and-so,' a rival pilot went up to inscribe the
word 'Don't' in front of it.

In 1950 it was announced that the words 'Pepsi-Cola' had been
written by as many as six aircraft in formation over 5,000 communities from Canada to Venezuela.

THE TORTURED AIR

WHEN G. K. Chesterton complained that man had vulgarized Infinity, he may have had in mind the words 'Daily Mail' traced in the firmament above the dome of St. Paul's, or he may have been thinking of the thousand unseen advertisements bombinating in the void—the radio messages flashing from beyond the sunset to warn mankind against pink toothbrush and athlete's foot.

In America, advertising on the ether began nervously, haphazardly, some thirty years ago. Now there is a long and impressive list of countries in which—to quote the tactful phrase of an advertising impresario—'the spoken word is at the advertiser's service.'[1] In Britain the story is largely one of how the advertiser was frustrated. Here it will be convenient to review, first, the growth of the American system.

At the outset, broadcasting on both sides of the Atlantic was the sport of amateurs. Even before the First World War ended, enthusiasts in America had begun playing gramophone records over the air, with or without credit to their local retailers. In 1920 came the event which roused Americans to the potentialities of the new toy: the broadcasting by Station KDKA (Pittsburg) of the presidential election results. The boom began. Within a year some 500 licences to operate broadcasting stations were requested and granted. A large proportion of these licences went to operators whose chief concern was to sell radio sets; others were taken up by educational and religious bodies, newspapers, and department stores. Notable in the throng was Station WEAF, operated by the American Telephone and Telegraph Company, which was willing

---

[1] These countries include Argentina, Austria, Australia, Brazil, Canada, Chile, Eire, Federated Malay States, Italy, Kenya, Mexico, New Zealand, Portugal, Spain, Union of South Africa.

to hire out its transmitter to any firm or organization wanting to provide a programme.

By 1923 there was near-chaos on the American ether, caused by nothing but the multiplicity of transmitters. In the listener's earphones sounded a crude charivari, a tumult of shouting and counter-shouting, of name-calling and deliberate jamming. The public had been assured that broadcasting was an invention not less important than printing, but at least printers did not print their messages on top of each other's sheets. Yet what redress had the listener? He had paid no licence fee, so he could not complain to his Government that he was being defrauded. At length the operators themselves grew tired of shouting each other down. There was only one course, and that a distasteful one: they themselves must ask the Government to intervene. Thereupon, President Harding appointed Mr. Herbert Hoover as arbiter of wavelengths, and some semblance of order was brought to the ether. 'Wave jumping' continued, however, until in 1927 a Federal Radio Commission was set up to enforce order and decency.

From the beginning, there was much wrangling as to whether advertising should be allowed. On one plane were those listeners who thought it blasphemy that the cry of the salesman should be allowed to beat against the very gates of heaven. Others were content to look on broadcasting as merely another amenity devised by science for man's amusement and advantage. It was only right, they argued, that a capitalist who met the heavy cost of a radio entertainment should be allowed to mention the product he manufactured. Opinions varied as to whether he should be allowed to give a sales talk about that product (even today there are firms which are content with the briefest mention, their concern being primarily to generate goodwill, as distinct from directly effecting sales). Others felt that a sponsor might be permitted to describe his product, but should be restrained from mentioning its price. Others again thought it permissible to include 'commericals' in daytime, but not in the evenings. Still others were prepared to tolerate a sponsor lauding his product, but drew the line at the non-sponsoring advertiser who leapt in, between changes in programme, with an irritating one-minute harangue.

What stimulated the growth of advertising on the air was the formation of networks, the first of which began to take shape in 1923–24. Many station operators had found that the maintenance of day-to-day programmes was a heavier commitment than they had expected, and were only too anxious to be taken under the wing of a resourceful parent body. As the 'hook-up' idea caught on, those national advertisers who had been reluctant to buy time from impecunious stations with no discernible following realized that there was a new mass public for the exploiting. In 1926 the National Broadcasting Corporation's network was set up, in the following year that of the Columbia Broadcasting System. The first big network show was the Eveready Hour, with a popular programme of light music and drama. Advertising agencies, which at first had displayed little interest in the possibilities of broadcasting, now began to recognize where the profits of the future lay.

One of the tasks of the Federal Radio Commission was to establish the principle that the ether was not a lake in which any American had the right to fish at whim. In fact, the lake was the property of the community and was to be fished in only by those holding a licence, and in accordance with strict rules. If any fisherman abused, or did not take advantage of, his privilege, his licence could be revoked. When it tried to enforce the decencies, the Federal Radio Commission soon found itself accused by the broadcasting interests of being harsh, meddlesome, and irresponsible; while those who still hoped to make an honest woman of broadcasting belaboured the Commission for irresolution and timidity in the face of vested interests. In its own time, and in its own way, the Commission began to tackle the seamier side of commercial broadcasting, in which it was assisted by the swindle-hunting Federal Trade Commission. The ether at an early stage had become a happy hunting-ground of the medicine men. Whereas the old-time quack had run the risk of being thrown into a horse trough if he overplayed his hand, his successor had merely to possess himself of a microphone and broadcast his humbug, with impunity, across a State. In 1930 the Federal Radio Commission was not the only official body to close in on John R. Brinkley, the 'goat gland specialist,' who for years had used his radio station at Milford, Kansas, to lure to his hospital persons willing to pay $750 for a 'rejuvenating' operation. In 1929 he began to prescribe treatments over the air for those who wrote in describing their symptoms. These patients were directed to druggists belonging to the Brinkley Pharmaceutical Association, an organization with 500 members in Kansas, Oklahoma, and Nebraska. Soon doctors began to lose their patients and Brinkley found himself under attack. His 'goat gland' operation was denounced as a fake. Brinkley was able to produce a long, indeed an endless, string of witnesses—including prominent figures in banking and oil—to testify that they had had their money's worth from the operation. Reluctantly, the State Medical Board agreed to watch Brinkley conduct two operations—from goat to user—but they revoked his licence to practise medicine next day without waiting to see the results of the operations. Then the Federal Radio Commission revoked his licence to operate a radio station. Brinkley, who had powerful supporters, announced that he would appeal to the public. To dramatize the issue, he decided to run as independent candidate for the governorship of Kansas, and it seemed probable that there would be a political upset of some magnitude. However, Brinkley eventually sold his station and crossed the Rio Grande into Mexico, where he continued to broadcast defiantly from a new station.

Another broadcaster to be disciplined by the Federal Radio Commission was one nicknamed 'the Oregon wildcat,' who in 1930 was alleged to have used 'indecent, obscene, profane and objectionable' language over station KVEP, in the course of nightly attacks on the chain stores. The Federal Radio Commission also attacked lottery organizers, fortune tellers, tipsters, and—as the *New York Times* had suggested—matrimonial racketeers. In 1934 the commission was reorganized and renamed the Federal Communications Commission, but still continued to draw abuse from both sides.

Even in the late 'twenties there were many and bitter complaints about the importunities of advertisers on the radio; but sponsors had begun to find new formulae of light entertainment which beguiled the masses to the extent that they were prepared to tolerate a certain measure of salesmanship in order to continue receiving it. Pioneer programmes in point were the Rudy Vallee show, in which well-known personalities were brought to the microphone by Fleishman's Yeast, and the Amos 'n' Andy programme, presented by Pepsodent. In the years immediately following came amateur talent shows, quizzes, and give-away programmes, all of which caught the popular imagination. Were not these entertainments brought to the home at no cost, whereas listeners in Britain were forced to pay a pound a year for programmes of notorious dullness? More serious-minded Americans, watching the give-away programmes grow into a national frenzy, suspected by now that they had been cheated. The radio industry was firmly in the hands of advertisers, and advertisers were concerned only to reach the largest mass audiences. It followed therefore that the great bulk of programmes would be light, popular, and unlikely to inspire thought or controversy. Radio, in short, was only a time-filling interval between bouts of salesmanship. True, the Columbia Broadcasting System could point to its New York Philharmonic Orchestra and the National Broadcasting Corporation could boast its Toscanini, but these were only the show pieces.

Llewellyn White, in *The American Radio*, sums up the conquest of the American ether by the advertiser as follows:

Like the beleaguered Czechs of ancient Bohemia, the broadcasters had cried out for succour. Like the Hapsburgs, the advertising men who came to rescue remained to rule. And, like many a philosophical Slav, the broadcasters accepted the conqueror's tongue.

When the 1929 crash came, the grip of the advertiser on the radio networks began to tighten. There were goods to be moved, and they *had* to be moved—even if it meant driving a coach and four through one Code of Ethics after another. Hitherto sales talk had been mostly straightforward, and not over-aggressive. Sometimes the announcer suggested, with elaborate diffidence, that if the audience had enjoyed the programme, they might like to show their appreciation by trying such-and-such next time they needed a toothpaste. Now the sales talk became brisker and brasher and highly supercharged, with that urgent, machine-gun delivery made familiar by the American sports commentator. To save their audiences from becoming punch-drunk under this kind of attack, some networks began to limit the number of words which could be spoken in a minute. A contrasting technique was to hire a voice which was lush, leisured, plummy, and avuncular, seemingly steeped in worldly wisdom.

Next came an attempt to dramatize the 'commercial,' to make it forceful or amusing in itself. Listeners heard the sound of a girl sobbing over a cancelled date, and a motherly voice tactfully counselling a change of face powder. Now, in all its horror, was heard the conversation at that blighted dinner party when the wife offered a cheap table napkin to her husband's boss. One excursion into dramatization was discouraged by the networks, however; the broadcasting of an after-dinner 'burp,' to point the need for taking somebody's cure for indigestion.

The trail-blazers began to show increasing effrontery in tying in the 'commercial' with the subject-matter of the programme—the 'integrated plug,' as it was elegantly called. This practice inspired a lesser volume of execration than it merited, and it persists to the present day. Sometimes the 'plug' itself was guyed, as in this excerpt from a comedy programme (quoted, with apparent approval, in *Advertising Copywriting*)[1]:

'Messieurs, ze duel shall begin now and shall end when you hear "*touché*." '
'What do you mean, *touché*?'
'I mean to shay that Swift's Premier Ham is the ham that's brown-sugar cured to give it a fine flavour. . . .'

From making a joke of the 'plug' it was only a short step to making a joke of the product, a fashion which has also continued to the present day. But 'ribbing the product' had its perils. Not every sponsor was a Henry Ford, willing to listen to a joke against himself, day in, day out.

In the early days the 'commercials' had been delivered by the sponsor's own hireling. Now the performers themselves were called upon to praise the product. Even popular (and high-salaried) idols like Bing Crosby and Gene Autry had to be ready and willing to sandwich in their patter items like this (again from *Advertising Copywriting*):

AUTRY: I won't interrupt you again.
CROSBY: Good! Because what I am going to say now is too important to interrupt. So listen closely. Friends, there is only one genuine Wrigley's Spearmint Gum and it always has the name Wrigley's clearly printed on the package. Look for it!
AUTRY: For my taste there's nothing else that can match the refreshin' Doublemint Flavour. It always gives me a welcome lift. And I get a lot of enjoyment out of Doublemint's pleasant, smooth chewin', too.

In 'tear-jerking' plays, characters who suffered ruin or sudden

[1] By Philip Ward Burton, Bowman Kreer and John B. Gray.

death would sometimes return to life a few moments later to take part in a commercial charade; which was as disruptive of mood as the lining-up of the corpses to take a bow at the close of *Hamlet*.

Not only popular entertainers were called upon to endorse the product; so were news announcers, military commentators, members of brains trusts, and counsellors on human problems. Much sophistry has been expended in an effort to justify the practice. The leader-writer, it is argued, writes what his employer tells him to write. Why should the broadcaster quarrel with his script? Perhaps the answer is that the leader-writer does not punctuate his diagnosis of the world's ills with praise of cures for 'draggle-top' and 'five o'clock shadow.'[1]

The attitude of many performers seemed to be: 'The show must go on, and we know it's a good show, so let's get the "plug" over as painlessly and entertainingly as possible.' Some artists found difficulty in delivering the more fatuous blurbs convincingly, and the impression—in the words of one critic—was that 'of a school bully reciting Mary's Little Lamb.' The surprising thing was that so many top-ranking performers contrived to say their lines as if they believed them.

The 'integrated plug' was not infrequently used in the 'soap operas' which began to go out over the air in the nineteen-thirties. These daytime serials, on which James Thurber has written long and devastatingly, were directed by the soap firms at the less intelligent housewife, who would listen to three or four of them daily as she went about her domestic chores. Churned out by battered cynics, the serials were designed to give frustrated wives the maximum opportunities for self-identification with the dreary, unhappy, and self-sacrificing heroines. The mental level of some of the listeners was such that they would send telegrams and bunches of grapes to the fictitious heroine when the writer involved her in a traffic accident. To the soap-sellers, it seemed a fair certainty that, if the heroine of a soap opera were made to endorse a certain soap, the listeners would carry self-identification to the point of imitation. Which they did.

Criticism of soap operas came from 'sophisticated urban

[1] In 1942, however, an association of news broadcasters passed a resolution calling on their members to refuse to interlard their news bulletins with 'commercials.'

elements,' but the soap firms could afford to ignore it; just as the manufacturers of 'yummy' or explosive breakfast foods could afford to ignore the criticism that they were corrupting the child listener, and filling a million homes with 'box-top jitters.'

At the end of the 'thirties, the networks surrendered unconditionally to the 'singing commercial.' A two-man team launched the craze with a verse in praise of Pepsi-Cola, fitted to a swing version of John Peel. This verse—

> Pepsi-Cola hits the spot,
> Two full bottles, that's a lot.
> Twice as much, and better, too—
> Pepsi-Cola is the drink for you!

was soon the scourge of the continent. In 1941 it was played 296,426 times over 469 stations. The public were even willing to put nickels into 'juke-boxes' in order to hear it. Soon the ether was full of maddening jingles, many of them composed by the same pair of writers. Few were so simple and catchy as Pepsi-Cola's. But the nation which had obstinately revelled in the 'singing telegram' had no intention of lightly forsaking the 'singing commercial.'

Another popular fashion was to give 'commercials' the Sonovox treatment. Anyone unfamiliar with this curious invention may find himself in the same predicament as a blind child listening to the description of a tree. In brief, Sonovox made birds, beasts, foghorns, and locomotives *talk*. It even went as far as to make them sing. On behalf of Lifebuoy, a foghorn achieved the noteworthy feat of enunciating 'Beeee Ooooh.' The manufacturers of Bromo-Seltzer, having been persuaded that the name of their product repeated over and over was the sort of noise a locomotive makes when it gathers speed, were further persuaded to allow the Sonovox experts a free hand. The result was a talking locomotive, which puffed into the programme to the delight of all small boys (who were the least likely, however, to be interested in the product itself).

Since the big advertiser likes to be confronted with charts and graphs showing that his appropriations are being scientifically spent, the most strenuous and ingenious efforts were made in America to measure 'listener reaction' to different programmes. Fan mail was too easily manufactured to be a reliable index to the popularity of a broadcast. In the mid-'thirties the firm of C. E. Hooper, Inc., organized a system whereby snap checks were made by telephone on listeners selected at random from the telephone directory. John Doe would be called to the telephone and asked, successively, whether he had been listening in, if so to what programme, and over which network, and finally, 'Who sponsored the programme?' Having satisfied the inquisition, he would be at liberty to return to his radio to hear the rest of the programme; though it was always possible that he might be called to the telephone again by a Hooper supervisor anxious to check that the firm's interviewers had been doing their job conscientiously.

Much importance began to be attached by radio advertisers to their 'Hooperatings.' But in due course other methods were devised of assessing the pull of radio advertising. The A. C. Nielsen Company fitted 'audimeters' to receiving sets in listeners' homes, and by this means obtained a traced record of all those periods during which the radio was in use. Another idea was to instal an 'ear' which could transmit the sound from a receiving set by telephone wire to a central switchboard, where monitors could check which programme was in most demand. Critics of these ingenious devices (which would appear to have a future in totalitarian lands) pointed out that there was no proof that anyone was *listening* to, or enjoying the radio during the periods when it was switched on. Possibly Junior was revelling in the programme while the rest of the family were writhing. But if these recorders showed that a large number of sets were switched on or off at a given time, appropriate conclusions could often be drawn.

It was one thing to check on the popularity of the programme after it had been broadcast. To some, the smart thing seemed to be to check on its merits *before* it was broadcast. Methods of pre-testing advertising copy have already been described in an earlier chapter. Radio advertisers also seated their guinea-pigs before buttons labelled 'like' and 'dislike' and played over the programme to them, afterwards analysing the synchronous record of pleasures and aversions. Not surprisingly this method of producing pre-digested entertainment has been a subject for satire, but it is not likely to be abandoned so long as there are sponsors—and there are many—whose chief consideration is that no programme shall cause offence to anybody.

The layman, glancing through text-books on American radio advertising, cannot but marvel at the lengths to which programme research and inquiry into consumers' habits are carried. He will find, for instance, charts showing what percentage of housewives in the Eastern Time Zone are engaged in ironing, washing-up, tending children or performing toilet at any time between 8 a.m. and 5 p.m.; or diagrams 'showing recall by New York women of advertising for gelatine desserts in various media in 1947'; also figures proving that mystery stories are more popular than serials in big cities, with the moral:

Consider how much more effective the mystery story would be for decaffeinated coffee (a big city product), and how much more efficient the serial would be for baking powder (a small town product).

There was a period when advertisers feared that intrusive 'commercials' might defeat their purpose by antagonizing listeners. Nowadays they worry no more. Expert after expert has assured them that there is nothing to be lost, and much to be gained, by annoying the listener. 'Some of the most effective radio selling has been, and is being, done by commercials that seem to get the most negative comment,' say the authors of *Advertising Copywriting*. In *Modern Radio Advertising* Charles Hull Wolfe says: 'Make your announcement either intensely liked or intensely disliked.' There is no need to worry, he says, when 'people repeat your commercial in slightly derisive mimicry.' In any case, irritation over 'commercials' is 'largely momentary.' Aesop Glim, in *Copy—The Core of Advertising*, warns that the technique of irritation should be employed only in a programme of high merit. 'The show creates its goodwill—and a corresponding degree of tolerance in the hearts of its audience. Then the droning commercials go to work—like drills. They are geared to eat up 70 per cent to 90 per cent of that tolerance, but are not supposed to pass 100 per cent.'

Be this as it may, there would appear to be a sufficient number of individuals with a dislike of 'commercials' to encourage inventors in the production of gadgets designed to tune out 'plugs,' or to switch off the set for one minute when a 'commercial' is imminent. The advertiser can afford to overlook these perverse inventions, for he can produce graphic evidence to show that some listeners (not necessarily children) prefer the 'commercials' to the programmes—just as thousands of persons prefer the advertisements in a magazine to the editorial contents. He can also produce statistics of polls showing that only a very small proportion of the American public would be willing to pay a licence fee rather than tolerate 'commercials.'

BRITANNIA DEFENSIVE

How did Britain contrive to thwart commercialism on the ether? There are some who believe that only the intransigence of Mr. J. C. W. (now Lord) Reith kept the advertiser at bay, in those early days at Savoy Hill. Others prefer to think that it was the innate decency and good sense of the British public that prevented the profanation of a new cultural medium. Captain P. P. Eckersley, one time Chief Engineer of the B.B.C., has another theory: 'Commercial broadcasting would undoubtedly have been instituted in Britain had it not been for the wavelength shortage.'[1]

In the aftermath of the First World War, broadcasting seems to have been regarded by the Government as a tiresome child which kept making exasperating noises while its elders were trying to speak. It had to be held sternly in check, and the Postmaster-General was the man answerable for its good behaviour. On sufferance, the Marconi Company was allowed to broadcast an amateur service, which amused the broadcasters as much as it did its audience. When, on a summer's day in 1920, the company broadcast the voice of Melba, the Postmaster-General's department is said to have complained that wireless telegraphy was being used for frivolous ends. Soon many requests began to be made for permission to set up broadcasting stations; among them were applications from big stores and national newspapers. These requests were flatly turned down. It is an interesting speculation how British broadcasting might have developed if, say, the *Daily Express* and the *Daily Mail* had been given permission to set up the stations they wished to operate.

The precocious infant could not be held back indefinitely, however, and eventually the decision was taken to allow the radio manufacturers, as being those most interested, to form a single broadcasting company, and to transmit programmes likely to

[1] *The Power Behind the Microphone.*

encourage the public to buy receiving sets. The question of advertising had been anxiously considered. Sir Henry Norman, who was chairman of the Wireless Sub-Committee of the Imperial Communications Committee, wrote in *The Times* of May 8–9, 1922: 'Of course every big retail house would like to shout the merits and low prices of its taffetas and tulles, its shirts and shoes. There is no room for this.' The British Broadcasting Company was set up later in the year, and Mr. J. C. W. Reith became its general manager in December.

In the following year the Sykes Committee on Broadcasting heard evidence on the desirability or otherwise of allowing advertising on the air. The newspaper proprietors had worked themselves up to a tense pitch on this topic. Lord Riddell, their spokesman, said that it was difficult to imagine anything more dreadful than that the atmosphere should be filled day and night with announcements of the merits of Beecham's or any other pills. If a firm gave a concert every night, and its name were mentioned each time, said Lord Riddell, that would be a valuable advertisement. 'The Press thinks that means should be devised to prevent this sort of thing. . . . If traders wish to advertise they should confine themselves to the existing methods.'

Lord Riddell even went so far as to claim that radio advertising would be an infringement of 'newspaper rights,' whatever those might be.

The Committee in their Report said:

In newspaper advertising the small advertiser as well as the big gets his chance, but this would not be the case in broadcasting. The time which could be devoted to advertising would in any case be very limited, and therefore exceedingly valuable; and the operating authorities who would want revenue would naturally prefer the big advertiser who was ready to pay highly, with the result that only he would get a chance of advertising. This would be too high a privilege to give to a few big advertisers at the risk of lowering the general standard of advertising.

The Committee thought there would be no objection to the broadcasting company being allowed to accept the gift of a concert and to name the donor; to broadcast the names of song publishers and the prices of their songs; or even to transmit commercial information in code, if it was necessary to augment revenue.

Contrary to the belief of many, sponsored broadcasts did take place in Britain, occasionally, in the early days of broadcasting. One of the first was by Harrod's, in 1923. One of the last was a fashion talk organized by Selfridges from the Eiffel Tower in 1925. Code advertising was never tried; but great liberties were given (and taken) in the naming of plays and theatres, cinemas and films, on the slenderest of pretexts—as indeed they still are.

The British Broadcasting Company became the British Broadcasting Corporation in 1927. Sponsored programmes were still permitted under the terms of its charter, but few if any were broadcast.

The newspaper proprietors were a little happier now. They had scotched, as they thought, a dangerous threat to their well-being. In the entertainment world there had been some apprehension that broadcast programmes of lively quality might keep people at home; but as private enterprise was discouraged from sponsoring programmes, it did not seem that much was to be feared from a sober-minded monopoly sworn to give the public only what was good for them. The public at large worried little over the advertising issue. It had heard that broadcasting in America was constantly and ludicrously interrupted by sales talk. Perhaps it was better to leave British broadcasting in the hands of a benevolent despot.

Potential advertisers were restless, however, and soon they got their chance. In 1930 Captain L. F. Plugge founded his International Broadcasting Company, which began to transmit commercial programmes in English from Radio Normandie. Three years later the Duchy of Luxembourg granted a concession to a French company to broadcast sponsored shows in such languages as it might wish. The Lucerne Convention offered Luxembourg a wavelength which was adequate for its internal needs, but the station 'pirated' a long wavelength which was lying idle. Both stations prospered, and despite a conspiracy of silence in the Press the news got round among the listening public that much livelier programmes of light entertainment were to be obtained, on Sundays especially, from the Continent of Europe. 'Pirate' stations began to multiply, and soon Britain was being bombarded with recorded programmes from a wide radius—from Athlone, Madrid, Hilversum, Toulouse and elsewhere. Many of the programmes were sponsored by well-known American firms, others by American religious bodies. One man who actively hunted radio concessions in Europe was the B.B.C.'s former Chief Engineer, Captain Eckersley. A radio station was an attractive proposition for those bijou states which had hitherto sustained their revenues only by repeatedly changing their stamps and coins; so the scouts were made welcome in places like Andorra and Liechtenstein.

At first the B.B.C. pretended that no one listened to programmes from the Continent, but by 1935 it was vigorously complaining to the Ullswater Committee about unfair competition. The Committee agreed that these foreign broadcasts were undesirable. So did the Postmaster-General; so, finally, did the Government. Then how, asked the critics in Parliament, did the Government propose to prevent the broadcasts?

The pages of *Hansard* in the 'thirties are strewn with question-and-answer on this topic. On February 10, 1936, for instance, Major G. C. Tryon, Postmaster-General, was asked whether he knew that in one recent week more than fifty hours of programmes obviously intended for British listeners had been beamed on this country from the Continent; that they were sponsored by seventy-five different business interests, seven of which were interested in encouraging people to bet. All Major Tryon could say was that the governments of the countries concerned had been asked whether they proposed to take any action. Here Captain L. F. Plugge made a characteristic interjection: 'Is the right hon. and gallant gentleman aware that 61 per cent of British listeners listen to these transmissions and like them?' There was no answer.[1]

On February 7, 1938, when Mr. Eden made a statement similar to that of Major Tryon, Mr. Robert Boothby suggested that it was unwarrantable interference with the liberty of the subject to prevent people from listening to any broadcast in English other than by the B.B.C., provided that it was not a propaganda broadcast. Mr. Eden said that this was not a matter for him.

Captain Eckersley makes acid comments on the efforts of the Foreign Office to persuade foreign governments to show 'a

[1] Captain Plugge's estimate was an optimistic one. Advertising interests put Radio Luxembourg's listening figure at about 4,000,000.
On November 29, 1951, Radio Luxembourg in an advertisement in the *Newspaper World* claimed 5,000,000 British listeners.

decent sort of spirit.' Only the outbreak of the Second World War, he says, interrupted the correspondence, which would otherwise have continued, 'probably on printed forms.' Occasionally there was acrimony between the representatives of Britain and other countries when the question of 'pirate' broadcasts came up at international conventions. At one stage the Postmaster-General had tried to scotch the offenders by withholding line facilities for relaying programmes from Britain. A quick counter-move was the recording of programmes on gramophone records (an arrangement which commended itself to the artists).

All this time the newspapers pretended that no foreign broadcasts were happening. Luxembourg was rarely, if ever, mentioned. The *Sunday Referee* broke the vow of silence and began printing the programmes of Continental stations, for which it suffered excommunication by the Newspaper Proprietors Association. This was a fate not lightly to be suffered (it meant, among other things, distributing editions by motor-cycle), and the newspaper, on promising to fall in line, was later readmitted. The British public continued to tune in Luxembourg and to hum such jingles as 'We are the Ovalteenies.'

The Second World War was hardly over before the controversy flared up anew. A Socialist Government took even graver exception to the broadcasts of the pirate stations. 'Sheer naked exploitation' was a phrase used in July 1946 by Mr. Herbert Morrison to describe the activities of Radio Luxembourg. 'We will do our best not to have commercial broadcasting directed at this country. We do not like this effort of a concern to set up a business in Luxembourg for the purpose of directing broadcasting at this country.' This was one of the many topics on which Mr. Morrison clashed with Mr. Winston Churchill.

Mr. Morrison's words were remembered by Radio Luxembourg and quoted, with due deprecation, in a memorandum to the Committee on Broadcasting in 1949. The directors pointed out that applications by firms to the Bank of England for permission to pay sterling to Radio Luxembourg had recently been blocked, doubtless in order to save foreign exchange, but they felt uneasy 'lest in the future either the Exchange Control or similar regulations be used as a means of gratifying the prejudice which it is known the B.B.C. Directorate entertain against Radio Luxembourg's sponsored programmes.'

Several big firms, notably Horlicks, Lever Brothers, Unilever and Rowntree, assured the Committee that it was essential for British advertisers to be able to go into radio if the export markets were to be developed. At present the manufacturer was 'working with one hand tied behind his back.' These firms did not want to see the B.B.C. displaced as such; all they wanted was a separate commercial network. The Institute of Incorporated Practitioners in Advertising thought that Britain should be in the van of those who create new techniques in distribution and selling, and that the introduction of sponsored radio 'would enable us to compete in the vitally important entertainment industry, which, through film and radio, has become a great international force and in which our present weakness is a national danger.'

The B.B.C. also submitted a memorandum to the Committee, pleading that

because competition in broadcasting must in the long run descend to a fight for the greatest possible number of listeners, it would be the lower forms of mass appetite which would more and more be catered for in programmes.

The B.B.C. estimated that the number of persons in Britain listening to Radio Luxembourg, between 1.30 p.m. and midnight on Sundays, was about half the audience of the Home Service and one-tenth that of the Light Programme.

The Committee, in its Report published in 1951, turned down—though not unanimously—the idea that broadcasting should 'become financially dependent on sponsoring as it is wholly in the United States and largely in Canada and Australia.' In the end this would only put control into the hands of those 'whose interest is not broadcasting but the selling of some other goods or services or the propagation of particular ideas. If the people of any country want broadcasting for its own sake they must be prepared to pay for it as listeners or viewers; they must not ask for it for nothing as an accompaniment of advertising some other commodity.'

To the general surprise, three members of the Committee—Lord Beveridge, Lady Megan Lloyd George, and Mrs. Mary Stocks—proposed a compromise course of allowing advertisements on the air at specified hours. 'Is there any decisive reason why the most pervasive of all means of communication should not be used at all for this legitimate purpose? . . . We believe that such advertising programmes at named hours, so far from causing offence to the public, would be welcomed by many of them.' This idea does not seem to have been received with any great enthusiasm by advertising interests.

There was another minority report, that of Mr. Selwyn Lloyd, who was in favour of sponsored programmes competing against the existing ones.

As for commercial broadcasts from abroad, the Committee thought 'the choice may come to lie between jamming them and making bargains to keep them under control.'

That seems a curiously short-sighted view, for the indications are that, with the development of very high frequency broadcasting, any listener in Britain will eventually be able to pick up, with clarity, any programme in Europe or America, or even farther afield. As Mr. F. P. Bishop has said, in his *Ethics of Advertising:*

What will the Government do then? Will it go farther along the totalitarian road and forbid the sale of sets that can pick up foreign stations?

TV—The 'Salesman's Dream'

Television had not long been invented before it was being hailed, in America, as the 'vacuum cleaner salesman's dream' and 'advertising's third dimension.' It was one thing to make the public read about a product; it was another to make them listen to the recited virtues of a product; but how much, how infinitely, better if they could be made to *see* the product, to watch it being demonstrated—and that in the comfort of their own homes. Moreover, a television audience would assuredly be one with superior 'buying power.'

On March 1, 1940, the Federal Communications Commission agreed to allow limited commercial operation of television as from September 1 of that year, with a rider that 'emphasis on the commercial aspects of the operation at the expense of programme research is to be avoided.'

During the war television progress was suspended but the public were fortified from time to time by advertisements which showed the bliss to come. General Electric were not too busy building death-dealing equipment to picture, for readers of the

T

Saturday Evening Post, a post-war family at dinner in their home, watching a more-than-life-size Lily Pons posturing on the wall of their dining-room. The advertisement told how baseball games, musical shows, fashions and new films would be brought into the home, and it did not omit to add: 'If you are a business man, you will introduce new automobiles, radio receivers, refrigerators, electrical appliances and airplanes by television.'

When the war ended there were half a dozen television stations in America; by the end of 1951 there were more than 100. In the same period the number of sets increased from 7,000 to 13,000,000. But the cost of running a television show was formidable and two things had become rapidly obvious: one, that only the wealthiest firms could stay the course; two, that there would have to be 'commercials' at painfully frequent intervals, if the pay-rolls were to be covered.

Though writers on advertising adjured announcers to remember 'You're in a living-room, not an auction-room,' some high-pressure selling was to be seen. Many housewives, it must be conceded, took a keen pleasure in watching the latest 'gadgets' demonstrated; the makers of a 'magic towel' which was advertised in this way—filthy one moment, clean the next—sold half a million in two months. Television offered a lucrative new scope for the suave-mannered professional 'pitchmen' who ordinarily performed at the rural fairs.

It was soon discovered that the most convenient way of introducing a 'commercial,' if it was a dramatization, was to film it first. Then all that had to be done was to fade out the programme at regular intervals and run the film. If this meant interrupting a comedian just as he was reaching the point of his joke, that was the fault of the producer for not timing the show properly. Some stations were particularly flagrant offenders. Not even old cowboy films could be watched without interruption. After fifteen minutes the film would be faded out and the camera would focus on an amiable young woman, who would say, brightly, 'Yes, it's quite an exciting film, isn't it? But before we go on, shall we have a word about——.' Then, fifteen minutes later, the same interruption would occur. Attempts to tie in the product with an incident or character in the film led to some excruciating lapses. One announcer was reported to have cut into the film 'Lady Hamilton' with a suggestion that the heroine would have been a happier woman if she had used a deodorant.

Even those case-hardened to the commercialization of the ether questioned the seemliness of allowing a private manufacturer to underwrite the televising of the United Nations in session. The possibilities of the 'integrated plug' in this field were fearful to contemplate. Happily the Ford Motor Company maintained its reputation for reticence on the air and was content with a simple mention at the beginning and end.

During 1951 most of the British national newspapers regaled their readers with descriptions of over-commercialized American television, under headings like 'Aren't You Lucky to Miss This?' (*Daily Mirror*, July 23). Mr. Collie Knox described in the *Daily Mail* of December 14 how he had watched the 'Kate Smith Hour':

She [Kate Smith] is on vision five days a week, on radio six days, and has a one-hour vision show at a theatre every Wednesday. During the 'Kate Smith Hour' I saw she sang only three songs and appeared in one sketch. The rest of the time she lauded commercial products to the skies. Eleven commercials had to be fitted in and the crush was fearful.

To a suggestion by Mr. Knox that these 'commercials' were ruining the artistic value of the programme, a director replied that the show cost $50,000 a week, and how else could the money be found?

It may be that not enough credit was given in the British Press to those American television shows which were less blatantly commercial. Some British visitors said they preferred the vigour and enterprise of American television, with all its high-power selling, to anything they had been accustomed to receive from Alexandra Palace. Yet even American observers were to be found rebelling at the advertiser's intrusion. Time after time the *New Yorker* television critic, Mr. Philip Hamburger, entered items like this in his log: 'The Lucky Strike Theatre's attempt a couple of weeks ago to compress Victoria Regina into an hour-long version can only be put down as a disaster . . . the persistent commercials (including the maddening jingle "Be Happy, Go Lucky, Be Happy, Go Lucky Strike; Be Happy, Go Lucky, Go Lucky Strike Today") made a mockery of the entire enterprise.' Another time he told how a scene from Thornton Wilder's *Our Town* was cut short in mid-speech. 'Apparently it had run overtime. "Better buy Bird's Eye! Better buy Bird's Eye!" screamed a demoniac voice.' And Mr. Hamburger wrote acidulously of an all-woman quiz in which each member of the brains trust ended up by saying a piece in favour of the sponsor's cigarette. On one occasion, however, he was candid enough to say that he found the 'commercial' the only soothing thing in an otherwise racking production of *A Comedy of Errors*.

Simultaneously, *New Yorker* cartoonists strafed television without respite. One television salesman in a shop was depicted saying to another, *apropos* a rapidly departing 'prospect': 'I had him sold right up to the second I turned the damn thing on.' The screen of the set showed three animated cartons dancing, arms linked.

But the classic joke about American television was not the invention of a professional humorist. According to *Time*, a flustered announcer (whose name was given) was required to say, 'Always demand the best in bread,' but spoonerized the phrase.

In 1951 commercialism went a stage further with the holding of daily television weddings over the Columbia network. The bride's gown and ring, the canteen of silver, the electric washing-machine, the car for the honeymoon and the hotel reservations—all were the gifts of advertisers. Only the parson was not mentioned by name.

In some quarters it had been urged that the choice of television programmes for children ought not to be left in advertisers' hands. Early in 1952 the Federal Communications Commission published the results of a check by a group of San Francisco mothers on children's hour entertainment. In four hours they logged (according to *Time*) '13 murders and assorted killings, four sluggings, six kidnappings, five hold-ups, three explosions, three instances of blackmail and extortion, three thefts, two armed robberies, two cases of arson, one lynching, one torture scene and one miscarriage. One mother clocked 104 gun shootings during a half-hour serial, and another found sudden death shudderingly described fourteen times in twenty minutes.'

*   *   *

In Britain, post-war television was operated on such a tight purse that many voices were heard calling for sponsored entertainment. Only in this way, it was argued, could better programmes be mounted.

The Committee on Broadcasting, reporting in 1951, held that television advertising would be a backward step. In their minority report, however, Lord Beveridge and his two associates thought that the public ought to have an opportunity at some stage of saying whether they would rather pay large fees in order to keep advertisements off the screen, or whether they would prefer to see some extra revenue raised by advertisements.

The issue was strenuously debated in Parliament and Press in the early part of 1952. A Conservative Party 'pressure group' had let it be known that they would strike as hard as they knew for the liberty of the advertiser. To the loudly expressed chagrin of the Socialists (and the dismay of some of their own supporters), the Churchill Government announced, in a White Paper issued in May, that they approved the principle of sponsored television—with reservations. Advertisers would have to build their own stations; there would be no 'commercials' over the B.B.C. network. Moreover, no commercial television would be allowed until the B.B.C. had completed its regional transmitters, and until much more research had been carried out in very high frequency broadcasting. The Socialists lost little time in announcing that if returned to office they would not tolerate advertising on television.

When the House of Lords debated this White Paper, no one was greatly surprised to hear Lord Reith class sponsored television with smallpox, bubonic plague and the black death. Two or three peers told of personal ordeals they had suffered on American television. Lord Macdonald of Gwaenysgor complained that the sponsor had cut into his televised discussion with Mrs. Roosevelt of the Colombo Plan for helping South-East Asia. Lord Simon had paid two dollars for the privilege of having a choice of five different television programmes in his hotel room. Once, on turning a knob, he heard the last questions and answers of an interview with a fellow countryman who was visiting America on behalf of the Travel Association. 'Sir Alexander, what do you think of Anglo-American relations?' the interviewer asked. Came the cautious reply: 'I think it very important that the two countries should be on good terms.' To this, the interrogator said, 'And so do I. And I hope when you travel about in America you will remember to recommend to your friends our cigarettes.' From Lord Brand came a useful retort to those who argued that advertisements on television would be no more distracting than advertisements in newspapers. Imagine, said his lordship, a man having his copy of *The Times* snatched away from under his eyes by an advertiser who said, 'You have to listen to me for three minutes before you can read the leader.'

Many advocates of sponsored television had argued that Britain need not imitate the worst excesses of American television. It was left to Sir David Maxwell Fyfe, supporting the Government's decision in the Commons, to say: 'We are a much more mature and sophisticated people.'

LAST WORD

THE last chapters have described how the advertiser has adapted old wiles to new forms of expression. It is probable that the future history of advertising will be a record of similar adaptations, for it is hard to believe that there can be any new wiles for cozening humanity still left in the bag. If the reader protests that, at this stage, it is equally hard to think of any new media which could be profaned by commerce, let him remember that a generation ago it did not seem likely that the advertiser would be in a position to intrude his voice into private houses, to demonstrate his wares at the family hearth, or even to scrawl his name across the heavens.

In his novel *The Richardson Story*, Mr. Francis Williams has conjured up an uncomfortably plausible picture of the next step in advertising—the grafting of inaudible ('supersonic') messages on to film sound tracks and radio recordings. These messages bombard the audience in its sub-conscious with a compulsive, hypnotic effect. As a try-out, the continent of America is induced to resort in its millions to a moribund quack medicine. *The Richardson Story* is the kind of novel the late H. G. Wells might have been tempted to write if he had survived with imagination and vigour unimpaired into the electronic era; as it was, he wrote *Tono-Bungay*. Inaudible suggestion is a pretty weapon for a medicine manufacturer; an even prettier one, as Mr. Williams indicates, for a tyrant.

Any advertising man who has read this far may demand to know why he alone of those who exploit human nature should be expected to head the procession along the road to absolute truth and honesty. It is a point he is entitled to make; on the other hand he may be willing to accept the responsibility. He may point out, with some justice, that his copy often observes a more scrupulous code of ethics than is observed in the editorial columns. He will shudder to read of the American advertising man who (allegedly) paid a murderer to eat peanuts on the way to the scaffold, but he will be piqued if he reads a shocked report of such a happening in a newspaper which stimulates its own sale by buying murderers' life stories.

The responsibility for raising the standards of advertising (as of the Press) lies partly with the public, but not wholly so, as many apologists pretend. Human nature, though glacially slow to improve, *has* responded on occasions to a lead; and today the advertising man, with his self-imposed code setting a standard higher than the law requires, can fairly claim to have given this lead. He must be encouraged to extend it (and in what better way, as the writer has already suggested, than by ceasing to solicit the socially prominent for testimonials?) His greatest difficulty in the future will be to prevent adventurers in his camp from betraying his standards; especially if newspaper competition again grows fierce and free.

INDEX